experimentation

matters

experimentation
matters

unlocking the potential of
new technologies for innovation

STEFAN H. THOMKE

HARVARD BUSINESS SCHOOL PRESS
Boston, Massachusetts

Copyright 2003 Harvard Business School Publishing Corporation
All rights reserved
Printed in the United States of America
07 06 05 04 03   5 4 3 2 1

Library of Congress Cataloging-in-Publication Data
Thomke, Stefan H.
    Experimentation matters : unlocking the potential of new technologies for innovation / Stefan H. Thomke.
        p. cm.
    ISBN 1-57851-750-8
    1. Technological innovations. 2. Technology—Experiments. I. Title.
    T173.8.T495 2003
    600—dc21

                                                                2002155998

To my family,

whose love and support

made this book possible.

contents

acknowledgments

Although experimentation has played an important role in the development of the ideas in this book, I have also benefited from the experience, wisdom, and generosity of many people. The work began in 1992 when I walked into Eric von Hippel's classroom at the Massachusetts Institute of Technology (MIT). At the time, I was a doctoral student in electrical engineering and was curious about why there was an entire course dedicated to understanding the process of technological innovation. Little did I know that I would later dedicate my career to researching the questions that Eric introduced in the course. Eric became not only my thesis advisor but a mentor, teacher, and coauthor whose support and friendship made possible the work that led to this book. I will be forever grateful for what he has done for me.

I am similarly indebted to my colleagues at Harvard Business School (HBS). Kim Clark, Dean of the Faculty, Roy Shapiro, and Jan Hammond were the heads of the Technology and Operations Management unit while most of the research for this book was being done, and I thank them for the support they have provided over the years. They encouraged me right from the start to think about the bigger managerial implications of my work and structured my assignments so that I could have the time and focus I needed to develop a strong body of scholarly research. Steven Wheelwright provided detailed feedback on some manuscripts that indirectly made it into this book. I would also like to thank the Harvard Business School Division of Research and my research directors over the past years—Dwight Crane, Srikant Datar,

Dorothy Leonard, and Gary Pisano—who ensured the necessary support for my extensive fieldwork.

I am grateful to many colleagues, managers, and students who spent time with me and provided the material and feedback necessary to shape the ideas presented here. David Bell, Amy Edmondson, Roland Franke, Takahiro Fujimoto, Fiona Lee, Christoph Loch, Don Reinertsen, Christian Terwiesch, and Eric von Hippel worked with me on instrumental papers that are the foundation of this book. My colleagues Kent Bowen, Marco Iansiti, Gary Pisano, Michael Tushman, and four anonymous reviewers carefully went through an early draft of the book and provided many useful suggestions. Tom Allen, Don Clausing, Steven Eppinger, Ralph Katz, Gordon Kaufman, and Ely Sachs supported my work as a graduate student at MIT and got me interested in the design and mathematics of experimentation. The book has also benefited enormously from discussions with, comments, and feedback from Paul Adler, Carliss Baldwin, Richard Bohmer, Felix Brück, Jim Cash, Hank Chesbrough, Clay Christensen, Michael Cusumano, Juan Enriquez, John Ettlie, Lee Fleming, David Garvin, Abbie Griffin, Alden Hayashi, Bob Hayes, Rebecca Henderson, Nitin Joglekar, Vish Krishnan, Walter Kuemmerle, Rajiv Lal, Alan MacCormack, Ashish Nanda, Kentaro Nobeoka, Ananth Raman, Christian Ramsauer, Kash Rangan, Andrew Robertson, Michael Schrage, Sandra Sucher, Phil Thomas, Karl Ulrich, David Upton, Michael Watkins, Charles Weber, Harry West, Daniel Whitney, Gerry Zaltman, and the participants of many seminars at HBS and elsewhere. There have been many more contributors, and I apologize for not having enough space to thank them individually.

I am also grateful to many students in M.B.A. and executive programs in which I have tested some of the ideas and frameworks discussed in this book. They patiently read, discussed, and listened to my ideas, and their comments, questions, and criticism have taught me what does and does not work.

Performing the fieldwork for this book took many years and involved hundreds of people from industries as diverse as automobiles, financial services, integrated circuits, and pharmaceuticals. Without their generous support, I could have never done the research that led to this book. I would like to particularly thank Chris Bangle, Julian Boyden, Warren Butler, Larry Dennison, Touraj Gholami, Martin Haslanger, John Heugle, Michael Holzner, David and Tom Kelley, Whitney Mortimer, Michael Pavia, Gerry Podesta, Paul Pospisil, Peter Ratz, Steven Sinofsky, Mary Sonnack, Ulrich Stuhec, and John Wright.

When I started this book, I had no idea how much work it would involve. Fortunately, some people have helped me along the way. Barbara Feinberg stands out as the prime contributor. Her advice, editorial suggestions, and encouragement deeply influenced the structure and concepts in this book. Ashok Nimgade worked with me on most of the case studies. Nathan Simon provided valuable research assistance with the automotive data in chapter 4. I would also like to thank Lisa Noonan and Christine Gaze for their help and Jeff Kehoe, Jill Connor, and the Harvard Business School Press staff for encouraging me to write this book and working hard to ensure a timely and smooth publication process.

I owe the most to my family. My grandparents and parents always encouraged me to learn and to pursue my ambitions and dreams. My wife, Savita, her parents, and our children, Arjun, Vikram, and Anjali, have given me the strength, happiness, and loving support that has made all my work possible. Our wonderful children taught me what good experimentation is about and that parents, by definition, are lousy experimenters. Meeting Savita more than sixteen years ago was the luckiest moment of my life, and this book exists because of her. My family is very special to me and I dedicate this book to them.

Stefan H. Thomke
Harvard Business School
Boston, Massachusetts
January 2003

introduction

Experimentation matters because it fuels the discovery and creation of knowledge and thereby leads to the development and improvement of products, processes, systems, and organizations. Put concretely, without experimentation, we might all still be living in caves and using rocks as tools. Anything we use today arrives through a process of organized experimentation, over time; improved tools, new processes, and alternative technologies all have arisen because they have been worked out in various structured ways.

But experimentation has often been expensive in terms of the time involved and the labor expended, even as it has been essential to innovation. What has changed, particularly given new technologies available, is that it is now possible to perform more experiments in an economically viable way while accelerating the drive toward innovation.

This book emphasizes not only why experimentation matters in the largest sense of its connection to innovation, but why and how new technologies are transforming its economics. Not only can more experiments be run today, the kinds of experiments possible are expanding. Never before has it been so economically feasible to ask "what-if" questions and generate preliminary answers. New technologies enable organizations to both challenge presumed answers and pose more questions. They amplify how innovators learn from experiments, creating the potential for higher research and development (R&D) performance and new ways of creating value for firms and their customers. At the same time, this book discusses companies that do not fully unlock that potential because how they design, organize, and manage their approach to innovation gets in the way. That is, even deploying new technology for experimentation, these organizations are not organized to capture its potential value—in experimentation or in innovation. Like any effective experiment, this book will reveal what does and does not work.

Experimentation encompasses success and failure; it is an iterative process of understanding what doesn't work and what does. Both results are equally important for learning, the goal of any experiment and of experimentation overall. Thus, a crash test that results in unacceptable safety for drivers, a software user interface that confuses customers, or a drug that is toxic can all be desirable outcomes of an experiment—provided these results are revealed early in an innovation process and can be subsequently reexamined. Because few resources have been committed in these early stages, decision making is still flexible, and other approaches can be experimented with quickly. In a nutshell, experiments that result in failure are not failed experiments, although they frequently are considered so when anything deviating from what was intended is deemed "failure."

Herein lies the managerial dilemma addressed in this book. A relentless organizational focus on success makes true experimentation all too rare. Because experiments that reveal what doesn't work are frequently deemed failures, tests may be delayed, rarely carried out, or simply labeled *verification,* implying that only finding out what works *is* the primary goal of an experiment. If there is a problem in the experiment (and there always is at least one!), it will, under this logic, be revealed very late in the game. But when feedback on what does not work comes so late, costs can spiral out of control; worse, opportunities for innovation are lost at that point—reinforcing the emphasis on getting it right the first time. By contrast, when managers understand that effective experiments are supposed to reveal what does not work *early,* they realize that the knowledge gained then can benefit the next round of experiments and lead to more innovative ideas and concepts—early "failures" *can* lead to more powerful successes faster. IDEO, a product development firm discussed in chapter 6, calls this "failing often to succeed sooner."

But organizing for more frequent, rapid feedback—as powered by these new technologies—is not trivial. Multiple issues can arise, for instance, the "problem" of greater experimental capacity. What do we do with the opportunity to experiment "more"? Consider the attempted integration of computer modeling and simulation—examples of new experimentation technologies discussed throughout the book—in the automotive industry. Car companies have spent hundreds of millions of dollars on computer-aided technologies and employ many engineers and specialists to improve the performance of their complex development processes. By replacing expensive physical testing with virtual models, management hopes not only to save costs and time but also to streamline decision making and coordination among team members.

The challenges of leveraging new experimentation capacity are best captured by the observations of two middle managers at different automotive companies.[1] The first manager heads a large department of computer-aided engineering (CAE) specialists intended to help project teams in the development of new cars:

While senior management agrees that the potential of CAE is impressive, my company simply doesn't take enough advantage of it. As simulation specialists, our input to important engineering decisions comes much too late. Few of my people are colocated with engineering teams and most of them talk to other simulation specialists. Project teams send us simulation jobs after hardware tests have been run and we are asked to verify their findings. Rarely do we get involved early in the process when learning what doesn't work can make a big difference. And when our results disagree with physical tests, project engineers usually question our models and assumptions rather than check if their tests have been done right. It will take time to change our culture and people's mind-sets. In the meantime, the company spends millions on additional technologies that we neither trust nor integrate into our processes.

Compare that frustration to the experience of another manager who headed a large group of engineers directly responsible for a new car project.

> *Many of our engineers were not ready to accept the results from simulated tests because they aren't [considered] real. When senior management decided to invest in new information technologies, simulation software and specialists, they anticipated substantial savings. But the more we simulated, the more physical prototypes were built to verify that simulation was accurate. No one was going to make a commitment and decision based on a computer model only. Because of simulation, we ended up spending more money on prototype testing than before.*

Both managers would admit that the potential of new technologies is great, but neither company fully recognizes that the problems encountered relate not to "the technology" but to how it must be integrated into product development activities and organizations surrounding them, and, more significantly, to what existing expectations are. In the first case, the assumption is that CAE is something "experts" perform, essentially off-line. Like consultants, these people are outside the "normal" process, not to be integrated: The technology's presumed benefits end up as potential liabilities. In the second case, the assumption is that by introducing simulation technology, other procedures would simply die off—and the very real cost saving that virtual modeling provides vis-à-vis "real" modeling would arise. But real modeling is integral to the experimentation process in this organization—and, moreover, it has decades of validity behind it. One does not simply substitute a new technology and hope that both behavior and economics will magically change.

But behavior and economics *can* change! Not by magic, of course, but by realizing that experimentation is not an isolated phenomenon but part of a larger organizational effort toward innovation. Clearly, this book starts from the perspective that experimentation is part and parcel of innovation—it *matters*. But the book is also cautionary, to the extent that new technologies for experimentation pose challenges for the organization of innovation. What follows is an overview of these challenges, capturing the principal arguments of the book.

Experimentation Matters to Innovation

When Albert Einstein noted that anyone who has never made a mistake has never tried anything new, he was undoubtedly referring to the need to experiment in the quest for discovering new things. Indeed, at the heart of every company's ability to innovate lies a process of experimentation that enables the organization to create and evaluate new ideas and concepts for products, services, business models, or strategies.

All companies have some experimentation process at work but not everyone organizes that process to invite innovation. In fact, as the book *In Search of Excellence* noted years ago:

> *The most important and visible outcropping of the action bias in the excellent companies is their willingness to try things out, to experiment. There is absolutely no magic in the experiment. It is simply a tiny completed action, a manageable test that helps you learn something, just as in high-school chemistry. But our experience has been that most big institutions have forgotten how to test and learn. They seem to prefer analysis and debate to trying something out, and they are paralyzed by fear of failure, however small.*[2]

Fear of failure holds especially in the development of new products and services, where no idea can become a product without having been shaped, to one degree or another, through the process of experimentation. Today, a development project can require literally thousands of experiments, all with the same objective: to learn whether the product or service concept holds promise for addressing a new need or problem, then incorporate the information in the next round of tests so that the best result can be achieved.

To establish the rigor and relevance of the ideas in this book, *Experimentation Matters* is divided into two parts. Part I, chapters 1 through 4, builds the intellectual foundation of why experimentation matters, where it matters, and how new technologies have the potential to transform innovation today and in the future. The chapters also draw from more than a decade of research and detailed case studies and show that tapping into the power of experimentation is a managerial problem: Companies must accommodate their processes, organization, and management of innovation to experimentation and the full effect of new technologies. Part II, chapters 5 through 7, shows senior and middle managers how to address this problem. Building on our understanding of experimentation and why it matters, the book introduces six principles for managing experimentation—including experimenting early and often and organizing for rapid iteration—that can unlock the potential for innovation *within* companies. The final chapter takes experimentation *beyond* organizations, using the technologies and ideas discussed throughout the book, and suggests how senior managers and entrepreneurs can potentially use their experimental capabilities to transcend their organizations.

The Central Theme: Learning by Experimentation

Central to experimentation is the use of models, prototypes, controlled environments, and computer simulations that allow innovators to reflect, improvise, and evaluate the many ideas that are generated in organizations: in short, to learn by trying things out. In an ideal experiment, managers and engineers separate an independent variable (the "cause") and a dependent variable (the "effect") and then manipulate the former to observe changes in the latter. The manipulation, followed by careful observation and analysis, then gives rise to learning about relationships between cause and effect, which ideally can be applied to or tested in other settings. In real-world experimentation, environments are constantly changing, linkages between variables are complex and poorly understood, and often the variables are uncertain or unknown themselves. The result is iteration: Innovators make progress through iterative experimentation that is guided by some insight where a solution might lie. In fact, *all* experimentation involves iteration sooner or later.

When all relevant variables are known, formal statistical techniques and protocols allow for the most efficient design and analysis of experiments. These techniques are used widely in many fields of process and product optimization today and can be traced to the first half of the twentieth century when the statistician and geneticist Sir Ronald Fisher first applied them to agricultural and biological science.[3] However, when independent and dependent variables themselves are uncertain, unknown, or difficult to measure, experimentation itself is much more informal or tentative. Iterative experimentation goes on all the time and is so much an integral part of innovation processes that it has become like breathing—we do it but are not fully aware of the fact that we are really experimenting. Moreover, good experimentation goes well beyond the individual or the experimental protocols but has implications for firms in the way they manage, organize, and structure innovation processes. It isn't just about generating information by itself but about how firms can learn from trial and error and structured experimentation.

Chapters 1 and 3 deepen our understanding of why and how experimentation matters to learning and innovation, and they explain how the development of products and services is being affected by new technologies. Specifically, chapter 3 addresses how the *rate* of learning possible is influenced by a number of factors, some affecting the process, others affecting how it is managed. Seven factors are addressed as they affect how learning through experimentation occurs (or does not occur): fidelity, cost, iteration time, capacity, sequential and parallel strategies, signal-to-noise ratio, and type of experiment all enhance the power of experimentation. It is through these factors that managers can change how their organizations learn from experiments.

The Potential

Traditionally, testing has been relatively expensive, so companies had to be parsimonious with the number of experimental iterations. To overcome this constriction, managers essentially have had two choices: Change the fundamental economics of experimentation through new technologies and process innovation or try to get more out of each experiment—in other words, make experiments more efficient. "Design of experiments" that employs sophisticated statistical methods has focused primarily on the latter and, as already mentioned, has had a significant impact on how R&D is done. By manipulating multiple variables in a single experiment while maintaining integrity in its data analysis, scientists and engineers have been able to get more learning out of their experiments than they could in the past. Experiments per se can often be made more efficient, of course: *Experimentation Matters* does not deny the importance of the many excellent methods derived from statistics theory.

Alternatively, new technologies that slash experimentation cost and time not only bring much-needed capacity but can also make possible "what-if" experiments that, up to now, have been either too expensive or nearly impossible to run. What if an airplane, a car, a drug, or a business were designed in a particular way? By employing new experimentation technologies, it's possible to explore the assumptions that underlie a design, how they could be changed, and what the consequences would be, positive and negative. Further, if consequences were positive, we can see implications for product, process, and system improvements. Indeed, these technologies hold the possibility of improving themselves, as has happened in the integrated circuit industry.

The latter sections of chapter 1 and all of chapter 2 show how new technologies can affect the development of products. Chapter 1 explores how new technologies such as computer modeling and simulation, rapid prototyping, and combinatorial chemistry allow companies to create more learning more rapidly; we see how that knowledge can be incorporated in more experiments at less expense. Indeed, new information-based technologies have driven down the marginal costs of experimentation, just as they have decreased the marginal costs in some production and distribution systems. Moreover, an experimental system that integrates new information-based technologies does more than lower costs; it also increases the opportunities for innovation. That is, some technologies can make existing experimental activities more efficient, while others introduce entirely new ways of discovering novel concepts and solutions. Chapter 2 provides hard evidence from the multibillion dollar integrated circuit industry, which has been transformed by new technologies more than once. In fact, the exponential performance gains of integrated circuits, accompanied by better models, have fueled dramatic advances in computer simulation and tools for design automation used in many fields. These advances have come full circle: Today's complex chips would be impossible to design and manufacture without the tools that they helped to create.

The changes have thus far affected businesses with high costs of product development, such as the pharmaceutical, automotive, semiconductor, and software industries. My ten years of research in these industries suggest that as the cost of computing and other combinatorial technologies keeps falling—thereby making complex calculations faster and cheaper—and as new combinatorial technologies and our knowledge of building models improve further, virtually all companies will discover that they have a greater capacity for rapid experimentation to investigate diverse concepts. Financial institutions, for example, now use computer simulations to test new financial instruments. In fact, the development of spreadsheet software itself has forever changed financial modeling; even novices can perform many sophisticated what-if experiments that were once prohibitively expensive.[4]

The enthusiasm for these technologies gets a dose of reality when we turn to how they are used in innovation processes. When knowing what does and doesn't work can happen much more rapidly and frequently, the promise these technologies hold is often diluted when they are not used to maximize the power of experimentation. In chapter 4, we learn about "realities" that get in the way of more effective experimentation. Drawing on years of research in the global automotive industry, the chapter shows how the introduction of computer-aided design and engineering (CAD and CAE) technologies has suffered from several predicaments. In particular, processes and people limit the impact of new technologies, organizational interfaces can get in the way of experimentation cycles, and technologies often change faster than human and organizational behavior.

What Managers Can Do to Unlock the Potential

The findings reported in chapters 1 through 4 paint a picture of both great opportunities and grave challenges for management. Experimentation matters because it is through learning equally what works and what doesn't work that people develop great new products, services, and entire businesses. But in spite of the lip service that is paid to "testing" and "learning from failure," today's organization, process, and management of innovation often impede experimentation. When new technologies amplify the impact of learning, managing experimentation becomes more important than ever before.

Chapters 5 through 7 propose that experimentation *can* be managed effectively by following some sensible principles that have been researched in diverse industries (figure I-1). On the surface, the experiments run in car companies, suburban bank branches, chip design

FIGURE I - 1

Unlocking the Potential of New Experimentation Technologies

The area of the triangle represents the experimentation technologies' potential contribution to R&D productivity, innovation, and value creation. Without rethinking and changing the process, organization, and management of innovation, much of the potential remains out of reach for companies.

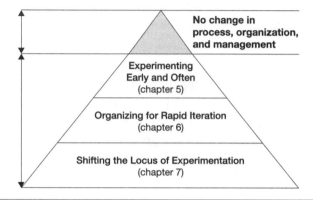

projects, and drug discovery firms could hardly look more dissimilar. Yet years of research have shown that they share a set of principles that maximize how learning by experimentation occurs (and does not occur). Not only do these principles address how companies ought to organize for experimentation, they also go the heart of human behavior in organizations: managerial biases, mental models, values, and incentives.

The following paragraphs summarize each principle and what managers can do to unlock the technologies' potential and accommodate them into their organizations.

Principle #1: Anticipate and Exploit Early Information Through "Front-Loaded" Innovation Processes

Large companies often spend millions of dollars to correct late-stage development problems but underestimate the savings of early experimentation. Moreover, enormous time and energy is expended on these problems, derailing schedules and budgets—taking away "opportunities" for companies to focus their precious resources on other projects.

New technologies are most powerful when they are deployed to test what works and what doesn't work as early as possible—the "front-loading" effect. These experiments are not as complete or perfect as late-stage tests, but they are able to direct early attention and integrated problem solving at potential downstream risks. Significantly, these experiments can reveal what does not work before substantial resources are committed and design decisions are locked in. With more experimentation capacity available during early development, teams are also more likely to experiment with many ideas and concepts that will ultimately result in better products and services. The early sections of chapter 5 show how this is done at companies such as Microsoft, Boeing, and Toyota.

Principle #2: Experiment Frequently but Do Not Overload Your Organization

With the benefits of front-loaded innovation processes, there remains the question of how frequently companies should run experiments. The quest for efficiency, combined with an incomplete understanding or measurement of the benefits of early problem solving, has been driving out experimentation. Money can be saved, so goes the logic, by lumping experiments into one big test or delaying them as long as possible until they are more likely to result in the verification of "success." In contrast, experimenting more frequently reveals what does and does not work with minimal delay and problems can be addressed right away, thus minimizing the cost of redesign. The middle section of chapter 5 thus suggests that a good experimentation strategy balances the value of early information against the cost of repeated testing.[5] Most companies find, however, that their accounting tracks the latter cost but little formal analysis is done on the former savings, shifting the balance toward too little experimentation. When new technologies dramatically drive down the cost of testing, understanding the need for frequent experimentation becomes more important than ever. As with many other changes, however, companies need also to prepare for the rapid increase in information that will result from more experimentation, information that has to be processed, evaluated, understood, and used in the planning of more experimentation.

Principle #3: Integrate New and Traditional Technologies to Unlock Performance

The new experimentation technologies discussed in this book should not be used in isolation; they need to be placed within an innovation system so that they enhance overall performance. While impressive in their potential, new technologies like computer simulation may not achieve more than 70 percent or 80 percent of their traditional counterpart's technical performance—but they can get there more quickly. Thus, by combining new and traditional technologies, organizations can avoid a performance gap while also enjoying the benefits of cheaper and faster experimentation. The later sections of chapter 5 show how the true potential of new technologies often lies in a company's ability to reconfigure its processes and organization to use them in concert with traditional technologies. In rare instances is the technology so advanced that it instantly displaces its traditional counterpart and all the development experience and engineering knowledge that goes with it. Eventually, a new technology can replace its traditional counterpart, but it then might be challenged by a newer technology that itself must be integrated.

Principle #4: Organize for Rapid Experimentation

Integral to innovation is the ability to experiment quickly: Rapid feedback shapes new ideas by reinforcing, modifying, or complementing existing knowledge. Indeed, rapid feedback is important to learning, yet far too many developers must wait days, weeks, or months before their ideas can be tested in experiments. Time passes and attention shifts, and when feedback finally arrives, momentum is lost, the link between cause and effect has been severed, and project decisions have been made. To prevent the trail of an idea or inspiration from growing cold, Thomas Alva Edison built and organized his famous West Orange, New Jersey laboratory around the concept of rapid experimentation. Supply rooms and machine shops were close to experimental rooms, libraries and storerooms had diverse supplies, and ample capacity made sure that delays could not slow down people's work and creativity.[6]

Chapter 6 shows how the German car company BMW leveraged advances in crash safety modeling and simulation to remove interfaces between functional groups in order to speed up learning from experimentation. The result was faster iterations and more ideas because much of the knowledge required about safety, design, simulation, and testing resided within the small group. In multiple instances, faster experimentation resulted in fundamentally new insights that ultimately made BMW cars much safer.

Principle #5: Fail Early and Often but Avoid "Mistakes"

When experiments reveal what does and does not work, the inevitable happens: Novel ideas and concepts fail. Early failures are not only desirable but also needed to eliminate unfavorable options quickly and build on the learning they generate. The faster the experimentation-failure cycle, the more feedback can be gathered and incorporated into new rounds of testing. The problem in many organizations is that knowing what doesn't work can go against a relentless focus on success. Failures expose gaps in knowledge and can lead to embarrassment, and the people "responsible" are unlikely to be promoted within traditional incentive systems. Ask yourself: How often are people rewarded for exposing failure early, thus saving their employer from investing precious resources in opportunities with little promise? This matters a great deal because in innovation processes, experiments that result in failure are not failed experiments. In fact, it was Edison, again, who noted that the "real measure of success is the number of experiments that be crowded into 24 hours."[7]

Chapter 6 suggests that failures, however, should not be confused with mistakes. Failure can be a desirable outcome of an experiment, whereas mistakes should be avoided as they produce little new or useful information and are therefore without value. Distinguishing between failures and mistakes thus becomes very important, particularly when organizations are integrating new technologies that will increase the number of experiments resulting in failure—in other words, learning what doesn't work. The chapter also presents research on what managers can do to *invite* experimentation into their companies.

Principle #6: Manage Projects as Experiments

A final principle for unlocking the potential of new technologies is that projects can be conceived of as experiments themselves. While senior management often considers portfolios of projects in the allocation and management of resources, it rarely applies the same logic to portfolios of experiments. This is somewhat surprising since projects are powerful mechanisms for managing change, knowledge creation, and the introduction of new technologies and processes. After all, how many organizations can point towards a set of fifteen to twenty ongoing and well-designed experiments that are either exploring new markets or are changing the organization itself? Chapter 6 explores how learning from projects can be maximized, using the same factors that drove learning *within* projects: fidelity, cost, iteration time, capacity, sequential and parallel strategies, signal-to-noise ratio, and type of experiment. Significantly, the chapter also addresses the delicate balance of managing dual objectives: finishing projects on time and budget *and* using the project as an experiment for learning. Research at Bank of America, BMW, and IDEO shows how this balance is achieved.

Shifting the Locus of Experimentation as a New Way to Create Value

Chapters 1 through 6 focus primarily on managing experimentation *within* companies: how to change the processes, organization, and management of innovation to tap into the power of experimentation and the opportunities that new technologies provide for. That in itself challenges most organizations, but the strong evidence from industries as diverse as automotive, financial, semiconductor, and software has shown that it can be done. The exciting part is that the changes are not just about raising productivity but also about fundamentally changing the kinds of products and services that are created, leading to innovations that simply weren't possible before.

Chapter 7 explores what would happen if we took the ideas of the book to another level—*beyond* organizations—where they can change the way companies create new products and services with customers and suppliers. Specifically, by putting experimentation technologies into the hands of customers, managers can tap into possibly the largest source of dormant experimentation capacity. Not only can shifting experimentation to customers result in faster development of products that are better suited to their needs, but their experimentation could also result in innovations we simply cannot imagine today.

The chapter explores how this was done by a number of companies, using an intriguing approach that takes advantage of experimentation technologies discussed throughout this book. Essentially, these companies have abandoned their efforts to understand exactly what products their customers want and have instead equipped their customers with tools to design and develop their own new products, ranging from minor modifications to major new innovations. The user-friendly tools, often integrated into a "toolkit" package, deploy new technologies (e.g., computer simulation and rapid prototyping) to make innovation faster, less expensive, and most important, better as customers run what-if experiments themselves.

A variety of industries have started to use this approach. Bush Boake Allen (BBA), a global supplier of specialty flavors that has recently been acquired by International Flavors and Fragrances (IFF), has developed a toolkit that will enable its customers to develop their own flavors, which BBA then manufactures. In the materials field, General Electric (GE) provides customers with Web-based tools for designing better plastic products. In software, a number of companies allow people to add custom-designed modules to their standard products and then commercialize the best of those components. Indeed, shifting experimentation and innovation to customers has the power to completely transform industries. In the semiconductor business, it has led to a custom chip market that has grown to more than $15 billion per annum over twenty years.

Tapping into the inventiveness and imagination of customers—not just R&D departments—can indeed generate tremendous value, but capturing the value is hardly a simple or straightforward process. Not only must companies develop the right design toolkit, they must also revamp their business models as well as their management mind-sets. When companies relinquish a fundamental task—such as designing a new product—to customers, the two parties must redefine their relationship, and this change can be risky. With custom computer chips, for instance, companies traditionally captured value by both designing and manufacturing innovative products. Now, with customers taking over more of the design task, companies must focus more intently on providing the best custom manufacturing and design tools. In other words, the location where value is created and captured changes, and companies must reconfigure their business models accordingly. Chapter 7 offers some lessons for companies preparing themselves to unlock the potential by managing experimentation beyond and between their organizations.

NOTES

1. The comments were made as part of a research project on global automotive development. Some of the study's findings are discussed in chapter 4.

2. Quoted from Peters and Waterman (1982), pages 134–135.

3. See Fisher (1921, 1923).

4. See Schrage (2000), chapter 2.

5. Thomke and Bell (2001) explore this tension in an analytical research paper.

6. Millard (1990) provides rich details on how Edison organized his West Orange laboratory for experimentation.

7. Quoted from Millard (1990), page 40.

Part I

why experimentation matters

1

new technologies for experimentation

At the heart of every company's ability to innovate lies a process of experimentation that enables the organization to create and refine its products. In fact, no product can be a product without first having been an idea subsequently shaped through experimentation. Today, a major development project involves literally thousands of experiments, all with the same objective: to learn, through rounds of organized testing, whether the product concept or proposed technical solution holds promise for addressing a need or problem. The information derived from each round is then incorporated into the next set of experiments, and so on until the final product ultimately results. In short, innovations do not arrive fully fledged but are nurtured through an experimentation process that takes place in laboratories and development organizations. All such groups have an experimentation process, but not every group organizes the process to invite innovation.

Experimentation is the lens through which we, in this book, shall look at several new technologies—simulation and computer modeling, and combinatorial technologies—that allow for the rapid and inexpensive generation and testing of new product possibilities. The enthusiasm for adopting these technologies comes partly from their potential to dramatically decrease the marginal cost of experimentation. When deployed to maximize the power of experimentation itself, however, they contribute to both higher R&D productivity and breakthrough innovations in addition to cost reduction.[1] Put alternatively, the promise these technologies hold is diluted if they are not used to maximize the power of experimentation.

At another level, the technologies can change how companies create value for customers and transform entire industries (chapter 7). What is also critical is that while the technologies are for experimentation—and achieve their power therefrom—they are at the same time new technologies. They are vulnerable to the problems of installation, integration, and adaptation that any and all new technologies face whenever they are introduced in an organization. In other words, the promise is not the reality, even in experimentation.

We begin this chapter by looking at the importance of experimentation in itself and to any organization; then we survey some new technologies that provide experimentation potential. We show "success" here, to preview the possibilities. Be aware that despite these success stories, the road is not smooth. Looking at the difficulties of integrating technology is never a pretty picture—and chapter 4 will fully lay out a cautionary picture to contemplate. What doesn't work is the basic message; what works is the message of chapters 5 and 6.

Why Experimentation Matters

The pursuit of knowledge is the rationale behind experimentation, and all experiments yield information that comes from understanding what does and what does not work. For centuries, researchers have relied on systematic experimentation, guided by their insight and intuition, as an instrumental source of new information and the advancement of knowledge. Famous experiments have been conducted to characterize naturally occurring processes, to decide among rival scientific hypotheses about matter, to find hidden mechanisms of known effects, to simulate what is difficult or impossible to research: in short, to establish scientific laws inductively.[2] Some of the most famous series of experiments have led to scientific breakthroughs or radically new innovations from which we still benefit today.

Louis Pasteur's discovery of artificial vaccines is one example. Pasteur had been struggling for years to understand the course of disease, in this case cholera, and ran extensive experiments to accumulate a knowledge base to help him make sense of what the experiments in his laboratory were yielding. In 1879, he returned from a summer vacation not realizing that chicken broth cultures, part of one ongoing experiment, had become infected. He thus injected his hens with the infected culture and followed that with injections of fresh, virulent microbes. What he discovered in this process was that the mild disease the infected cultures gave rise to forestalled the deadly form from occurring. Pasteur was able to compare the results of previous experiments with recent ones and thereby draw accurate conclusions based on the knowledge accumulated over the course of all these experiments.[3]

Nearly a century later, the discovery of 3M's Post-It adhesive demonstrated the role of experimentation in the discovery of both technical solutions and new market needs. The story began in 1964, when 3M chemist Spencer Silver started a series of experiments aimed at developing polymer-based adhesives.[4] As Silver recalled:

> *The key to the Post-It adhesive was doing the experiment. If I had sat down and factored it out beforehand, and thought about it, I wouldn't have done the experiment. If I had limited my thinking only to what the literature said, I would have stopped. The literature was full of examples that said that you can't do this.*[5]

Although Silver's discovery of a new polymer with adhesive properties departed from predictions of current theories about polymers, it was at least another five years before 3M determined a market for the new adhesive. Silver kept trying to sell his glue to other departments at 3M, but they were focused on finding a stronger glue that formed an unbreakable bond, not a weaker glue that supported only a piece of paper. Market tests with different concepts (i.e., a sticky bulletin board) were telling 3M that the Post-It concept was hopeless—until Silver met Arthur Fry. Fry, a chemist and choir director, observed that members of his choir would frequently drop bookmarks when switching between songs. "Gee," wondered Fry, "if I had a little adhesive on these bookmarks, that would be just the ticket." This "Eureka" moment launched a series of experiments with the new polymer adhesive that broadened its applicability and ultimately led to a paper product that could be attached and removed without damaging the original surface. In other words, repeated experimentation was instrumental in finding the now obvious solution once the Eureka moment occurred.

Although Eureka moments make for memorable history, they do not give a complete account of the various experimentation strategies, technologies, processes, and history that lead to scientific or innovative breakthroughs. After all, such moments are usually the result of many failed experiments and accumulated learning that prepare the experimenter to take advantage of the unexpected. "Chance," noted Louis Pasteur, "favors only the prepared mind."[6] Consider what the authors of a careful study of Thomas Alva Edison's invention of the electric light bulb concluded:

> *This invention [the electric light], like most inventions, was the accomplishment of men guided largely by their common sense and their past experience, taking advantage of whatever knowledge and news should come their way, willing to try many things that didn't work, but knowing just how to learn from failures to build up gradually the base of facts, observations, and insights that allow the occasional lucky guess—some would call it inspiration—to effect success.*[7]

When firms aim for breakthrough innovations, however, they cannot rely on luck or even lucky guesses alone; experimentation must be organized and managed as an explicit part of a strategy for pursuing innovation itself (chapter 3). At the same time, as we shall see throughout this book, the serendipitous may be more likely when an effective experimentation process is in place and new experimentation technologies are integrated into it. The serendipitous is also more likely when experimenters are clear that understanding what does not work is as important to learning as knowing what does.

If we attempt to add up all the significant experiments that have been carried out since the Greeks began systematic scientific studies around 400 BC until the nineteenth century, we can probably say that the number is in the millions. If we then include experiments initiated in industrial R&D laboratories since the nineteenth century, the number perhaps reaches several hundred million. That number, in turn, will be dwarfed by the billions or trillions of experiments we will run with computers, combinatorial technologies, and other methods in the coming decade alone, fundamentally challenging how innovation will happen. The sheer quantity of inexpensive experimentation possible with these new technologies, along with the knowledge gained from them, will make the "lucky guess" much more likely as long as companies are willing to fundamentally rethink how they research and develop new products and create value for their customers.

Failure, Success, and Uncertainty

As noted, all experimentation—whether conducted in ancient Greece, in Edison's laboratory, or in the presence of simulation or other sophisticated technology today—generates knowledge. The knowledge, however, comes as much from failure as it does from success. Innovators learn from failure: Again, understanding what doesn't work is as important as understanding what does. The next round of experimentation should benefit equally from either result. Further, knowledge of either failure or success itself can be stockpiled, providing a resource that, if not applicable to one set of experiments, can be used for subsequent inquiries.

For example, IDEO Product Development, a leading design firm, maintains a Tech Box for stockpiling experiments from finished and ongoing projects. This giant "shoebox" for cataloging and electronically documenting materials, objects, and interesting gadgets is used to inspire innovators in new development projects. A curator organizes and manages the content of the Tech Box and duplicates its contents for other IDEO offices—and occasionally for other companies—throughout the world. Designers and engineers can rummage through the box and play with an assortment of switches, buttons, and odd materials that were all part of successful or failed experiments.[8] The Tech Box underscores the fact that one can never fully anticipate what tools and materials would be required in a development project that involves great novelty. Edison learned this lesson early in his career and later tried to have everything at hand in his West Orange laboratory. Thus, when Edison noted that "the most important part of an experimental laboratory is a big scrap heap," he leveraged a well-stocked storeroom and a collection of apparatus, equipment, and materials that came from previous experiments. The larger the scrap heap, the wider the search space for Edison and his experimenters and the more likely it was that somewhere in this pile the solution would be found.[9]

Similarly, pharmaceutical companies stockpile very small quantities of discrete chemical compounds in "chemical libraries," which are used in the search for new drugs.[10] Many of these compounds were generated in prior drug development projects and showed therapeutic promise in complex experiments involving either simple screening procedures or living organisms. Consisting of several hundred thousand compounds and information on their specific properties, these libraries are used to find leads in new drug projects where access to chemical diversity is an important competitive advantage. Such libraries and the associated information on how and where to use them represent a long history of investments in scientific research, experimentation, and strategic commitment; *The Economist* has referred to them as one of the "most carefully guarded assets" of pharmaceutical companies.[11]

The fact is, when pharmaceutical companies such as Eli Lilly launch new drugs or automotive firms like BMW introduce new cars, the products are the result of as many failed experiments as successful ones. An innovation process, overall, should ensure the gradual accumulation of new knowledge that will guide the path of development itself. This new knowledge, however, is at least partially based on "accumulated failure" that has been carefully understood.[12]

The reason why experiments inevitably fail as part of product development has to do with the uncertain nature of the innovation process itself. When teams undertake the development of products or services—particularly novel or complex ones, they rarely know in advance whether a particular concept will work as intended. That means they have to find ways of rapidly discarding dysfunctional ideas while retaining others that show promise. At the same time, the dysfunctional ideas themselves have generated knowledge and should, as such, be captured. Edison understood this very well when he noted, "Just because something doesn't do what you planned it to do doesn't mean it's useless. Reverses should be an incentive to great accomplishment. Results? Why, man, I have gotten lots of results! If I find 10,000 ways something won't work, I haven't failed. I am not discouraged, because every wrong attempt discarded is just one more step forward."[13] A century later, academic research on R&D organizations showed these insights to be more relevant than ever: Project teams spent an average of 77 percent of their time on experimentation and related analysis activities to resolve uncertainty.[14]

Not all uncertainty is alike, however. *Technical uncertainty* arises from the exploration of solutions (e.g., materials) that have not been used before or have not been combined in "this" way before or have not been miniaturized in such a way before. As such, it often relates to product functionality and can be managed through rigorous prototype testing throughout development. *Production uncertainty* exists when we do not know if a technical solution that works well in prototypes can also be produced cost-effectively. What may work in small quantities may not be feasible when production ramps up: The entire manufacturing process itself may need to be revised. At every stage of R&D, technical and production uncertainty exists and needs to be managed, in part through a systematic process of experimentation.

Beyond technical and production uncertainty, rapidly changing customer demands create *need uncertainty*, another critical reason for rigorous experimentation. Customers are rarely able to fully specify all their needs because they either face uncertainty themselves or cannot articulate their needs on products that do not yet exist. If they have neither seen nor used such a product before, they themselves will have to experiment before arriving at a recommendation. Finally, when innovations are "disruptive," as research has shown, *market uncertainty* can be so significant that firms are reluctant to allocate sufficient resources to the development of products for those markets.[15] In such cases, the composition and needs of new markets evolve themselves and are either difficult to assess or change so quickly that they can catch good management by surprise. To successfully harness the opportunities of disruptive change, successful managers rely in part on experimentation.[16] According to the research, such managers "planned to fail early and inexpensively in the search for the market for a disruptive technology. They found that their markets generally coalesced through an iterative process of trial, learning, and trial again."[17] The principles for unlocking the potential of new experimentation technologies thus apply at all levels of uncertainty—technical, production, customer, and market—and will be delved into throughout the book.

New Technologies for Experimentation

Despite the critical role that experimentation plays in innovation, complex experiments have traditionally been costly and time consuming to run, and companies have been parsimonious in expenditures to provide for them. Two interrelated consequences followed. Experimentation capacity has been constrained and the number of experimental iterations limited. More subtly, the notion of experimentation has often been confined to verification of known outcomes; testing at the end of development programs is managed to find late-stage problems. And when the test itself becomes a high-profile event, such as the preliminary evaluation of a new and expensive weapon system, companies regard a successful outcome as one that results in no new information or surprises and, hence, in no learning at all.

Thus, given the costs and time heretofore associated with running experiments—particularly complex ones—as much as experimentation itself can generate learning, not learning can be a consequence, too. As we have seen, "failure" is a prime source of learning, enabling experimenters quickly to sort what works from what doesn't; such efforts also stockpile knowledge—along with the bits and pieces (as we saw with IDEO and Edison)—available for future inspiration. Indeed, in the absence of learning from failure, because of experimental capacity constraints and/or the number of iterations possible, experimentation itself—its insufficiencies—ironically becomes a bottleneck to innovation.

To make more capacity available, essentially two choices are available: Either we change the fundamental economics of experimentation through new technologies and process innovations, or we must try to get more out of each experiment itself—make experiments more efficient. Statistical methods for designing experiments have focused primarily on the latter and have had a big impact on industrial R&D.[18] By manipulating multiple variables in a single experiment, while maintaining integrity in its statistical analysis, scientists and engineers have been able to get more learning out of their experiments than their professional peers were able to do a few hundred years earlier. However, even more structured methods cannot overcome all the limitations that scarce experimentation capacity poses.

Alternatively, new technologies that slash experimentation cost and time would not only bring much-needed capacity but could also make possible what-if experiments that, up to now, have been either prohibitively expensive or nearly impossible to run: What if an airplane, a car, a drug, or a business were designed in a particular way? Such technologies could potentially provide not only new knowledge about how nature works but they could also fundamentally change how the fruits of that design effort are harvested in innovations, process improvements, and ultimately, the new technologies themselves.

The Promise of New Experimentation Technologies

New technologies now enable more learning to be created more rapidly, and the results can be incorporated in even more experiments at less expense. In other words, information-based technologies drive down the marginal costs of experimentation just as they have decreased the marginal costs in many production and distribution systems. Moreover, an experimental system that integrates new information-based technologies effectively does more than lower costs; it also increases the opportunities for learning and innovation. Thus, some technologies can make existing experimental activities more efficient, while others introduce entirely new ways of discovering novel concepts and/or solutions.

Businesses that have benefited the most from these technologies—businesses in the pharmaceutical, automotive, and software industries in particular—have high product development costs. Examining how technologies influence experimentation in these industries lets us draw lessons that are applicable to other industries. As the cost of computing keeps falling, thereby making all sorts of complex calculations faster and cheaper, and as new technologies emerge, virtually all companies will discover that they have a greater capacity for rapid experimentation to investigate diverse product concepts. At the same time, deeper knowledge of the underlying phenomena has led to much better experimentation models, thus providing us with results that are closer to reality. Financial institutions, for example, now use computer simulations to test new financial instruments. In fact, the development of spreadsheet software itself has forever changed financial modeling; even novices can perform many sophisticated what-if experiments that were once prohibitively expensive.[19]

The remainder of this chapter surveys two important areas where advances in technology have dramatically decreased the marginal cost of experimentation: computer modeling and simulation, and combinatorial and high-throughput testing technologies. Understanding these technologies and their advances is important in itself. But the value of the understanding is intensified when we examine the technologies in action in a number of innovation settings. At the end of the chapter, we shall look at one company that is putting these technologies to work and discovering along the way that unlocking their potential requires a fundamental rethinking of how R&D is done. Put simply, not only do these technologies have the potential to dramatically raise development productivity, but they also require new ways of organizing and managing innovation processes.

Computer Modeling and Simulation

Without the knowledge that came from computer-based modeling and simulation, many scientific breakthroughs, products, and even services that we take for granted today simply would not exist.[20] Once the first prototype computer became operable around 1945 and Monte Carlo methods for numerical simulation had been introduced, computer-generated artificial worlds and experiments were essential to the development of the first hydrogen bomb and many scientific discoveries ever since.[21] The rapid emergence of the semiconductor industry then accelerated the trend toward low-cost "digital" experiments and the advancement of tools and methodologies. The steady decrease in computational cost, following Moore's Law, and the associated knowledge in modeling complex phenomena allowed for rapid increases in simulation capacity, whereas the design of integrated circuits themselves demanded tools and models for complex experiments that in turn benefited many other fields of engineering (figure 1-1).

At the same time, research organizations supported by the Department of Defense continued to advance their capacity for running computer-based simulation for applications such as missile design and

FIGURE 1 - 1

Advances in Problems Being Solved by Computer Simulation

The graph shows the growth of computer technology since 1955, including advances in average commercial performance and milestone events. Problems that are solvable in reasonable times at the indicated level of computer performance are shown in brackets. Approximate system prices are shown in dollars at the time.

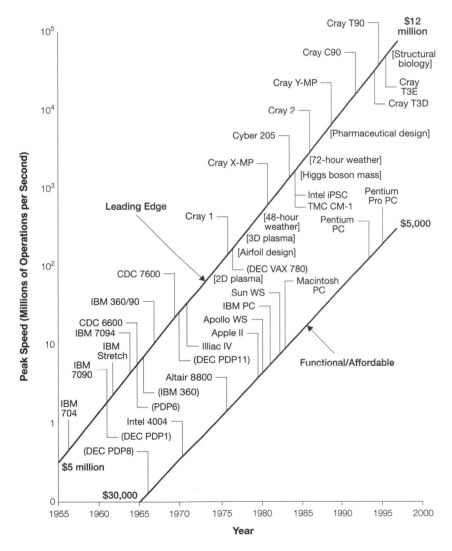

Source: Redrawn with modifications from A. Brenner, "The Computer Revolution and the Physics Community," *Physics Today* 46, 24–39, 1996.

warfare.[22] Today, the ability to run massive experiments via simulation has become critical in many fields, ranging from the sequencing and analysis of the human genome and the design of modern airplanes and automobiles to understanding the flow of fluids in the development of baby diapers. The potential impact that simulation and other experimentation technologies have had and will have in the future is limited only by imagination. Scientists and engineers are already joining forces to model regulatory mechanisms of genes and eventually entire cells, tissues, and organs in the human body. These simulation models will not only allow researchers to run experiments "in silico" faster and cheaper but will also make possible experiments that cannot be done today because of practical or ethical limitations.[23] Building the complex computer models necessary to run simulations will continue to advance our knowledge itself, perhaps in ways that we cannot anticipate today (box 1-1). Indeed, one area that has already benefited from simulation is crash safety, one of the most difficult problems in the development of new cars.

Car Crashes in Silicon

If you live in a developed country, chances are you ride in a car every day without thinking much about the risks. Several factors have made car travel safer since the mid-1980s: The inclusion of air bags and other design improvements in vehicles, the use of seat belts, and even the increasing maturity of the driving population have combined to lower the fatality rate on U.S. highways by nearly one third since 1987. Nevertheless, driving remains relatively risky. In the United States alone, accidents killed more than 42,000 and injured about 3 million people in 2001, according to the National Highway Traffic Safety Administration (NHTSA). In addition to this incalculable loss of life, there are enormous economic costs. In 1994, the NHTSA estimated that the annual cost of motor vehicle crashes exceeded a staggering $150 billion.

Cars that are better designed to protect their human occupants in crashes are a major reason the rate of fatalities is lower today than it was in the mid-1980s. Unfortunately, though, competitive pressures in the automobile industry are forcing most companies to spend less money and time developing new automobiles. As a result, when customers and

BOX 1-1: COMPUTER SIMULATION: HOW IT WORKS

Computer simulation involves representing experimental objects and experimental environments in digital form (via numerical models) and then simulating their interaction within a computer in a type of virtual experiment. For example, one might model an automobile and a crash barrier inside the computer, simulate the crash of the model car into the model barrier, and then calculate the effects of the crash on the structure of the car via finite element analysis. The results of this virtual experiment would then be assessed by viewing a visual representation of the "crashed" car on a video display and/or by looking at detailed calculations of the forces and accelerations generated during the simulated crash and their effects on the car's structure and passengers.

The ability to usefully substitute a simulation for a "real" experiment of course requires more than advanced computer equipment: It needs simulation models that are accurate for a given experimental purpose. A simulation model may not be fully accurate in ways that later turn out to matter, and when this is recognized, various combinations of virtual and physical experiments may be conducted to combat the source of error or to be certain that what happened virtually will translate into reality. Thus, auto designers supplement data gathered from virtual car crash experiments with information from real crash experiments using real cars to assure themselves that results of the virtual experiments also hold true in the real world. This automotive crash example illustrates some of the general advances in experimentation that modern computer simulation offers to many firms today.

For more information on how simulation works and its use in automotive safety, see S. Thomke, M. Holzner, and T. Gholami, "The Crash in the Machine," *Scientific American*, March 1999, 92–97.

governments alike are demanding safer cars, the budgets to design them are shrinking. An increased use of computer simulation helps auto manufacturers deal with this dilemma. Traditional crash tests—characterized by running heavily instrumented prototype cars into concrete barriers—are being replaced by "virtual" crashes: High-performance computers simulate collisions. Over the past ten years, tremendous

FIGURE 1 - 2

Advances in Crash Simulation

The cost and time to carry out crashworthiness experiments via computer simulation has decreased by orders of magnitude in twenty years.

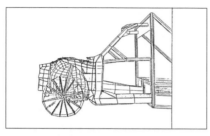

1982: Simulation model using CRASHMAS software (3,000 finite elements)

Run time nearly three months

No real significance in design decisions

2002: Simulation model of BMW X5 using PAMCRASH software (about 700,000 finite elements)

Run time less than thirty hours (at less than $10 per hour)

Drives important design decisions in automotive development

Source: Courtesy of BMW AG.

---

increases in computer speed and improved software models have advanced crash simulation to the point where results are trusted with a high degree of confidence (figure 1-2). The resulting surge in the use of computers is revolutionizing the way vehicles are designed.

Quicker and Cheaper Experiments

Consider how much time and money crash simulation saves. Traditional crash testing begins with building a prototype vehicle, which usually takes anywhere from four to six months and costs hundreds of thousands of dollars. The prototype is then outfitted with several crash-test dummies—costing around $65,000 apiece—that contain electronic sensors to record acceleration. Various instruments, including high-speed cameras, record the crash. However, glass and other debris from the crash itself frequently obstruct the view—and the dummies may accelerate through interior regions of the vehicle that are not covered by the cameras. As such, the postcrash films usually offer little to engineers hoping to improve the car's design (table 1-1).

TABLE 1 - 1

Contrasting Experimentation Strategies in Car Safety Design

Traditional Prototype Crashes	Crash Modeling and Simulation
Primarily design verification because of late and slow feedback	Learning and experimentation through early and fast feedback
Costly and time-consuming construction of each crash prototype	Cheap, fast generation of virtual prototypes after initial model is "built"
Destructive testing difficult to analyze	Simulation testing allows for careful and deep analysis
Experiments minimized because of high cost	Experiments maximized with diverse concepts
Experimental conditions limited to standard laboratory set up	Experimental conditions can be changed easily
Prototypes are closer to reality for some crashes	Models are approximations of reality and may be too complex for some tests
Interaction with humans more natural because it is physical	Requires better human-machine interfaces to maximize acceptance and learning

Actual differences between technologies vary and are intended for illustrative purposes only.

By contrast, a simulated test can be conceived, programmed on a computer, then carried out in days or weeks; the main expense is for the simulation engineers' salaries. Yes, the computers are typically either top-of-the-line workstations costing tens of thousands of dollars or supercomputers that cost millions. But unlike the crash-test prototype vehicles, the computers and their software and models are used over and over and sometimes have other applications within a company apart from verifying "crashworthiness." (See appendix 1-1 for a detailed description of how crash simulation works.) Perhaps most important, computer simulations let design engineers work in ways that would be otherwise impossible. In a relatively short period, for example, they can carry out a barrage of tests aimed at improving a structural piece—like one of the pillars connecting the car's roof to the chassis below the window—that affects the crashworthiness of the entire vehicle. They can replay a simulation as slowly as they like and zoom in on any structural element or even on a small piece of it to see how it reacts. Such capabilities not only generate a wealth of useful detail, they also enable engineers to learn and make the most of the expensive prototype collision tests. And some of their learning flows back into improved computer models, which are essential to making simulation experiments useful to designers. With a good set of simulated crashes, the development team can reduce the chances that an actual prototype crash test will go poorly and trigger another round of costly redesign and retesting.

Opportunities for Learning and Innovation

The power of simulation—beyond overall reduction of costs and increases in speed—comes from introducing a new capacity for innovation. A project at the German car company BMW (discussed in detail in chapter 6) illustrates this well. Initiated in 1995, it included a "simulation specialist," a test engineer, and several design engineers from different functional areas, who were attempting to develop technical concepts that would improve the side-impact safety for all BMW vehicles. The team set out to explore the potential of simulation (using the PAM-CRASH program—see appendix 1-1), and decided to limit prototype testing to only two crashes at the end to verify final design concepts.

An existing production model served as the project's starting point. After each simulation, the team met, analyzed results, and designed another experiment. As expected, the team enjoyed quick feedback, enabling the members to try out an idea and accept or reject it within days. The surprise was that as the trials began to accrue, the whole was more than the sum of the iterations; the group was increasing its fundamental understanding of the underlying mechanics.

A fruitful example involved the B pillar, one of six structural elements connecting the roof to the chassis below the windows (there are three pillars on each side of the car, labeled A, B, and C from front to back). By analyzing the records of prototype side-impact crashes from earlier development projects, engineers on the team had learned that in crash after crash, a small section of the B pillar folded. And when a pillar buckled, its use as a barrier was compromised and the probability of injury to passengers rose.

Although the engineers assumed that adding metal would strengthen the bottom of the pillar, making the car more resistant to penetration from the side, no one felt it necessary to test the assumption. One development team member, however, insisted on verification, pointing out that it would be neither difficult nor expensive to do this via computer simulation. When the program was run, the group was shocked to discover that strengthening the folded area actually decreased crashworthiness. But what caused that phenomenon? After more iterations and careful analysis, they found out. Reinforcing the lower part of the B pillar made the part higher up—above the reinforced part—prone to buckling. So the passenger compartment would be more vulnerable to being penetrated higher up—closer to passengers' midsections, chests, and heads. As such, the solution to the folding–B-pillar problem turned out to be completely counterintuitive: Weaken it rather than reinforce it. Equipped with that knowledge, the group reevaluated all the reinforced areas in the bodies of all BMW vehicles then in production or under development. The project improved to varying degrees the crashworthiness of all those automobiles.

When the team finished its work, it had carried out ninety-one virtual accidents and two prototype crashes in about a year. For the developmental vehicles that were redesigned, side-impact crashworthiness advanced an average of 30 percent over the initial design, measured in various ways, for example, calculating and comparing simulated and dummy acceleration in both virtual and real crashes. Significantly, the two prototype crashes at the end of the project strongly confirmed the simulation results and also the economics of testing: At a total of about $300,000, the two prototypes cost more to build, prepare, and test than did the entire series of ninety-one virtual crashes. But to obtain the full benefits of simulation technologies, BMW had to undertake sweeping changes in process, organization, and attitudes—changes that took long to accomplish and will be discussed in chapters 5 and 6.

Limits to Simulation

As is evident, computer simulations, despite their cost advantages and flexibility and their growing share of the design and development process, complement rather than completely replace traditional crash tests for the foreseeable future. For one thing, government traffic safety agencies in most developed countries still require data from traditional tests. In the United States, the NHTSA works with other organizations to develop safety regulations that carmakers must meet in order to sell vehicles. In Europe the specific regulations are somewhat different, but the legislative process is similar. For another thing, despite steady increases in knowledge about crash dynamics and computer processing power that let programmers achieve a remarkable level of accuracy and detail, simulations have inherent limitations.

Significantly, the questions that simulation can answer today are limited by the range of phenomena that can be modeled. So it is difficult to simulate and predict the outcome of rollover accidents, for instance. A rollover can take a full three seconds, as opposed to 100 to 150 milliseconds for a more typical smashup, and simulating that much time requires prodigious computer power. The behavior of a car in a rollover can also be difficult to predict, because it depends on road friction and other factors external to the car. It is also essentially impossible to use computers to discover whether any parts of the car will present a fire hazard in an accident—for example, whether a fuel tank is likely to explode.

Advances in Rapid Prototyping and Combinatorial Technologies

While computer modeling and simulation have the potential to fundamentally revolutionize innovation, there have been parallel advances in the physical world that will complement the power of simulation.[24] According to Peter Schultz, director of the Genomics Institute of the Norvartis Research Foundation and a professor at the Scripps Research Institute in La Jolla, California,

> The [other] revolution that has occurred during the last 10 years in the biological and physical sciences is the way in which we carry out experimental science. There has been a tremendous increase in our ability to design, implement and analyze experiments—to carry them out not one at a time but thousands or millions at a time. That has made been made possible by combinatorial technologies, computational tools and advances in engineering and miniaturization—the kind of tools and processes that revolutionized the semiconductor industry are being moved over into the biological and physical sciences.[25]

All these combinatorial technologies have dramatically reduced the cost and time of generating physical artifacts of an idea or concept (prototypes), thus allowing for many combinations to be generated over a short period of time. Developers use these rapid prototyping technologies to quickly generate an inexpensive, easy-to-modify prototype that can be tested against the actual use environment, allowing for experimentation under real—as opposed to virtual—conditions. Such technologies can be found in areas ranging from mechanical designs to the design of integrated circuits (see chapter 2 for a detailed discussion). Rapid prototyping, therefore, is usually an inexpensive and fast way to build models that preserve the advantages of working in the physical world and thus overcome any limitations that simulation may have. Thus, a high-quality prototype of a connector that links computers to external devices like scanners or printers can be "plugged" into a real system, generating immediate feedback from customers. Uncertainty about technical and customer needs can be resolved quickly via a process of iterative trial and error experimentation.

A case in point is stereolithography, a technology that allows companies to create three-dimensional plastic objects from CAD drawings in a matter of hours, thus providing a quick and cheap way to turn design concepts into real and testable objects. In the past, it could take weeks or months and possibly tens or hundreds of thousands of dollars to prototype a high-quality plastics part because injection molding has been optimized for low-variable production cost but requires the high fixed cost of building the necessary tooling. Similarly, three-dimensional printing technology developed at MIT allows for the rapid production of physical prototype parts of any geometry, out of any material, including ceramics, metals, polymers, and composites.[26] Taken together, these technologies allow for more rapid and low-cost experimentation and thus are already having an impact on how new products are developed.

Perhaps some of the most important changes are occurring in the discovery of new drugs where the cost and time of generating some drug candidate and its related testing have dropped by orders of magnitude. Instead of painstakingly creating compound "prototypes" of a drug one at a time, combinatorial chemistry and high-throughput screening methods now allow drug developers to quickly generate numerous variations simultaneously and screen them at a small cost fraction of traditional tests, which were slow and fraught with logistical difficulties, high expense, and statistical variation. However, to fully understand the opportunities that these combinatorial technologies may eventually provide, we need to take a closer look at how drugs are developed.

Drug Discovery Challenges Faced by Pharmaceutical Firms

If dramatic changes in the economics of experimentation are important to any firm, they are compelling to those in the pharmaceutical industry. In fact, new technologies, methods, and breakthroughs such as the sequencing of the human genome offer companies the potential to transform how drugs are developed. At the same time, finding new drugs to cure or ameliorate increasingly complex diseases ranging from cancer to heart disease is becoming more costly while public pressure to control prices is mounting.

A widely cited study of pharmaceutical drugs developed between 1972 and 1987 found that the expected capitalized development cost per marketed drug was on average $230.8 million (1987), with total development times well above ten years. Various other studies have shown a trend that has caused much concern in the pharmaceutical industry: The cost and time of new drug development have increased significantly, reaching about $800 million in a recently released study by the Tufts Center for the Study of Drug Development, primarily due to increases in the costs of running expensive clinical trials.[27] Besides the impact of lower R&D productivity on firm cost and profitability, longer development times have also raised important public policy concerns. As the industry remains the dominant provider of life-saving and life-prolonging medicines, it is in the public interest to have promising new drugs available to patients as quickly as possible.

To appreciate the problems pharmaceutical companies face, we need a brief understanding of drug development itself. In the late nineteenth century and for much of the twentieth century, drug development occurred through a process of systematic trial-and-error experiments. Scientists would start with little or no knowledge about a particular disease and try out numerous candidate molecules, many from their company's chemical libraries, until they found one that happened to work. Drugs can be likened to keys that need to fit the locks of targets, such as the specific nerve cell receptors associated with central nervous diseases. Metaphorically, then, chemists were once blind or at least semiblind locksmiths who had to make up thousands of different keys to find the one that matched. Doing so entailed synthesizing compounds one at a time, each of which usually required several days at a cost from $5,000 to $10,000.

The three-phase drug development and approval process begins with a so-called preclinical research phase devoted to the discovery and optimization of one or a few "lead" chemical compounds that appear to hold sufficient promise as drugs to merit investment in clinical testing (see appendix 1-2). The second phase, clinical development, typically comprises three clinical stages that determine and document the safety and efficacy of the proposed drugs. The final phase involves regulatory New Drug Approval (NDA) review processes of the clinical trial outcome. Typically, for each successful drug that makes it to market, a firm investigates roughly 10,000 starting candidates. Of those, only 1,000 compounds make it to more extensive trials in vitro (outside living organisms in settings such as test tubes), of which twenty are then tested even more extensively in vivo (in the body of a living organism such as a mouse), of which less than ten make it to clinical trials with humans. The entire process represents a long and costly commitment.

Addressing the Experimentation Bottleneck

In the late 1980s, leading pharmaceutical firms could test and analyze perhaps twenty chemical compounds per week against a disease target. As the synthesis of compound prototypes was very costly and time-consuming, the rate of twenty per week was perhaps sufficient to test promising newly generated drug candidates, but it was hardly enough to tap into the large libraries of older but potentially valuable chemicals. In other words, the cost of generating and testing new drug candidates, combined with the limited capacity to search through precious compound libraries, represented a serious bottleneck to drug discovery. At that same time, the average U.S. pharmaceutical company synthesized and evaluated roughly 6,000 chemical compounds for each

BOX 1-2: WHAT ARE COMBINATORIAL CHEMISTRY METHODS?

Combinatorial chemistry methods and technologies consist of several new chemical synthesis strategies for the efficient and fast generation of a large number of related chemical compounds. This large number of chemical compounds, also called compound libraries, is subsequently used in pharmaceutical drug screening projects. The term "combinatorial" originates from chemical synthesis methods applied to most of these libraries. In 1998, combinatorial chemistry was recognized by the influential journal *Science* as one of ten discoveries that transformed our ideas about the natural world and also offered potential benefits to society.[28]

Following is a brief description of some process technologies that enable a large number of parallel experiments to be generated quickly and at low cost:

- BIOCHIP LIBRARIES: Photolithographic synthesis methods are used for the creation of compound libraries on the surface of a silicon chip. Thousands of individual compounds can be synthesized on a silicon chip with little more than one square centimeter surface area.

- SOLUTION LIBRARIES: Mixtures of compounds react chemically in a carefully designed system to form solution libraries with tens to thousands of different compounds within a few hours.

successful drug that made it to the market—a number well below the average library size of up to 150,000 discrete chemical compounds that large firms possessed around the same time.[29]

In the last ten years, new technologies have significantly increased the efficiency and speed at which companies can generate and screen chemical compounds. Using combinatorial technologies known as combinatorial chemistry ("combichem"), researchers no longer need to painstakingly create one compound at a time (box 1-2). Instead, they can quickly generate numerous variations simultaneously around a few promising lead compounds, just as locksmiths can make thousands of

- RAPID PARALLEL SYNTHESIS LIBRARIES: Robotic equipment is custom-tailored to dispense chemicals into individual reaction chambers, carry out many individual chemical reactions in parallel, and extract and purify the reaction products automatically. Although this process is significantly slower than the other three technologies, it results in individually purified compounds at quantities sufficiently large for elaborate second-round screening. (The other methods may require chemical resynthesis, which can cause a small but significant time delay.)
- SOLID SUPPORT LIBRARIES: Compounds are synthesized on the surface of polymer beads. This method allows the chemist to attach a certain type of molecule to the beads and split and mix the pool of beads to continue with different synthesis steps. As opposed to parallel synthesis, in which each compound remains in one container, this method produces a mixture of related compounds in each vessel. The result is a reduction in containers and a rapid increase in the number of generated compounds, easily exceeding millions, but also the problem of identifying, tracking, and testing these compounds.

For additional information on combinatorial chemistry methods, see M. Plunkert and J. Ellman, "Combinatorial Chemistry and New Drugs," *Scientific American*, April 1997, 68–73.

keys from a dozen basic shapes, thereby reducing the cost of a compound from thousands of dollars to a few dollars or less (table 1-2).

In practice, however, combichem methods have disrupted well-established routines in laboratories. For one thing, the rapid synthesis of drug candidates has led to a new problem: how to screen those compounds quickly. Traditionally, potential drugs were tested in live animals—an activity fraught with logistical difficulties, high expense, and considerable statistical variation.

So laboratories developed test-tube-based screening methodologies that could then be automated. This technology, called high-throughput

TABLE 1 - 2

Contrasting Experimentation Strategies in Drug Discovery

Traditional (Medicinal) Chemistry and Testing	Combinatorial Chemistry and High-Throughput Screening
Primarily sequential experimentation with few compounds per round	Primarily parallel experimentation with many compounds per round
Costly, slow generation of "prototype" compounds	Cheap, fast generation of "prototype" compounds
Small testing capacity	Large testing capacity through automated screening
High "solution" diversity through proven compounds in chemical libraries	Limited "solution" diversity but expected to grow in the future
Nearly perfect chemical purity and thus high confidence in results	Lower chemical purity and thus less reliable results
Focus on the craft of perfection	Focus on the science of production
Bottleneck is generating and testing new compounds	Bottleneck is ability to process and understand massive amounts of data

Actual differences between technologies vary and are intended for illustrative purposes only.

screening, has required significant innovations in equipment (high-speed precision robotics, for one) and in the screening process itself to let researchers conduct a series of biological tests, or assays, on members of a chemical library virtually simultaneously. At the same time, these high-throughput screening technologies have also enabled firms to test their entire chemical libraries for promising new leads, thus tapping into knowledge and information that has been accumulated over decades from other projects in the form of diverse chemicals. Moreover, the availability of new experimentation technologies is challenging the traditional structure of drug discovery. A fundamental challenge is that many discovery activities will be done in parallel, thus requiring companies to rethink how information is managed and integrated across groups and process steps.

Because of the radically different economics and speed of generating and testing drug "prototypes," most large companies have entered strategic alliances to gain access to these new technologies. The indica-

FIGURE 1 - 3

Emergence of Combinatorial Chemistry and High-Throughput Screening

The number of scientific publications and technology alliances between companies involving combinatorial chemistry and high-throughput screening rose rapidly in the 1990s.

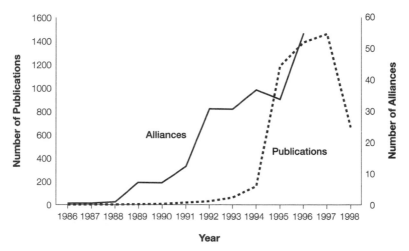

Source: Data from S. Thomke and W. Kuemmerle, "Asset Accumulation, Interdependence and Technological Change: Evidence from Pharmaceutical Drug Discovery," *Strategic Management Journal* 23, no. 7 (2002).

tions are not only a rapid rise of publications but also an increase in alliance activity involving access to combinatorial chemistry and high-throughput screening (figure 1-3).

Complementing New and Traditional Technologies

Similar to crash simulation, combinatorial chemistry will complement rather than completely replace traditional chemistry in the immediate future. For one, the purity and diversity of compounds generated via combichem have been lower when compared to traditional synthetic chemistry, and most applications so far have focused on the optimization rather than generation of promising drug candidates. But if future combinatorial chemistry achieves levels of purity and diversity comparable to the compounds in a library, companies will increasingly try to use it during earlier phases of drug discovery. In fact, all major pharmaceutical companies are using combichem and traditional synthesis in concert with other technologies, and the companies that are best able to manage the new and mature technologies together so that they fully complement each other have the greatest opportunity to achieve the highest gains in productivity and innovation.

Moreover, new methods utilizing such scientific advances as X-ray crystallography and/or nuclear-magnetic resonance (NMR) spectroscopy to determine the three-dimensional shape of a receptor or an enzyme via computer-aided modeling and simulation will also continue to be a significant factor in determining the best experimental space in the search for a new drug. Developers would enter the structure of this receptor into a computer software package containing information on the configuration and strengths of the chemical bonds that could form between atoms. This software would then allow the developers to use simulation to design drug molecules that bind properly to the target receptor. Chemists in the laboratory would then create real molecules, as specified by the computer modeling exercise, to be tested for the desired pharmaceutical effect. However, molecular modeling of a drug requires very accurate data on the structure of the target receptor, and the required degree of accuracy is often very difficult for researchers to attain using present-day methods. Moreover, some real-world mechanisms (i.e., what happens when the target receptor changes as a result of a drug inserted into its "binding pocket") are simply too complex to be modeled by current-day simulation tools. As a consequence, computer-based molecular modeling exercises need to be complemented with many experiments involving "real" drug candidates such as the ones generated by combichem and synthetic chemistry.

Not only do the technologies described here suggest radically different ways of discovering drugs, they have already led to firms whose business is developing the technology itself. Such firms then build alliances with other companies to sell their technology to larger partners or may become integrated pharmaceutical companies themselves. One example is Millennium Pharmaceuticals, founded in 1993. To close this chapter we shall look at how the company has tried to leverage a platform of different experimentation technologies for the development of new drugs. Along the way, however, Millennium's senior management had to fundamentally rethink the way they organize and manage the drug discovery process. How this is done will be discussed in chapters 5 through 7.

Technology Platforms for Experimentation

The combination of new and traditional experimentation technologies and methods allows for the creation of so-called technology platforms, which makes the whole much greater than the proverbial sum of its parts. If carefully optimized and deployed, technology platforms can raise the promise of R&D to entirely new levels, as the experience of several companies has shown (see chapter 2 for evidence from the semiconductor industry).

One company, Millennium Pharmaceuticals in Cambridge, Massachusetts, was started in 1993 with $8.5 million in venture capital funding and a vision to build a technology platform that would marry molecular biology with automation and informatics. Along with major drug companies such as Eli Lilly, Merck, and Pfizer, Millennium would harvest findings emerging from the Human Genome Project, an ambitious international effort to identify and map every bit of human DNA (which in its entirety is termed the "genome").[30] These findings would allow for discovering and processing huge amounts of information about genes, making thousands of new drug targets possible. A dramatic increase in targets would also require quicker screening technologies in order to test many more compounds, which would be generated by new combinatorial methods. Proprietary lab technology included software for analyzing gene function and machines that decode DNA sequences. Remarking on the background of Millennium's founder, Mark Levin, as a chemical engineer, *The Economist* noted:

> *Whereas biologists tend to see biotech as the search for a compound, Mr. Levin thinks of it as a complex production process. While they concentrate on the bio, he also thinks hard about the technology. Mr. Levin focuses on trying to make each link in the discovery chain as efficient as possible. . . . He has assembled an impressive array of technologies—including robotics and information systems as well as molecular biology. He then enhances them and links them together in*

novel ways to create what the engineer in him likes to call "technology platforms," [which] should help drug searchers to travel rapidly on their long and tortuous journey from gene to treatment. And Mr. Levin is prepared—keen, even—to use or buy other people's technology to help in the struggle to keep up to date. One observer has called him the "Mao Zedong" of biotech, a believer in continuous revolution in both technology and organization.[31]

New technologies promised a shortcut for finding cures for human genetic diseases. It allowed for skirting the traditional time-consuming study of family trees of diseased individuals in order to track down the responsible genes. Since these genes could be anywhere along the vast expanse of human DNA, some firms tried to take advantage of rulings that allowed for filing patents on naturally occurring gene sequences as fast as they could find them.

"The important thing is to get California instead of Appalachia" in this pharmaceutical land grab, according to former Millennium executive John Maraganore. To find these prime pieces of genetic real estate, researchers analyzed hundreds of gene sequences simultaneously using miniature "DNA probes" that could ferret out promising stretches of DNA. These probes were derived through research on samples from people suffering from diseases of particular interest.

The pharmaceutical industry's genomics-based approach reversed the traditional process by first identifying and understanding the role of genes implicated in causing a disease. This should allow for selecting drug candidates based on their ability to intervene in disease initiation and progression—thus targeting the genetic root of illness. The industry's challenge, however, was not just designing integrated technology platforms but also addressing the dramatic changes required for organizing and managing the science of discovery. Commenting on the impact on experimentation and knowledge creation, Edward Scolnick, president of Merck Research Laboratories, noted:

In traditional biology, you start with a hypothesis about how a specific biological process works. You then do an experiment to collect data to test your hypotheses. You essentially try to understand a system by building up your knowledge one component at a time. The difficult part was in understanding how one biological process might be related to another. Genomics essentially turns the process on its head. We can now measure the expression of 10,000 genes all at once and use software algorithms to sort through the data to identify what's related to what. This is referred to as "systems biology." The problem is that nobody is trained in this stuff. And it takes an entirely different mind-set and skill set than how we have traditionally done basic research.[32]

Creating such a new mind-set and rethinking how drugs could be developed with new experimentation technologies has been fundamental to Millennium's strategy from its beginning.

Rethinking Product Development from the Ground Up

In 1997, Levin hired Michael Pavia, a pioneer in combinatorial chemistry, as chief technology officer with the charter to fundamentally rethink how new drugs could be discovered. As Pavia translated his charter for industrializing the drug discovery process, "the only way to achieve such an aggressive goal is to question everything and to hire people that challenge assumptions held by the industry for decades."[33] He knew from the beginning that even the best technology by itself would not be sufficient to reach the company's goals.

Millennium was by no means the only company thinking along these bold lines. Most large pharmaceutical firms had initiatives under way to shorten the development cycle significantly and make drug development more predictable. Current practice seemed unsustainable. Pharmaceutical firms would bring several successful drugs to market each year and bear the cost of failure in the very long and expensive clinical phase where only one out of ten drug candidates would make it to the market.

To fundamentally rethink drug development, Millennium, along with other companies, aggressively approached its task using the following approaches: Speed up individual experiments, including rapid feedback on critical tests such as toxicology; carry out serial experiments in parallel whenever possible; front-load drug failure modes through the use of new technologies.

Speed Up Individual Experiments

For the early research phase of drug discovery, scientists and engineers sought to speed up the various steps involved in isolating, characterizing, and understanding DNA. By drawing on automation experts and engineers with manufacturing experience, Millennium sought to automate truly complex process steps and create an industrial R&D "factory," using robots and other equipment often used in advanced production of other products. To achieve these goals, engineers opportunistically outsourced and modified emerging technologies, often creating machines envied even by leading universities. Like other companies, Millennium also planned to use combinatorial chemistry and high-throughput screening to reduce the time required in the laborious traditional random search process for drug candidates. Interestingly, no matter how much each step was sped up, however, a crucial bottleneck in the entire R&D process remained: the difficulty of assimilating and making sense of the staggering amount of information made available. To address this problem, an increased focus on the rapidly growing field of bioinformatics was essential for the company.

Carry Out Sequential Experiments in Parallel Whenever Possible

Early in 1999, the company established a group that reviewed the entire drug development process, using basic principles of operations management, for ways to compress the drug development timeline by allowing more experiments to be conducted in parallel. This shift in thinking could save considerable time during drug discovery when drug developers evaluated each candidate compound for target validity, organ-specificity (i.e., was the target specific to the organ of interest), bioavailability (i.e., would the compound be absorbed appropriately by the body), and toxicity. Rather than addressing each of these issues one by one in the traditional sequential fashion, Millennium decided it would seek to do a series of several "quick and dirty" tests on minute quantities of each candidate compound in a fairly simultaneous fashion to see if a candidate was even in the ballpark. This task was analogous to prescreening job candidates over the telephone in parallel so that only a smaller batch of higher-yield candidates would be invited in for in-depth interviews.

Find New Technologies That Could Front-Load the Downstream Failure of Drug Candidates

In the late 1990s, between one and two out of ten drug candidates typically made it through clinical development—by far the costliest phase of drug development. Senior management wanted to improve these odds significantly. Its staff sought to diminish this wastage by try-ing to find the potential failure modes through, for instance, prescreen-ing drug candidates, as discussed. Gaining information about, say, the toxicological profile of a drug early on could significantly improve the predictability of its likely success. Management also decided that it would systematically seek to use other failed drug candidates to see if new technologies could indeed pick up these "failures" earlier. This included the scouring of conventions and trade fairs for cutting-edge technologies that would provide earlier feedback on candidate drugs. The point was not necessarily to avoid failure but to shift failures ("attrition") to earlier phases in the process.

Thus, in terms of reducing the product development cycle, much potential for technological improvement existed alongside the uncer-tainties inherent in all drug development projects. Like most of the major pharmaceutical firms aiming to shorten the drug development cycle, Millennium realized it would have to focus on many, if not all, links in the drug development process. Focusing on just early drug development through combinatorial chemistry and high-throughput screening, for instance, could save an estimated half-year to year. Thus, downstream phases would also need to be shortened. These downstream changes could be achieved through administrative as well as technologi-cal changes. For instance, reviewing toxicology data as they were gener-ated might compress the traditional nine-month cycle for a toxicology review into as little as a month. Millennium's Levin described the chal-lenges and potential of new experimentation technologies:

> [C]ompanies must find new ways to make the entire drug develop-ment process—finding and testing leads—much faster and more

cost-effective. That's what our R&D technology can do. We've already dramatically accelerated the process of identifying leads. It wasn't too long ago that a scientist might spend half a year working on just one lead. She'd sit at a bench, do a few experiments, and report the results six months later. But thanks to our technology, our scientists can spend their time designing automated experiments and analyzing results rather than carrying out the experiments manually. Indeed, if you go into any Millennium-run laboratory, you're not going to see a lot of scientists at work because the process has become so automated that most of the actual experimentation is carried out by robots. One scientist can now look at dozens of experiments in the space of a week rather than just the one she did.[34]

Millennium Pharmaceuticals is one example of how new technology platforms for experimentation can form the basis for fundamentally rethinking innovation processes. Throughout its young history, the company has reinvented itself multiple times to take advantage of the constant change and upheavals in the pharmaceutical industry. How much it will participate and succeed in downstream drug development remains to be seen, but their technology platform and its role in re-thinking drug development will remain an integral part of Millennium's strategy.

Conclusion

A company's ability to innovate depends in part on a process of experimentation in which new products and services are created and new ones are improved. Traditionally, the high cost of experimentation has limited innovation. Statistical methods for designing experiments have helped companies to get more out of each experiment, making them more efficient. Alternatively, new technologies such as computer simulation and modeling are lifting the cost constraint by changing the economics of experimentation. These technologies are not only slashing cost and time to free up testing capacity but also making possible what-if experiments that have been either prohibitively expensive or nearly impossible to carry out. They amplify the impact of learning, thus creating the potential for higher R&D performance and breakthrough products.

To unlock the potential, however, managers must not only understand the power of new technologies for experimentation but also how they impact the processes, organization, and management of innovation. Significantly, Millennium was entirely dedicated to this endeavor from the outset; it never has had to experience the very difficult organizational challenge of moving from one innovation system to another—a challenge that established companies face as they are trying to integrate the same experimentation technologies. Just how difficult such a revolution can be will be taken up in chapter 4. Before we look at these difficulties, however, we shall learn how one industry (integrated circuits) has been and continues to be transformed by new experimentation technologies (chapter 2), followed by what good experimentation entails regardless of the technologies involved (chapter 3). By understanding what has worked in integrated circuits and the underlying principles of how to maximize learning from experimentation, we are better prepared to look at how it can go awry and to understand how to make it work for companies (chapters 5 and 6).

APPENDIX 1-1

How Crash Simulation Works

To understand how designers use crash data to make cars safer requires some knowledge of the physics of collisions.[35] An automobile accident is basically a transformation of energy from the kinetic energy of the moving vehicles to the energy used in deforming the bodies of the driver and passengers during the crash. The single most influential characteristic is the vehicle's speed at impact, because the absorbed crash energy goes up with the square of velocity (a crash at 90 kilometers per hour is four times more energetic than a crash at 45 kilometers per hour).

Weight is another key factor. Although weight is a disadvantage in a single-vehicle crash, it can be a plus in a multivehicle accident. When heavy and light vehicles collide, passengers in the heavy ones generally fare better—unless the light vehicles are built with stiffer materials, relative to the heavy cars, in key impact areas. In fact, this issue points to an unfortunate situation: government-mandated prototype crash tests require crashworthiness to be evaluated in isolation, despite the fact that about 60 percent of all fatal crashes involve two or more vehicles. If automakers had to minimize the damage to all the vehicles in a crash—for example, by balancing weight and stiffness—sport utility and other relatively heavy passenger vehicles would be built with materials that were somewhat pliant. Indeed, a few automakers are just now starting to incorporate this principle into their designs.

Basically, all injuries that occur in an accident can be traced to one of two causes: the human body's collision with objects—the steering wheel, for one—resulting in external injuries such as bruises or punctures or the body's sudden acceleration during the crash, which causes injuries inside the body such as bone fractures and organ ruptures accompanied by internal bleeding. In a prototype crash test, sensors in the dummies record peak acceleration; a lower acceleration indicates better crash-worthiness and thus a lower probability of death or severe injury.

The acceleration comes from momentum, which the vehicle and whatever it hits transfer to each other in a collision. For safety purposes, one of the most significant factors is the rate at which the momentum is transferred to the vehicle. This factor in turn depends on many variables; in the vehicle, material strength and stiffness, structural supports, the position of the engine, and the rigidity of the steering wheel column—to name a few of many design parameters—can all influence the degree to which a collision causes injury.

The computer programs that model all these parameters are based on an algorithmic technique known as finite element analysis. With this method, programmers represent each piece of the structure as a group of finite elements; each element is a polygon that has an associated mathematical description of its physical and material properties, such as stiffness and tensile strength. For a crash test, the complete model generally consists of several components: the body of the vehicle, the seats, the engine, and the passengers. Each component is further broken down. The vehicle, for example, consists of door panels, windows, pillars, struts, and other parts; programmers represent each part as a group of finite elements.

The more finite elements in the model, the more closely it simulates reality. Currently engineers use high-end workstations or supercomputers, which are powerful enough to simulate a vehicle model with 200,000 to 300,000 finite elements. The seats, engine, and passengers can add another 100,000 to 200,000 polygons. Limitations in computer power have forced programmers to model the passengers as rigid, jointed figures, much like crash dummies; this is still the industry's standard practice. But higher computing speeds are finally enabling some university researchers to simulate occupants with more realistic features, such as soft tissue and bones. The work is important because as computers continue to become more powerful, it will only be a matter of time before simulation engineers can compute the acceleration of specific organs in the body during a crash. This capability would be another significant advantage for computer-based simulations, because although crash-test dummies have embedded accelerometers, these sensors merely measure the increase in speed of parts of the dummy. They cannot predict how a specific organ suspended in the body, a largely fluid medium, will move.

To generate the many thousands of finite elements in a model, engineers use data from the computer-aided design programs that are created early in the development process. Then they associate with each element the physical properties (mass, density, stiffness, and so on) and contact conditions relative to the elements that surround it. As they connect the elements to create a model, including the passenger modules, engineers fine-tune it, making sure that the mass distribution and the resulting center of gravity represent reality as closely as possible. The finished model is a complex piece of software that computes how kinetic energy is transformed into deformations, acceleration forces, and other parameters during a collision.

Before a simulation, engineers create the crash conditions by setting the velocities, just before impact, for the vehicle and whatever it hits. On impact, the kinetic energy is converted into deformation energy according to the laws of Newtonian physics. Calculating the conversion from kinetic to deformation involves representing the movement within and between the many finite elements, using simple relations. In effect, the programs sum the forces over all the elements, which results in a system of equations that is solved using various mathematical and numerical methods. The stress within the elements is determined using standard principles of material behavior. The simulation is time-dependent, meaning that the system of equations is solved over and over again, each time updating the position and stress levels of every element. Each new iteration takes as its initial conditions the results of the previous iteration. The conversion goes on, iteration after iteration, until there is no more kinetic energy left to convert—or, in other words, until all moving pieces have come to rest.

During the simulation, programmers can determine the velocities and deformations at the vertices of the finite element polygons. They can then use these values to determine the stress to which each finite element is subjected. For the passenger components of the model (the "software dummies"), they measure accelerations, movements, and forces rather than levels of stress. The three major simulation programs used by auto firms today are PAMCRASH, LS-DYNA3D, and RADIOSS. All three are based on programs that were developed in the late 1960s for military purposes in the United States. They all work on the finite element principles just outlined and differ from one another subtly in the assortment of materials they can easily simulate, the way they handle the simulated surfaces that come into "contact" with one another in the collision, and the software support they provide during model-building (preprocessing) and crash-analysis (postprocessing) phases.

APPENDIX 1-2

How Drug Discovery Works

The following simple explanation describes a process that is in reality very complex and possibly poses one of the most difficult R&D problems of our day.[36] Drugs achieve their effect by binding with very specific molecular receptors or enzymes or biologically important molecules that are present in the human body or on/in disease-causing agents such as bacteria, fungi, and viruses. The goal of drug discovery or drug design is therefore to discover or create a molecule that will in fact bind to a particular, say, receptor with a required degree of tenacity (binding affinity) and that will at the same time not bind to other receptors that may be structurally similar but have different functions.

The drug discovery process can involve either or a combination of two basic approaches: (1) One can start with little or no knowledge about the structure of a disease target (receptor, enzyme, molecule) associated with a particular disease and simply try out many candidate molecules until one finds one that happens to bind properly with the target receptor. (2) One can strive to determine the structure of the relevant receptor with biophysical methods and then attempt to design or select a molecule that will bind to it.

Until the 1970s, methods of drug discovery necessarily relied on the first of the two approaches because the technical ability to determine the molecular structure of a protein receptor did not yet exist. Researchers at early pharmaceutical firms (often subsidiaries of chemical manufacturing firms) implemented this approach by setting up a systematic trial-and-error drug discovery system known as the mass screening system, which is still used today.

The mass screening system begins with the selection or design of a "screen"—for example, a disease-causing bacterium or an isolated receptor that is known to be associated with the disease under study. "Masses" of chemical compounds are then applied to this screen (one at a time) with the goal of identifying compounds that cause the screen to display a desired effect (e.g., killing of the disease-causing bacterium or evidence of binding to the receptor).

Traditionally, there have been two different sources of input materials to the discovery process. The first source is proprietary archival libraries of known chemical compounds that have been collected by chemical and pharmaceutical firms over the years. A given major firm might have an archival library of perhaps a few hundred thousand known compounds. The second source is extracts of plants, microorganisms and animals, each of which may contain perhaps up to 100,000 unknown chemical compounds.

The screening process proceeds differently depending on which type of input is used. In the case of archival libraries, the known compounds are tested against the disease target screen one by one, and the effect of each compound on the screen is observed. In the case of natural extracts, the entire extract is tested against the screen. If a desired effect is observed, the compound responsible for that effect must then be isolated via a complex series of fractionations and retestings.

As an illustration for the natural compound process, consider the development of antibiotics based on "magainins," natural antimicrobial compounds named after the Hebrew word "magain" meaning shield. When researchers noticed that frogs living in bacteria-contaminated water did not appear to get skin infections, they suspected that a new and useful antibiotic compound in a frog's skin might be involved. To identify it, they began by grinding up frog skin and subjecting the whole mixture—consisting of literally hundreds of thousands of different compounds—to mass screening tests for antibiotic activity. When the tests indicated antibiotic activity, the researchers next had to identify which compound(s) in the complex mixture was (were) the source of the activity. They did so by biochemically separating the compounds found in frog skin into fractions, followed by a test of each fraction for the presence of antibiotic activity. The active fraction was then subjected to further cycles of fractionation and test until finally the active compound was isolated.

When an active compound is finally identified via screening, it generally does not meet all the criteria required to make it a lead candidate for a new drug. For example, it may display the needed medical effect very powerfully, but at the same time it may display unacceptable side effects, such as toxicity or mutagenic effects in animals, or it may not become available in the bloodstream after ingestion or injection. Therefore, the lead optimization process in the drug discovery process is to create and test a number of variations ("analogs") of the originally identified molecule in order to find one or more that appear to have all the attributes needed for a successful new drug. One lead compound is then advanced into the clinical development phase where its effects are tested on humans.

To create analogs to the original compound, medicinal chemists (specialized organic chemists employed by pharmaceutical firms) maintain the basic structure of the compound but add, exchange, or remove chemical groups from it. On average, it has taken seven to ten days and approximately $5,000 to $10,000 to synthesize one such analog and many thousands are needed before a drug can be tested on humans. According to the Centre for Medicines Research, the average American pharmaceutical company synthesized approximately 6,100 chemical compounds for each successful drug that made it to the market—a number well below the average library size of 150,000 discrete chemical compounds that large firms possessed in 1992.[37]

The reason it is necessary to develop so many potential solutions to the receptor problem is that many drugs must be precisely tailored to discriminate sharply between very similar receptors. For example, researchers working to develop a drug for Alzheimer's disease are targeting a particular muscarinic receptor located in the brain. However, five subtypes to this muscarinic receptor are known to exist in the gut and elsewhere, and the desired drug must not affect them. Compounds displaying the needed selectivity can be very difficult to find without extensive analoging.

NOTES

1. "Productivity" and "efficiency" are often used imprecisely. They are, in fact, two sides of the same coin. Productivity refers to the output per unit of effort, while efficiency measures the use of inputs (e.g., time, money, resources) dedicated to that effort. As such, efficiency gains can be applied to either producing more or saving more (on inputs). For example, an automotive company generally applies a reduction in engineering hours (input) per car project to an increase in the number of cars it develops (output). In short, an increase in engineering efficiency can result in higher R&D productivity.

2. For a discussion of the development of scientific theory and laws, see Kuhn (1962), Hare (1981), and Galison (1987).

3. Hare (1981), page 106.

4. The following account is based on Nayak and Ketteringham (1997).

5. Nayak and Ketteringham (1997), page 368.

6. Quoted from Hare (1981), page 106.

7. Quoted from Friedel and Israel (1987), page xiii.

8. A full article describing IDEO's Tech Box can be found in "For a Seller of Innovation, a Bag of Technotricks," *New York Times,* 11 February 1999.

9. Millard (1990), page 15.

10. The role of chemical libraries in the drug discovery is discussed more extensively in Thomke and Kuemmerle (2002).

11. Quoted from *The Economist* (1998), pages 9–10.

12. The notion of failure as an important element of learning and innovation is also discussed in Sitkin (1992), Leonard-Barton (1995, chapter 5), and Garvin (2000, chapter 2).

13. Quoted from, "Thomas Edison 'Quotes'," <http://www.thomasedison.com/edquote.htm> (accessed January 2003).

14. Allen (1977), chapter 4.

15. The work on disruptive technology and its role in why firms fail is discussed in Christensen (1997).

16. Garvin (2002) notes that new business or ventures can be regarded as experiments where direct contact with the marketplace is essential to exploration and validation, particularly for radically new businesses where the usual sources of knowledge provide only limited insight.

17. Quoted from Christensen (1997), page 99.

18. For example, see Box, Hunter, and Hunter (1978), Box and Draper (1987), Fisher (1921, 1923, 1966), Montgomery (1991), Phadke (1989), and Taguchi and Clausing (1990).

19. A more complete description of how the financial spreadsheet has slashed the cost of financial modeling and changed the way business professionals experiment can be found in Schrage (2000), chapter 2.

20. This section draws extensively from Thomke (1998b) and Thomke, Holzner, and Gholami (1999). Both publications contain more detailed discussions of the ideas and issues described here. While the word "simulation" is used in many contexts, I adhere to the following definition: *Simulation* is the representation of selected characteristics of the behavior of one physical or abstract system by another system. In a digital computer system, simulation is done by software that uses mathematical equations and/or approximations that represent the behavior of the system.

21. The history of Monte Carlo methods and their role in the development of nuclear weapons, particularly the hydrogen bomb in the late 1940s and early 1950s, also provides us with an account of the importance of simulation in physics more than fifty years ago. An excellent description and analysis of this history can be found in Galison (1997), chapter 8. For a history of numerical simulation, see also Brenner (1996) and Seidel (1996).

22. On 21 June 1991, the Undersecretary of Defense for Acquisition established the Defense Modeling and Simulation Office (DMSO) to provide a full-time focal point for activities in modeling and simulation. More information on the DMSO's extensive use of simulation can be found at <http://www.dmso.mil> (accessed January 2003).

23. See Gary Taubes, "The Virtual Cell," *Technology Review* (2002), pages 63–70.

24. The interested reader can find more detail on these technologies in Thomke, von Hippel, and Franke (1998) and Thomke and Kuemmerle (2002).

25. Quoted from *Technology Review* (2000), page 96.

26. For an early description of three-dimensional printing technologies, see Sachs (1992).

27. For published data on drug development economics, see DiMasi, Hansen, Grabowski, and Lasagna (1995). DiMasi and his colleagues have recently completed a new study, and early findings have been made available in a press release by the Tufts Center for the Study of Drug Development.

28. Reported in, "Breakthrough of the Year," *Science* (1998), pages 2156–2161.

29. The data come from an empirical study published in Thomke and Kuemmerle (2002).

30. Genes causing disease could prove potential targets for drug development. These targets could then be used to develop families of new drugs the world has never seen before. Mapping the human genome "may be the most important step we've taken in science," according to Nobel laureate James Watson, codiscoverer of the structure of DNA. Since every disease has a genetic component, deciphering the "book of life," as some scientists refer to the genome, promised to revolutionize medical research over decades to follow. Specifically, researchers have estimated that current drug therapy is based on less than 500 molecular targets, but there are somewhere between 5,000 to 10,000 targets that could potentially lead to new drugs (Drews (2000)). In other words, there are at least ten times as many molecular drug targets than what has been used in the last 100 years of medicine.

31. Quoted from, "Millennium's Bugs," *The Economist* (1998), page 70.

32. Quoted from Pisano et al. (2002), page 4.

33. Quoted from Thomke and Nimgade (1999), page 11.

34. Quoted from Champion (2001), page 114.

35. This appendix draws extensively from Thomke, Holzner, and Gholami (1999).

36. This appendix draws extensively from Thomke, von Hippel, and Franke (1998).

37. See Thomke and Kuemmerle (2002) for data on the size of chemical libraries.

2

new technologies at work

the integrated circuit industry

The introduction of new experimentation technologies has had no greater impact on the development of new products than in the integrated circuits industry. Not only was this industry a pioneer in advances in computer modeling and simulation, it also gave rise to a new prototyping technology, field-programmable logic devices, which led to fundamental changes in the creation of custom integrated circuits. In 2000, these chips represented more than $5 billion in revenues and made possible numerous product innovations. This chapter not only presents compelling and detailed evidence that new experimentation technologies can have a dramatic impact on development strategy, process, and performance, it also shows that introducing the technologies can affect an industry already considered a leader in the use of advanced design tools and technologies. The integrated circuit industry had already been revolutionized through advances in computer-aided design and simulation, which made possible most chips that we use today.

The introduction of field-programmable logic devices started with a radical idea: What if chips could be made so flexible that changing them would be as simple as modifying a computer model? Such chips would preserve the advantages of having experimentation models that were close to reality, but they would do so without the high cost and time delays of building production prototypes. That the process of chip design could be changed again with new technologies was a revolutionary concept.

In addition, the introduction of field-programmable logic devices provided a "natural" experiment for me whereby the effects of the technology change could be understood and measured empirically, thus validating the technology's impact.[1] As a colleague of mine once put it, "Always look for [business] experiments where your observations are not obscured by too much 'noise.' Real-world business settings are complex and constantly changing, which makes it difficult to draw meaningful conclusions from the most careful observations." Scientists constantly seek natural experiments to test and refine theories. Their learning is maximized when they can link cause and effect while minimizing the impact of noise and other factors that obscure the phenomena they are interested in. In chapter 3, we shall discuss experimentation for effective learning and the impact of factors such as "noise."

As I embarked on a study of the industry, I realized that contrasting development projects where the cost of building and modifying of prototypes was *high* with comparable projects where—because of new technologies—the cost was *low* would be precisely the kind of powerful experiment that my colleague described. My investigation led me to the following hypothesis: Development strategies are optimized around the cost and time of making design iterations and changes. Environments in which iterations are difficult and costly *inhibit* experimentation and foster strategies that emphasize planning and risk minimization. In contrast, the ability to iterate and make changes quickly and at low cost *invites* experimentation and tolerates risk and rapid change.

As we shall see throughout the chapter, the evidence strongly supports this hypothesis. An analysis of about eighty chip design projects shows that when new field programmable technologies lowered the cost and time of iterations, experimentation-driven development strategies not only resulted in fundamentally different design processes and cultures, they also doubled project performance and challenged fundamental assumptions about best industry practice.

Custom Integrated Circuits:
How They Have Been Traditionally Developed

In 1959, when Jack Kilby and Robert Noyce independently invented what would become the integrated circuit (IC), it was not evident that they had created the foundation of most modern technologies. They had found a way to place electronic components such as transistors, resistors, capacitors, and wiring onto a single miniaturized chip. Heretofore, standard components (known as discrete devices) were used to design complex electronic systems, resulting in significant compromises in speed, size, and economy. By the turn of the millennium, based on Kilby's and Noyce's invention, Intel's Pentium 4 processor could fit about 42 million transistors into a space the size of a dime—at a price low enough for mass markets; worldwide sales of semiconductors exceeded $200 billion in 2000.[2] Indeed, ICs are everywhere. The performance gains of integrated circuits roughly followed the prediction of Moore's Law, named after Intel's cofounder, Gordon Moore, that transistor density on a chip would increase exponentially each year while keeping cost constant. These gains, accompanied by increased knowledge of modeling, have fueled dramatic advances in simulation and the development and use of automated design tools. Fascinatingly, these advances have come full circle: Today's complex chips are impossible to design without the tools they have helped to create!

While there are many ways to classify the different kinds of chips currently in use, a simple taxonomy divides them by range of application. *Standard ICs,* such as microprocessors and memory chips, can be deployed in a wide array of products and are useful to many customers. In contrast, *custom ICs* are designed for a narrower range of applications and customers, making them suitable only to either a single customer like an automotive supplier of electronic brakes or a narrow application. Custom ICs developed for specific customers are commonly referred to as ASICs (short for "application-specific integrated circuits").

In a complex production process involving 500 or more individual steps, modern ICs are generally built onto the surface of a thin, flat silicon wafer. The process steps are carried out in ultraclean fabrication environments, using some of the world's most sophisticated production equipment, and are designed to either add or remove very thin layers of semiconducting or insulating materials.[3] The resulting structure consists of standard electronic components (e.g., transistors or capacitors) that are interconnected via lines of metal that are invisible to the human eye. The most fundamental building block of a digital chip is often referred to as a "gate," which might require a few transistors and other related electronic components such as diodes and resistors. In the case of *custom* chips, engineers convert product specifications into a description of such interconnected gates or cells using computer-automated design tools. Errors in design or production are found via computer simulation and extensive tests of physical chip prototypes manufactured in a semiconductor foundry.

Custom Chip Development

In the beginning, custom electronic circuitry was designed and built by combining standard integrated circuits with discrete electronic components and connecting them on a printed circuit board; the boards became part of larger systems such as computers and telecommunications and military equipment. With increasing demands on technical performance (for complexity, speed, and reliability), power consumption, integration density, and lower cost, firms began to ask for custom chips that could integrate many (more) standard components onto a much smaller area. Starting in the late 1960s, some chip suppliers offered to design and manufacture specific chips for select customers with large-volume needs, and thus the ASICs business was born.[4]

Today, the design of such chips (box 2-1) usually begins with a detailed specification of the chip's purpose that is then converted into a functional description entered into a software design tool. The tool converts the information into a description of interconnected logic elements that provide the specified function and ensures that the design falls within the so-called design rules that guide manufacturing. The design then is tested using sophisticated simulation models. Any errors in the design logic cause the simulation to not perform as intended, and the designer uses these results to detect and then, usually in multiple iterations, correct the errors using capabilities of the simulation and design tools.

BOX 2-1: CUSTOM-INTEGRATED CIRCUITS: HOW THEY ARE DEVELOPED

The development of high-volume custom chips usually involves a phased development process aimed at minimizing development risk.

Design specification: Development begins with the formulation of design requirements and specifications, followed by chip-level decisions such as estimates of pin counts, and it involves multiple meetings between supplier and customer. During these meetings, technical issues that relate to the interdependence between design and fabrication are discussed, technical and economic trade-offs are considered, and contractual agreements between the two parties are made. Good specifications lower the probability of costly design changes due to miscommunication.

Design development: After an agreement is signed, the supplier usually provides software design libraries that are specific to its production technology. These libraries are needed to start the low-level design. In very complex projects, designers often write a completed set of design documentation before starting the actual design development. Only then do engineers develop the chip according to specifications and with the aid of either schematic entry tools or higher level design synthesis tools.

Design verification: After a design block is completed, designers develop a set of functional test patterns and run simulated tests. If a functional error is detected, it is analyzed for its cause and design changes are made. This process iterates until minimal functional errors are detected. Functional tests are followed by more complex simulations (e.g., timing) and again designers iterate until no errors are detected within a specified time period. Since the chip has not been "laid out or routed" (a process where the supplier converts the design into a manufacturable and process-specific circuit architecture), simulation models are only rough approximations of actual production conditions. As a consequence, some complex simulations have to be repeated when the routed design is available.[5]

Design prototyping: After receiving a signed release approval from the customer, the supplier generates the final design database, which is used to create pattern-generation tapes (also know as tape-out). The tapes are used to manufacture photolithography masks, which are used to fabricate integrated circuits in a complex and costly process. The first prototypes

(continued)

> *(continued)*
>
> are tested and packaged by the supplier and delivered to the customer for in-system verification and evaluation.
>
> *Design evaluation:* Finally, the development team determines whether the prototype works without problems. If an error is detected, costly prototype modifications are necessary unless a hardware or software workaround can be found. If a workaround is not possible, the chip design has to be modified and many of the earlier design and sign-off-related steps are repeated. After the prototype performs as intended, a prototype approval is signed and volume production can begin. Due to the high cost of correcting design errors in conventional technologies, chip designers rely heavily on simulation to get the prototype "right the first time."
>
> For more information on the process of developing custom chips or other references, see S. Thomke, "Managing Experimentation in the Design of New Products," *Management Science* 44, no. 6 (June 1998): 743–762.

Next, the designer—an external or internal customer—transfers the corrected logical description to the supplier, where other tools are used to lay out the chip's physical geometry so that it is compatible with the supplier's production process. Information from this step is sent back to the designer, who resimulates the design, looking for and correcting more errors (so-called timing errors) created by the conversion of the design from a functional representation into an actual physical chip to be produced by a specific process. The revised design is then sent back to the supplier for building special tooling ("masks"), resulting in substantial fixed and setup costs for initial production runs. Finally, the first manufactured prototype is tested by the supplier and customer for final acceptance. As is evident, first-time design acceptance is a critical success criterion of experimentation strategies, process phases, and interactions among design groups or customers.

Although greatly simplified as described here, the process has been used for most design and production technologies and is still being followed today. Over the years, however, fundamental changes have occurred at the design level itself (e.g., how cells and libraries are being used) and as a result of new design and production technologies themselves.

Full-Custom, Standard Cell, and Gate-Array Technologies

Until the late 1970s, "full-custom" methods like those described were the only alternative to using standard devices or chips. Since each design was treated as unique, the approach was relatively slow and expensive. Highly skilled design engineers would work closely with production personnel and customers to optimize chip speed and levels of integration to achieve the highest performance possible. Not surprisingly, the method has been relatively expensive and only makes sense when very large numbers of custom chips are required. The cost and time required to build a first physical prototype are very high. Today, only the most advanced custom chips (e.g., some microprocessors) still utilize this approach.

Alternatively, customers can specify arrangements of predefined and tested subcircuits (called cells) that are developed using software-based design tools. Customers usually receive libraries of standard cells and some of the design tools from their IC supplier. This standard cell approach became widely available in the early 1980s and simplified chip development a great deal, yet it maintained some of the advantages of integration and performance. Because nonrecurring engineering and manufacturing costs are still high, the development process is carefully designed to avoid repeated iterations of physical chip prototypes.

Around the same time that standard cell methods became available to more customers, such custom IC pioneers as LSI Logic Corporation (founded in 1981) marketed so-called gate-array-based chips. In this technology, a standard array or matrix of logic gates are prefabricated, which in turn lowers the cost and time of production customization. The customer's desired functionality is achieved by linking these gates via layers of metal lines. Computer software and libraries of standard gate-array modules allow developers to design and test chips before committing to physical prototypes with production runs that are still costly and time-consuming.

In the remainder of the chapter, chip projects using full-custom, gate-array, or standard cell technologies are often referred to as "ASIC technologies." The name implies only that these chips were developed for a particular application (initiated by a chip customer or as a product) and were designed using one of the three technologies.[6] While these technologies differ substantially in technical dimensions, they all share the high costs and time of producing the first prototype in silicon.

Field-Programmable Logic for Low-Cost and Fast Iterations

Toward the mid-1980s, companies such as California-based Altera Corporation and Xilinx, Inc. introduced new field-programmable logic devices (FPLDs) that were significantly different from ASIC technologies. FPLDs are off-the-shelf logic chips that a customer—not the manufacturer—programs to perform a particular function. Design automation tools used by customers already contain the most accurate simulation models available since no custom production is required. Suppliers provide these standard yet flexible chips with links between components that can be either created or "melted," in the case of fuse technologies, or simply programmed, in the case of erasable memory technologies. As a result, suppliers do not have to be involved in the customer's design process and physical prototypes needed for testing can be prepared at very little cost or time (table 2-1 compares different technologies).

Initially, FPLDs could be used only for designs of little complexity and thus complemented rather than competed against conventional standard cell or gate-array technologies. Because no initial production run was necessary for each customer chip, they were particularly attractive for low-volume applications. By the mid-1990s, however, Altera and Xilinx had made such significant advances that programmable technologies became an attractive alternative to the lower-volume segment of the custom integrated circuit segment. One programmable technology—field-programmable gate arrays (FPGAs)—became particularly successful since it allowed designers to erase and reprogram a chip instantly and at no cost.

The coexistence of different technologies that could be used for a similar chip design thus became a natural experiment for research. The impact of technology on development strategy, process, and performance could be directly compared across many projects using: (1) full-custom, standard cell, or gate-array technologies (or ASIC technologies), where the cost and time of building and modifying a prototype is *high,* and (2) field-programmable logic devices (FPLDs), where the cost and time of building and modifying a prototype is *low.*

The technology choice is in part affected by the expected volume of chips produced and, of course, the design's complexity. As production volumes rise, the lower fixed cost of programmable logic tends to be offset by lower variable costs of gate arrays, standard cells, and

TABLE 2 - 1

Technologies for Custom Chip Development

Technology	Full Custom	Standard Cells	Gate Arrays	Programmable Logic
Cost to Build Prototype Chip	Highest (more than $50,000)	High	High	Lowest (less than $1,000)
Time to Build Prototype Chip	Highest (more than 8 weeks)	High	Medium	Lowest (minutes)
Variable Cost of Each Chip Unit	Lowest	Lower	Medium	Highest
Chip Complexity and Performance	Highest	Higher	Medium	Lowest
Market (2000)	Less than $10 billion	$9.5 billion	$2.7 billion	$5.4 billion

Time and cost are very rough author estimates based on interviews and can vary widely, depending on chip complexity, technological change, and level of service provided by suppliers. The market data come from World Semiconductor Trade Statistics 2000.

full-custom—although specialist firms now offer "upgrade" paths that allow customers to convert designs from one to another of these technologies. Similar, very complex designs cannot be accomplished with programmable logic. For the large customer base with low-to-moderate complexity needs, however, all technologies represent possible development options. This difference in iteration cost, in turn, enabled me to test my earlier hypothesis: Development strategies are optimized around the cost and time of making design iterations and changes.

The remainder of this chapter reports on the compelling evidence from this research project. A description of how the data were collected can be found in appendix 2-1.

Major Changes in Development Process and Performance

Most advances in integrated circuit design had focused on better and faster design and simulation tools and models that were aimed at avoiding costly experiments with chip prototypes.[7] Without any doubt, these advances were instrumental in making possible the most complex integrated circuit designs today. However, the instability of design requirements and the comparative speed and fidelity advantage of "real" silicon makes some prototype testing not only desirable but unavoidable.[8] The innovation of field-programmable technologies thus addressed two market needs: radically reducing the cost and time of building prototypes to allow for experimentation with real silicon and providing robust and easy-to-use design toolkits that would require no involvement from the chip supplier. The use of design toolkits for experimentation and its impact on the integrated circuit industry will be discussed in depth in chapter 7.

To test the impact of experimentation cost and time on process and project performance, I carried out a research program that compared the use of ASIC technologies (full-custom, standard cell, or gate-array) against programmable devices such as FPGAs. Access to raw data on nearly 400 development projects, with an even split between systems designed with ASIC and programmable technologies, formed a database for comparison.

Before I could compare differences, however, the data had to be adjusted for product complexity. Project teams using ASIC technologies such as gate arrays also worked on more complex chip design than teams using FPLDs. These are interesting choices in their own right, but to gauge changes in process and performance, I needed a better "apples-to-apples" comparison. After all, I wanted to understand differences if firms chose different experimentation technologies but worked on similar products. Fortunately, the database was very large and contained multiple measures of chip complexity that could be used to extract two samples—one for each technology—where teams worked on projects of similar complexity.[9] This adjustment reduced the database to about ninety projects but guaranteed an apples-to-apples comparison.

Experimentation Technologies Matter: Development Performance

To measure performance, I asked designers to indicate the amount of total effort that went into their project and to break it out into five distinct phases. Since many projects involved a very small number of designers, effort was not only a good measure of productivity but also a proxy for elapsed time from specification to final design approval. The study findings shown in figure 2-1 are quite striking: not only did FPLDs help development teams to be more than twice as productive, but almost all the differences were found in the first three out of five

FIGURE 2 - 1

Chip Development Performance

Data comes from seventy-eight similar development projects, each involving the design of custom chips using different technologies. The symbols * and ** mean that the differences are statistically significant at the 5 percent and 1 percent level, respectively.

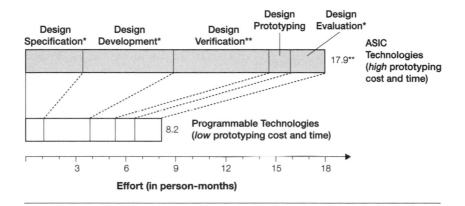

phases. On average, teams employing programmable technology required 8.2 person-months to completion, which was less than half the 17.9 person-months reported by the other teams using ASIC technologies. (Statistical analysis showed that there was only a 1-in-165 probability that the difference was a result of chance alone.)

The use of advanced computer simulation and design tools was instrumental in all projects in developing a custom chip of low complexity. What accounted for most of the difference, however, was how their experimentation strategies took advantage of the combined power of simulation and prototyping and how it affected the development process.

Experimentation Versus Specification: Getting It "Wrong" the First Time

The high cost and time of producing the first prototype made experimental changes in "silicon" an undesirable feature of chip development when ASIC technologies such as standard cells and gate arrays were used. Good management and design methodologies minimize the risk of such changes. Not surprisingly, nearly one quarter of the productivity difference could be attributed to the *design specification* phase, where information on customer needs is gathered and detailed requirements are determined. Teams using programmable logic invested less than one third as much design time in specification than the teams using ASIC technologies. This difference, of course, is a rational response to the expected cost and time of making prototype changes. Developers who face *low* cost and time of making changes spend *less* time on the clear and precise understanding of customer requirements and definition of detailed specifications, several of which were likely to be modified anyway as the design evolved. In contrast, developers facing high cost have an incentive to spend much time up front and to clearly understand, specify, and document requirements, since prototype changes could jeopardize the success of the project.

This difference also affected the second phase, *design development.* Designers using ASIC technologies put in about twice as much effort on designing their circuits. Company interviews indicated that fear of finding a problem in the first prototype made them more cautious: To minimize the risk of first-time failure, much more design documentation was prepared, which, in turn, required additional time. The combined effect was an increase in development time and effort. In contrast, designers using programmable logic could come up with a design solution and quickly move to an experimental trial (via simulation or prototype testing) as a means of getting rapid feedback from internal testing and customers.

The observed differences suggested two different development approaches that also give rise to different R&D cultures. In one culture, the risk of change is eschewed and frozen specifications drive incremental experiments that are confined to computer simulation. This linear *specification-driven* development is a rational response to the constraints that technology—in this case, gate array and standard cells—poses: Changes are costly and should be avoided. In the other culture, changes are considered natural and experimentation is invited as a way of resolving customer and technical uncertainty. This evolutionary *experimentation-driven* development starts with a specification that is good enough and uses computer simulation combined with frequent prototype iterations to address problems quickly as they occur. A typical characteristic of this philosophy is more frequent prototyping, also found in my study.[10] Programmable technology resulted in an average of 14 hardware iterations per project whereas conventional technologies led to 1.5—clearly a shift from a specification to a more experimentation-driven development approach and culture (figure 2-2).[11]

FIGURE 2 - 2

Role of Prototype Iterations

Data come from eighty-four similar projects. Prototype changes were defined as changes that were made to any part of the physical design prototype and that were subsequently verified by the designer. The difference is statistically significant (at the 1 percent level).

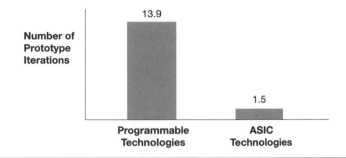

This shift is particularly important when product requirements are unstable—as they usually are. A recent study surveyed more than 200 product developers and found that fewer than 5 percent had a complete specification before beginning product design.[12] On average, only 58 percent of requirements were specified before design activities began. The inevitable result is changes. Academic research in the area of technological innovation has shown that a significant part of these changes can be attributed to (a) the coevolution of technical solutions in components that are part of a larger system and (b) customers' inherent difficulty in accurately specifying their needs at the outset of a design project system.[13]

Individual designs are often part of larger systems, and their requirements are derived from their role in such systems. As designers at the system and subsystem level engage in problem solving, they can alter interfaces within the system. Since these interfaces are in reality the product requirements for subsystems, the subsystems in turn are subject to changing requirements. These findings have been supported by academic research on engineering problem solving and the related evolution of the technical solution path in the design of a number of aerospace systems (figure 2-3).[14]

The study found that design engineers who were developing an aerospace subsystem conceived of and evaluated a number of design alternatives and selected the one judged best. The designers' preferences

FIGURE 2-3

Instability of Subsystem Solutions

A solution development record of an engineering team designing an antenna radiation subsystem shows a rapid change over time in the probability that one of the three technical approaches (A, B, and C) will be adopted. These records are based on data from real-time monitoring of problem-solving processes in R&D.

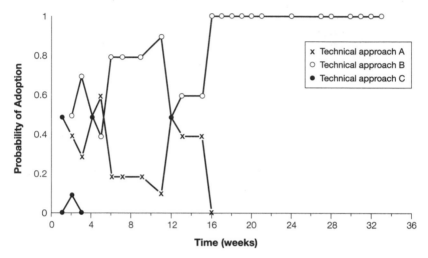

Source: Data from T. J. Allen, "Studies of the Problem-Solving Process in Engineering Design," *IEEE Transactions on Engineering Management* 13, no. 2 (1966): 72–83.

for these alternatives, however, changed frequently and quickly as the design evolved, and it would have been very difficult to conclusively determine the best alternative at the outset of the project. Moreover, the different alternatives required different subsystem components or interfaces to other system components—resulting in rapidly changing product requirements (or specifications) as the development project evolved.

At the system level, requirements are driven by rapidly evolving customer needs, an additional source of instability. Research has shown that familiarity with existing product attributes can interfere with an individual's ability to express needs for novel products.[15] In other words, it is hard for inexperienced customers to accurately describe their needs. Needs become more refined (or change) as the customer comes in direct contact with the product and starts to use it. This happens quite often in systems that involve human-machine interactions, resulting in responses such as the familiar "I'm really not sure what I want, but I'll know it when I see it." For example, designers of applications software sometimes find that customers significantly revise requirements after they use their software for the first time, leading to very costly and time-consuming redesigns of an otherwise functional product.

The advantage of experimentation-driven approaches is that they can tolerate the risk that comes with the instability of fast-moving environments much more effectively. Instead of being engaged in expensive and time-consuming activities (e.g., "overspecifying" requirements that are likely to change) that aim at minimizing the risk of change, frequent experiments elicit feedback from customers and changes are quickly incorporated in designs.[16]

Combined Effect of Computer Simulation and Rapid Prototyping

In most R&D organizations, teams have multiple modes of experimentation at their disposal. Mental simulations aided by paper and pencil, physical yet simple mock-ups, simulation models and functional prototypes all constitute alternatives through which developers test their ideas, concepts, and design solutions. An important part of an experimentation strategy is therefore the switching between different modes so as to maximize learning from experimentation.[17]

Projects usually begin with the mode that is best under initial conditions. Simple paper-and-pencil consideration can be effective since it provides immediate feedback. As the returns from experimentation in a particular mode diminish, switching to another mode (e.g., computer simulation) makes sense since not much more can be gained. Since R&D is hardly a linear process, switching back can sometimes be beneficial when design alternatives are dismissed or substantially changed. However, when one experimentation mode becomes very costly—as in the case of prototype changes for gate arrays and standard cells—its power for experimentation is no longer attractive. The result is excessive simulation that could have been carried out much faster in real silicon. This is particularly true for an important group of tests that evaluate the speed at which a chip can perform. In such cases, computer simulation can take orders of magnitude longer than real silicon.[18]

This occurrence is what happened when I compared the *design verification* phases of different project teams. It turned out that more than 40 percent of the productivity difference had to do with the extent to

FIGURE 2 - 4

Switching Between Experimentation Modes

With decreasing returns, developers will switch to ASIC technologies when their problem-solving productivity exceeds computer simulation. With programmable technologies, the trajectory shifts up, and switching earlier to prototype testing thus raises overall problem-solving productivity.

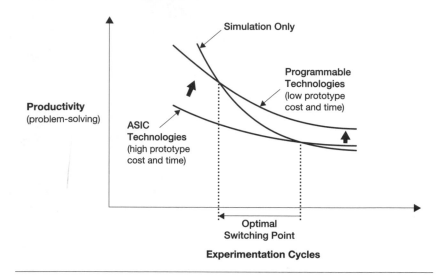

which teams simulated (and resimulated) their designs. Because prototype iterations are considered undesirable and designs had to be resimulated after better computer models became available from the supplier (after laying out a chip's geometry), the use of ASIC technology such as gate arrays or standard cells resulted in significantly longer verification time. In contrast, developers using programmable logic took advantage of cheap redesigns: after having performed some degree of experimentation by simulation, they quickly moved to prototype testing (shown in figure 2-4). Interestingly, less simulation did not lead to significantly higher effort during *design evaluation*—the phase where most prototype testing occurs.

Early Experimentation with Better Models

Clearly, experimentation-driven development resulted in better development performance for teams that used programmable technologies. The findings in the previous section also suggest a fundamental shift in when experimentation modes were used. Shifting the balance toward more prototype iterations also implied that test models of reality were used earlier, thus forcing some problem solving to earlier stages of development.

To test this hypothesis even further, I divided my dataset into two groups: (1) early switching—stop simulation and start prototype testing while design problems remain (and, to some extent, can be identified via simulation)—and (2) late switching—start prototype testing after being extremely confident that no design problems remain. Developers then responded to these questions by problem category since my research indicated that model fidelity could best be approximated by problem categories. In the case of logic errors, the fidelity of simulation is very high; it is somewhat lower for timing errors and significantly lower for errors due to signal quality problems.[19] The data show that R&D teams that used programmable technology also prototyped much earlier in the process, particularly when the fidelity of simulation models was the lowest (timing and signal quality problems; table 2-2).

TABLE 2 - 2

Early Experimentation with Chip Prototypes

Problem Category	PROGRAMMABLE TECHNOLOGIES			ASIC TECHNOLOGIES			Statistical Significance
	SWITCH			SWITCH			
	Late	Early	Total	Late	Early	Total	
Logic	91 (46.7%)	104 (53.3%)	195 (100%)	105 (57.1%)	79 (42.9%)	184 (100%)	0.051
Timing	59 (30.3%)	136 (69.7%)	195 (100%)	102 (57.0%)	77 (43.0%)	179 (100%)	0.000
Signal Quality	17 (8.7%)	178 (91.3%)	195 (100%)	38 (21.1%)	142 (78.9%)	180 (100%)	0.001

Values of 0.05 or below are considered to be statistically significant (two-tailed Fisher's exact test). Designers switch to prototype testing early if (a) the cost and time of prototype changes decrease (from ASIC to programmable), or (b) the fidelity of simulation models decrease (from logic to signal quality).

Source: Data from S. Thomke, "Managing Experimentation in the Design of New Products," *Management Science* 44, no. 6 (1998): 743–762.

The reason early experimentation with chip prototypes was so powerful had to do with its relative efficiency advantage over the diminishing returns of computer simulation. While simulation was much more effective during most of development, rapid prototyping technologies increased the attractiveness of hardware, which, of course, had its advantages and disadvantages as well. But only by switching earlier to prototype testing were teams able to reap the full benefits of new programmable technologies (figure 2-5).

To demonstrate the importance of the right experimentation strategy with a simple example, consider the effect of rapid prototyping on a hypothetical development process, CHIP, which consists of only two phases: (1) experimentation with computer simulation and (2) experimentation with prototypes (figure 2-6). Before the introduction of the rapid prototyping technology, CHIP faces very high costs of building and modifying design prototypes. Thus a good experimentation strategy

FIGURE 2 - 5

The Sources of Technology Potential

With new programmable technologies, the lower iteration cost and time result in a baseline gain even when experimentation with prototypes does not happen earlier. An additional and very significant source of productivity gain, however, can be unlocked if programmable technologies are used earlier in the development process.

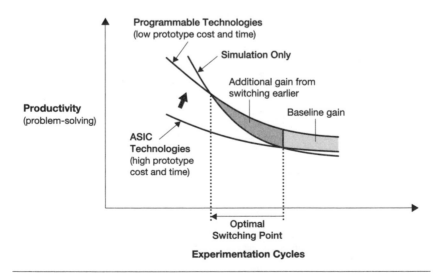

FIGURE 2 - 6

Tapping into the Potential of Rapid Prototyping Technologies

Before low-cost prototyping technology is available, chip projects switch to prototype testing relatively late (case A). After the technology is available, some productivity gains can be realized without any changes in development process and organization (case B). The full potential, however, can be unlocked if management makes some fundamental changes to its innovation process (case C).

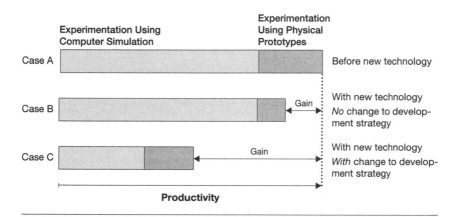

includes the simulation of a design until the conclusion can be reached with a high degree of certainty that the first prototype will operate without failure (case A in figure 2-6). Good management practice in this first case would include a development schedule with ample simulation time and resources and perhaps performance feedback, such as a "prototype-works-right-the-first-time" design award.

Now consider the availability of rapid prototyping that allows a designer to build (and modify) a prototype at a lower cost and time (case B in figure 2-6). The use of rapid prototyping would most certainly reduce the total cost and time required for prototype testing, even if the managerial actions from case A were left in place and the development strategy and process remained unchanged.

However, the findings in this chapter suggest that additional opportunities for productivity gains would remain untapped unless management understands the impact of rapid prototyping on early experimentation and takes action accordingly. In this instance, it would imply an earlier switching from simulation to prototype testing and, as a result, a change of the managerial actions that were appropriate for case A. For example, the "prototype-works-right-the-first-time" design award would certainly motivate designers to follow experimentation practices that emphasize first-prototype success; after all, it was appropriate before the availability of rapid prototyping. Thus management should replace the award with some incentive that would motivate designers to switch from simulation to prototype testing before being very certain that no errors remain in their designs. This behavior, though somewhat counterintuitive, often results in designers getting the prototype wrong the first time but at the same time being able to further increase development performance significantly (case C in figure 2-6).

As we shall also see later in this book, however, early experimentation requires much more than just incentives, since it challenges how R&D organizations have been traditionally organized and managed. It requires rethinking many things from the ground up, including coordination of specialized R&D departments and groups, the role of rapid iterations in design processes, and a fundamental culture shift toward the acceptance of early and fast failure—changes that will be discussed in depth in chapter 6.

Implications for the Integrated Circuit Industry

Finally, why would any designers *not* choose programmable technologies, given that it is a feasible technology alternative? The possible reasons are subtle. First, there may be technical considerations that make FPLDs infeasible, given the speed, size, or power requirements of a complex integrated circuit. Second, designers may choose to stay with full-custom, standard cell, or gate-array technologies because at large-volume production, lower variable cost would provide significant savings that are traded off against a more inefficient and slower development process. This reason is supported by data from the two subsamples analyzed: on average, designers using programmables eventually produced 1,581 units whereas other designers had average production volumes of 113,232 units. However, a number of firms have recognized this opportunity and started to specialize in supplying a conversion path from programmables to standard ASIC designs. (Designers would use programmables to develop their integrated circuits, have a specialized firm convert it to another chip technology, and then run volume production in a traditional chip foundry.) And third, designers are reluctant to switch to a technology they may consider inferior; doing so requires them to make an investment in acquiring different skills and, if they use programmables, often a career track with lower pay, less peer recognition, and fewer opportunities to grow (e.g., moving into high-end design projects). This apprehension of designers was especially true when FPLDs became available for the first time.

The fact is that a rapidly increasing proportion of companies has indeed changed the way they developed chips, and programmable technologies have been the fastest-growing sector in the custom chip business in the last ten years.[20] As a result, the changes in experimentation strategies and development performance have already affected hundreds of thousands of users and will continue to be a very important force in the integrated circuit industry, as shown in figure 2-7. We shall revisit these changes in chapter 7 where custom products and design tools are discussed in detail.

FIGURE 2-7

Creating Value Through New Experimentation Technologies

Figures are from World Semiconductor Trade Statistics for custom metal oxide semi-conductor (MOS) logic, a dominant technology for digital circuits. The total shaded area equals the cumulative billings of these technologies over time. CAGR stands for compound annual growth rate.

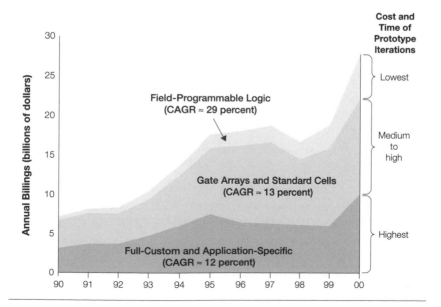

Conclusion

The results from the integrated circuit development study make a compelling case for the importance of new experimentation technologies and their potential to fundamentally change how new products and service are developed. Significantly, the research has shown that field-programmable technologies not only lowered the cost and time of prototype iterations but also gave rise to differences in development strategy, process, and performance.

In the traditional ASIC setting, the risk of change is eschewed and frozen specifications drive incremental experiments that are confined to computer simulation. We have seen that this *specification-driven* development is a rational response to the constraints that technology—in this case, gate array and standard cells—poses: Changes are costly and should be avoided. When FPLDs are used, changes are considered natural and experimentation is invited as a way of rapidly resolving uncertainty. This *experimentation-driven* development starts with a specification that is good enough and uses computer simulation combined with frequent prototype iterations to address and solve problems quickly. That approach, in turn, requires a fundamental rethinking of the process, organization, and management of design.

The chapter also shows that opportunities to improve performance can be found in industries that are already considered to be leaders in the use of new technologies, such as CAD and simulation tools for chip design. In the following chapters, we shall see how other industries are affected by the changing economics of experimentation and the problems that companies have in introducing and integrating new technologies. Before we move into these issues, however, chapter 3 will look at what good experimentation entails and how companies can maximize learning from it.

APPENDIX 2-1

how the study data were gathered

Empirical data on experimentation and development performance and strategies were collected in a two-stage process. First, I conducted a field study at a Cambridge high-technology firm. Over a period of three months, I conducted over thirty extensive interviews with system and chip designers and constructed a database with twenty-four design error case histories. The interviews and the data allowed me to verify the significance of experimentation strategies in integrated circuit design and to develop an in-depth technical understanding of simulation and prototype testing in design practice. Second, I applied my learning from the field to developing a detailed questionnaire that was used to collect data on experimentation strategies from nearly 400 chip projects throughout the United States. The data analysis employed statistical methods to determine whether in fact the differences in prototyping cost and time resulted in different experimentation strategies and if so, whether it had an impact on overall development cost and time.

A pretest of the questionnaire was conducted with the support of two networking technology design groups at a large company in Maryland and a detailed discussion of their responses ensured that designers in both groups understood the questions as they were intended. The questionnaire was then sent to 1,000 designers who were selected from the subscriber database of a leading technical industry journal. The study sample was divided into two groups (500 projects using full-custom, standard cells, or gate arrays and 500 projects using programmable logic) that were randomly chosen from a pool of designers who worked in a large variety of industries, ranging from communications systems to medical electronic equipment. In sixteen cases, the addressee could not be reached or had left the company. Of the 984 designers reached, 463 returned the questionnaire. Of these, sixty-one had to be discarded because the designers felt that their background and experiences did not allow them to answer the questions with high confidence. The eleven questionnaires that arrived after the analysis had been completed were not included in the study. The remaining 391 yielded a total response rate of 39.7 percent, which was divided between programmable logic (40.9 percent) and full-custom, gate-array, and standard cell technologies (38.5 percent). A comparison of the respondents' length of design experience resulted in no significant difference between the groups—both had been designing integrated circuits and systems for an average of ten years.

As projects based on programmable logic were on average less complex than full-custom, standard cell, or gate-array-based chips (ASICs), I needed to make sure that the study made an apples-to-apples comparison. To achieve a fair comparison, I extracted two project sub-samples that were compared along six complexity measures (see note 9). A comparison of chip projects in the two subsamples showed no significant difference in development project complexity. Using input from design engineers, the subsamples were carefully selected to occupy a complexity and performance spectrum where ASIC and FPLD technologies were feasible choices for designers. Even though the subsamples represented designs that were considered of lower complexity and speed, they accounted for 30.5 percent of the research study's FPLD and 25.2 percent of all ASIC-based designs. Thus it was reasonable to assume that projects from both subsamples were of similar complexity and that an objective comparison of project performance could be conducted. Where appropriate, results of the study were compared using these subsamples only.

NOTES

1. In a meaningful experiment, managers or engineers separate independent and dependent variables and then manipulate the former to observe changes in the latter, with minimal interference or other changes to maximize learning. In a *natural experiment*, the manipulation has already happened (e.g., the introduction of a new technology), much to the benefit of the experimenter, as long as learning is not obscured by other changes or poor access to information. We will discuss experimentation and learning in chapter 3.

2. Semiconductor Industry Association, Press Release, 5 February 2001.

3. For details on the fabrication of integration circuits, see Sze (1988).

4. See Walker (1992).

5. After the design is verified with the aid of computer simulation, the designers have to prepare a design package for the ASIC vendor. Such a design package normally includes (1) a set of test patterns used by the vendor to verify the fabricated ASIC for physical functionality, (2) the translated design files (in a standard format), (3) copies of error reports, and (4) a copy of a "design floorplan." Upon receipt of the design package, the ASIC vendor reviews the material and prepares a design specification document

that has to be approved and signed by the customer. The handover of a signed specification document is often referred to as the first sign-off. After receiving the signed document, the vendor develops a design layout and routes the array interconnects (in the case of gate arrays), which are highly dependent on the fabrication process. The actual lengths of metal interconnects are extracted and used to create an interconnect-delay file, which is returned to the customer. In addition, the vendor normally runs its own simulations to verify the manufacturability of the design. Using the interconnect-delay file, the customer can rerun timing simulations with higher modeling accuracy and check for errors that passed earlier timing simulations. If errors are found, the design has to be modified and part of the design process has to be repeated. Once the customer is satisfied with the design, it is formally released to the vendor by signing a release-to-manufacturing approval (often referred to as the second sign-off). The process of resimulating with more accurate models can still be regarded as part of "design verification" (or better, "design reverification").

6. Classifications of custom integrated circuits vary widely, depending on the firm's perspective. A silicon foundry that also provides design services usually differentiates between three types of designs: ASICs (*application-specific integrated circuits,* where the design is requested and paid by a customer), ASSP (*application-specific standard products,* where the design may or may not be initiated by a group of customers but is paid by the foundry), and COT (*customer-owned tooling,* where the customers design the chip and use a foundry only for production purposes). In contrast, the Semiconductor Industry Association (SIA) uses yet another classification that makes distinction along chip technologies and end application rather than locus of design. The SIA classifications are available at <http://www.semichips.org> (accessed December 2002).

7. The following sections draw extensively from Thomke (1998a).

8. The meaning of "fidelity" is discussed in chapter 3. It signifies the extent to which a model represents a product, process, or service in experimentation.

9. Based on the analysis of complexity clusters in a histogram of gate densities, the subsamples were selected to contain all designs with densities between 5,000 gates and 25,000 gates (today, the relevant gate densities would be much higher as very complex programmable chips are available). In

addition, other measures that could influence complexity were used. The *first* variable (design size) measured the number of gates that were used in the design. The *second* variable (percentage of design copied) accounted for the possibility that some designs have a high gate count but are of little complexity because most of the design is copied or replicated. (E.g., a memory cell can be repeated many times, quickly increasing the gate count with little incremental effort.) The *third* variable (type) captured to what degree the design was a mix of analog and digital components. If there was a significant difference in "type," one would have to analyze its impact on design complexity. The *fourth* variable (has done similar designs before) measured the degree of similar design projects that designers had completed previously. The *fifth* variable (run speed was pushed to limit) and the *sixth* variable (high degree of logic complexity) captured rated design speed and logic complexity, respectively. In summary, respondents provided six measures that all relate to design complexity.

10. As Schrage (2000) points out in his work on innovation cultures, specification and prototyping can be mutually reinforcing or can prove implacable enemies. Successful innovators actively manage the dialogue between specification and prototypes. Similarly, Bowen et al. (1994b), Leonard-Barton (1995), Ulrich and Eppinger (1994), and Wheelwright and Clark (1992) all emphasize the importance of frequent prototyping for innovation.

11. The difference was significant at less than 0.1 percent using a t-test.

12. See Thomke and Reinertsen (1998).

13. In my field research, I discovered the following two examples of unstable requirements (see also Thomke, 1997): (1) *Changes in technology:* Personal computer circuit boards normally consist of an array of chips. The central processing unit (CPU) is the "brain" of a computer, and the remaining chips usually execute support functions, such as controlling external and internal devices. A design engineer's group had the task of integrating a large number of these supporting chips onto a single device. A critical feature in the design was the CPU's clock frequency because it determined the speed at which the design had to operate. Well into the design process, the manufacturer of CPUs (Intel) introduced a revised microprocessor that ran at a 50 percent higher clock rate. The new processor had a serious impact on the design and integration of supporting chips and led to a com-

plete redesign that eventually added 15 percent to their total development time. (2) *Changes in user needs:* In another interview, a designer of a video board reported an experience where customers changed their needs after using the product for the first time. Before the design project was started, customers were interviewed about their color preferences in a video application. Customers indicated that they preferred the color blue. However, after the first prototype was available and customers actually saw the color blue on a screen, they felt that their selection was poor and changed the color requirement, which resulted in an expensive and time-consuming design change to the video board.

14. See Allen (1966, 1977).

15. See von Hippel (1988), page 104.

16. Eisenhard and Tabrizi (1995) and Iansiti (1995) identify adaptive processes in high-velocity or turbulent environments as an important feature of successful product innovation.

17. Pisano (1997) uses "learning before doing" and "learning by doing" as a strategic process development framework for determining the optimal point when firms switch from a laboratory or small-scale pilot facility to a full-scale factory.

18. These tests verify the timing of chips where the relative difference in run times between simulation models and prototypes can be several orders of magnitude. While increasing computer speed will certainly help in closing that gap, it is still a very significant obstacle to full verification by simulation only.

19. In my research, I found that designers typically categorize errors as follows: (1) *logic problems* due to faulty logic behavior of a design (e.g., reversed select lines of a decoder; inversion of an input signal); (2) *timing problems* due to faulty temporal behavior of a design (e.g., insufficient setup and hold times in a digital circuit); (3) *signal quality problems* due to the degradation of signal quality during signal transmission (e.g., introduction of noise in high-frequency applications due to excessive line proximity on printed circuit boards). Designers typically have different simulation tools available that focus on the detection and analysis of one of these problem categories. Because of the varying difficulty of modeling the underlying

error-related behavior, different simulation tools vary in effectiveness and probability of adoption during the design process. Models for logic simulation are usually very accurate whereas signal quality can be modeled only with difficulty.

20. Today's commercially available programmable logic chips allow for design complexities that were thought of as unattainable ten years ago. The ability to configure and customize chip hardware without additional production steps has also stimulated other fascinating research such as the Raw microchip of the Oxygen project at MIT. Researchers are working on an entirely new kind of microprocessor that will provide unprecedented performance, energy efficiency, and cost-effectiveness because of its flexible design. As opposed to "hard-wiring" functionality into microprocessor chips, as it is done today, researchers anticipate that the Raw chip architecture will allow software to program "wires" as needed by their application (Agarwal, 1999).

3
experimentation and learning

All experiments, by definition, generate information, which at a minimum becomes an input to additional experiments or is applied to the result—the intent of the experiment itself—or both. An experimentation process, however, can do more than generate information useful to the process itself. When well structured and integrated into an organization, experimentation generates learning that has implications far beyond the "laboratory." As we saw in chapter 2, the changes in learning from experiments in custom chips ended up transforming an industry, indeed creating a new multibillion-dollar segment: programmable logic technologies. In chapter 1, we saw how looking at the results of experiments as more than information helped change both the thinking about crashworthiness and BMW's approach to car design.

At the same time, the *rate* of learning is influenced by a number of factors, some affecting the process, others affecting how the process is managed. Both sets of factors are equally important. What constitutes good experimentation has been known for a long time. For more than a hundred years, experimentation organized as a group activity has also been codified. A pioneer in codification was Edison. He may be popularly known as the Wizard of Menlo Park, but his West Orange industrial laboratory—built in 1887 on fourteen acres and subsequently extended well beyond that—showed how group experimentation could work. Hundreds and eventually thousands of people were employed at Edison's self-styled invention factory—then the largest in the world—and its organization and the thinking behind it remain salient today. Edison stressed *learning* as critical for practical and scientific endeavors:

> *Edison's invention factories were the pioneers of industrial research because they carried out organized, systematic research directed toward practical goals. Their work encompassed a broad range of activities . . . . The laboratory notebooks kept at West Orange provide evidence of Edison and his leading experimenters theorizing about fundamental principles, making deductions from these principles, and testing the results by experimentation.*[1]

In this chapter we shall look at what is basic to any experimentation process. At a core level, we shall see that the various, time-tested "stages" of activities are ordered to maximize the amount of information a test can yield. We shall also look at what impedes the yield—the managerial and organizational factors that inhibit not only clarity of information but potential learning. Woven through this discussion is the exciting "case" of *Black Magic,* Team New Zealand's stunning winner of the 1995 America's Cup. By integrating new experimentation technologies with tried-and-true methods and capturing the results in its organization, Team New Zealand showed how learning by experimentation works. At the end of the chapter, Bank of America's experience with managing experimentation for learning shows us how service innovation, not only products or processes, can benefit as well.

As exciting and recent as these cases are, we should not forget the Wizard. A hallmark of Team New Zealand's approach was the rapid iteration of experimentation "steps." Consider what Edison said more than 100 years ago: "The real measure of success is the number of experiments that can be crowded into twenty-four hours."[2]

Types of Experiments

When managers, engineers and scientists want to go beyond the passive learning through observation or exploration, they may choose to carry out experiments. Such experiments require a directed effort to manipulate or change variables of interest. In contrast, observers wait for changes to be induced and then carefully study what has been presented to them. Exploration assumes a more proactive role but still lacks the manipulative character of an experiment.[3] In the sciences, astronomers are perhaps the most patient observers, while anatomists take on a more active role when they dissect plants or living organisms (figure 3-1).[4]

In an ideal experiment, innovators separate an independent (the cause) and dependent (the effect) variable and then manipulate the independent variable to observe changes in the dependent variable. The manipulation, followed by careful observation and analysis, then gives rise to learning about relationships between cause and effect which, ideally, can be applied to or tested in other settings. In the real world, however, things are much more complex. Environments are constantly changing, linkages between variables are complex and poorly understood, and often the variables are themselves uncertain or unknown. We must therefore not only move between observation, exploration, and experimentation but also iterate between experiments.

FIGURE 3 - 1

How Scientists Learn

To find out about nature, scientists often use a combination of observation, exploration, and experimentation.

Degree of Intervention	Activity	Example
High	Experimentation	The chemist who manipulates compounds to achieve a particular reaction
Some	Exploration	The anatomist who dissects plants and living organisms
None	Observation	The astronomer who observes processes in the heavens

---

When all relevant variables are known, formal statistical techniques and protocols allow for the most efficient design and analysis of experiments. These techniques are used widely in many fields of process and product optimization today and can be traced to the first half of the twentieth century when the statistician and geneticist Sir Ronald Aylmer Fisher first applied them to agricultural and biological science.[5] Today, these *structured* experiments are being used for both incremental process optimization and studies where large solution spaces are investigated to find an optimal response of a process.[6] In more recent years, these techniques have also formed the basis for improving the robustness of production processes and new products.[7]

However, when independent and dependent variables themselves are uncertain, unknown, or difficult to measure, experimentation itself is much more informal or tentative. A manager may be interested in whether manipulating the incentives of an employee improves her productivity or a software designer wants to know if changing a line of code removes a software error. These *trial-and-error* experiments go on all the time and are so much an integral part of innovation processes that they become like breathing—we do them but are not fully aware of the fact that they are experiments. Moreover, good experimentation goes well beyond the individual or the experimental protocols but has implications for firms in the way they manage, organize and structure innovation processes. It isn't just about generating information by itself but about how firms can learn from trial and error and structured experimentation.

Framework for Experimentation

All experimentation consists of iterating attempts to find the direction in which a solution might lie.[8] The process of experimentation typically begins by selecting or creating one or more possible solution concepts, which may or may not include the best possible solutions—no one knows what the best solutions are in advance. Solution concepts are then tested against an array of requirements and constraints. These efforts (the trials) yield new information and learning, in particular about aspects of the outcome the experimenter did not (or was not able to) know or foresee in advance: the errors. Test outcomes are used to revise and refine the solutions under development, and progress is made in this way toward an acceptable result.

When Team New Zealand developed their winning racing yacht, the design team began with different concepts that were based on prior experience, expertise, and creativity (for background information, see box 3-1; note 9). These solutions were tested with the aid of one-quarter

BOX 3-1: TEAM NEW ZEALAND AND THE AMERICA'S CUP

The America's Cup began in 1851 when the Royal Squadron of England offered a trophy to the winner of a sailing race around the Isle of Wight, a small island off the English coast. Because the race was won by the schooner *America* of the New York Yacht Club, the race became known as the America's Cup. Over the years, the race has become a high-profile international sports event that challenges teams not only for their sailing skills but also the ability to design, engineer, and produce the most capable boats. Even though the rules of competition place strict limits on how boats are constructed, the teams with large R&D budgets have had a historical advantage because of the impact on engineering capacity and prototyping and testing of novel design concepts. Limiting the number of race boats to two per team has had only a marginal impact on expenses: In the 1995 campaign, it was estimated that the seven challengers and three defenders spent nearly a total of $200 million. The 1995 competition consisted of three races. In the first two, the defenders from the country of the cup holders and the challengers from all other nations simultaneously competed for the right to enter the third race. In May 1995, the winning challenger team competed against the winning defender team for the America's Cup trophy. Boat designs were allowed to change between races until the start of the final race, and time differences between first- and second-place boats were often less than one minute. Team New Zealand was headed by Peter Blake, one of the finest ocean sailors in the world, who adopted a low-key and team-oriented approach that was in direct contrast to the more directive styles of other contenders. Blake's team consisted of about fifty people, and activities were divided between team management, design, and the crew, skippered by Olympic gold medalist Russel Coutts.[9]

scale models in wind tunnels and towing tanks. Team New Zealand's design team was headed by Doug Peterson, an American whose experience spanned more than thirty years and thousands of boats, including the winning boat of the 1992 America's Cup race, for which he ran over sixty-five prototype tests and iterations alone. However, in 1995, Peterson planned to tap into the power of computer-aided design, modeling, and simulation tools, which required him to hire experts in these areas as well. Under Peterson's and Blake's leadership, the team followed a disciplined process of experimentation that emphasized rapid learning. Specifically, such experimentation comprises four-step iterative cycles (figure 3-2).[10]

FIGURE 3-2

Experimentation as Four-Step Iterative Cycles

Experimentation cycles are repeated many times and the steps may involve coordination among multiple individuals, groups, or departments.

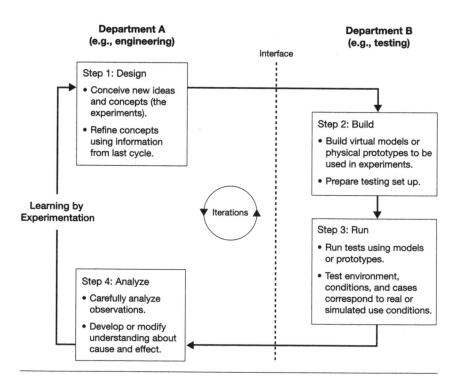

Step 1: Design

During the design step, individuals or teams define what they expect to learn from the experiment. Existing data, observations, and prior experiments are reviewed, new ideas are generated through brainstorming, and hypotheses are formulated based on prior knowledge. The team then selects a set of experiments to be carried out in parallel and analyzed.

In Team New Zealand's case, the team had to design a light boat with as little drag in the water as possible. At the same time, the structure had to be strong and flexible enough to withstand the harshest conditions: strong winds and a highly variable sea. While mast and sails were important boat elements, most of the team focused on the shape of the hull and the keel. The hull would define a boat's architecture and thus had the potential for big jumps in performance and also catastrophic structural failures. (In fact, the Australian team did sink one of its boats when it competed against Team New Zealand in an early race.) In contrast, the keel sitting below the hull could be optimized carefully and gradually, which could still lead to big gains that were sufficient to win a race.

During the design step, the team thus brainstormed on different design alternatives that could enhance the performance of the boat. At the start of their development process, these alternatives tended to be more radical departures from known designs (e.g., new hull concepts), but as time passed by and deadlines loomed, the focus shifted to more incremental improvements on prior experimental iterations (e.g., tweaking the wing of a keel).

Step 2: Build

At this point, one builds (physical or virtual) prototypes and testing apparatus—models—that are needed to conduct an experiment. In yacht design at the time, teams would build a one-quarter scale (twenty feet) version of the boat at an expense of about $50,000 and several months of construction time. It wasn't unusual to build five to six boats in parallel per iteration and repeat this process three to four times.

Step 3: Run

The experiment is then conducted in either laboratory conditions or a real setting. In yacht design, wind tunnels and towing tanks simulate the varying conditions of the sea, with the advantage that designers have control over the settings. Storms and high waves can be created without having to wait for the real weather to change. Of course, the trade-off is that laboratory conditions aren't real and a test apparatus is often designed for certain purposes. True errors may go undetected or false errors show up because of unique conditions under which the experiment is carried out. For example, the apparatus designed to measure the speed of an airbag deployment in the design of a car is unlikely to be able to detect unanticipated toxicity in the gas used to inflate the airbag, even though information regarding this "error" would presumably be of great interest to a car company.

Step 4: Analyze

The experimenter analyzes the result, compares it against the expected outcome, and adjusts his or her understanding of what is under investigation. During this step, most of the learning can happen and forms the basis of experiments in the next cycle. At a minimum, the developer can disqualify failed experiments from the potential solution space and continue the search by going to step 1 of another cycle. In many cases, however, an error or a failed experiment can help someone to adjust mental, computer, or physical models to reflect what has been observed. The result is a deeper understanding and less uncertainty about cause and effect.

If the results of a first experimental cycle (steps 1 through 4) are satisfactory or address the hypothesis in question, one stops.[11] However if, as is usually the case, analysis shows that the results of the initial experiment are not satisfactory, one may elect to modify one's experiment and "iterate"—try again. Modifications may involve the experimental design, the experimental conditions, or even the nature of the desired solution. For example, a researcher may design an experiment with the goal of identifying a new cardiovascular drug. However, experimental results obtained on a given compound might suggest a different therapeutic use and cause researchers to change their view of an acceptable or desirable solution accordingly.[12]

FIGURE 3-3

Automotive Development As Nested Experimentation Cycles

Experimentation cycles can occur at many different levels and are deeply embedded in innovation processes. They are a fundamental activity used to resolve uncertainty, and with advances in technologies, they can occur tens of thousands of times in large development projects.

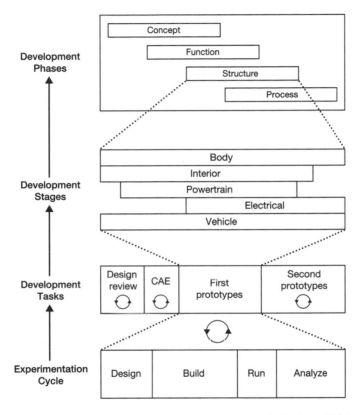

Source: Reprinted from *The Journal of Product Innovation Management* 17, S. Thomke and T. Fujimoto, "The Effects of 'Front-Loading' Problem-Solving on Product Development Performance," Copyright 2000, with permission from Elsevier Science.

Experimentation iterations like those noted are performed by individuals and teams across different functional departments; in large development projects such as in automotive development, there can be tens of thousands of such cycles (figure 3-3)—even small projects can involve many iterations. How firms link experimentation activities to major process phases, system stages, and development tasks, therefore, is an essential part of effective management practice. We shall explore these issues in chapters 5 and 6.

As projects progress and designs mature, cycles tend to include models of increasing fidelity, or representativeness, gradually moving toward functional prototypes and pilot vehicles. These models are used to test decisions affecting design appearance, function, structure, and manufacturability.

However, real-world experimentation with higher-fidelity models such as physical prototypes is often limited by time and budget constraints, as the following quote from Team New Zealand lead designer Peterson illustrates very well:

> *The tank and tunnel method is a design process where experimentation occurs in bursts. Every couple of months, you get back the results of your experiments. As a result, there is a limit to the number of design iterations you can perform. A typical project can rarely afford more than twenty prototypes, due to time and money constraints. In each design cycle, you have to rely on big gains in performance.*[13]

The attractiveness of using computer simulation to Team New Zealand and many firms developing new products can be found in the higher speed and efficiency of carrying out experimental cycles. Within their time and budget constraints, the additional use of simulation thus offers the potential to learn at a higher rate within these cycles. That, in turn, provides great innovation potential because these cycles can run thousands of times for even a single project.

How Learning by Experimentation Happens

The objective of any experiment is to *learn* from the experiment. Information gleaned ultimately (ideally) leads to the development of new products, processes, and services that in turn will benefit the firm. The rate at which a company can learn by experimentation depends on many factors that require strategic and managerial commitment and organizational flexibility. These characteristics do not happen overnight, but they do happen! Although learning from particular experiments can be affected by multiple firm-specific conditions, seven *factors* are common to learning across all experimentation: Fidelity, cost, itera-

TABLE 3 - 1

Factors That Affect Learning by Experimentation

Factor	Definition
Fidelity of Experiments	The degree to which a model and its testing conditions represent a final product, process, or service under actual use conditions
Cost of Experiments	The total cost of designing, building, running, and analyzing an experiment, including expenses for prototypes, laboratory use, and so on
Iteration Time (all four steps)	The time from planning experiments to when the analyzed results are available and used for planning another iteration
Capacity	The number of same fidelity experiments that can be carried out per unit time
Strategy	The extent to which experiments are run in parallel or series
Signal-to-Noise Ratio	The extent to which the variable of interest is obscured by experimental noise
Type of Experiment	The degree of variable manipulation (incremental versus radical changes); no manipulation results in observations only

tion time, capacity, sequential and parallel strategies, signal-to-noise ratio, and type of experiment all influence learning and, ultimately, innovation processes (table 3-1).[14] These seven factors dictate, in general, how learning through experimentation occurs (or does not occur). As we shall see in this chapter and the remainder of the book, new technologies for experimentation have a very significant impact on all the factors.

Fidelity of Experimentation Models Affects Learning

Experimentation is often carried out using simplified versions (models) of the eventually intended test object and/or test environment. For example, aircraft designers usually conduct experiments on a possible aircraft design by testing a scale model of the design in a wind tunnel—an apparatus that creates high wind velocities that partially simulate the aircraft's intended operating environment. The value of using models in experimentation is twofold: to reduce investment in aspects of the real that are irrelevant for the experiment and to "control out" some aspects of the real that would affect the experiment in order to simplify analysis of the results. Thus, models of an aircraft subjected to wind tunnel experiments generally include no internal design details such as the layout of the cabins. Such details are both costly to model and typically irrelevant to the outcome of wind tunnel tests, which are focused on the interaction between rapidly moving air and the model's exterior surface.

Models used in experimentation can be physical in nature, as in the example just given, or they can be represented in other forms, for example, by computer simulation. Sometimes designers test a real experimental object in a real experimental context only after experimenting with several generations of models that isolate different aspects of "reality" and/or that gradually encompass increasing amounts of model complexity.[15]

In Team New Zealand's case, the design team—a multidisciplinary group of naval architects, designers, engineering researchers, analysts, and sailors—relied on complementing tank and tunnel tests with computer models and simulation. Structural characteristics were analyzed using finite element analysis (FEA), the flow of water over the yacht's critical surfaces was optimized using computational fluid dynamics (CFD), and the velocity of the boat design under particular wind and sea conditions was predicted by velocity prediction programs (VPP). Originally developed for the nuclear and aerospace industries (see also chapter 1), these tools allowed for cheaper and faster experimentation cycles than partial or full-scale prototype boats. Equipped with these tools, the team realized that the experimentation bottleneck had shifted from step 2 (build) of a cycle to step 4 (analysis), where most of the learning happens. They also realized that the tools fundamentally changed how they learned; alternative design choices could be compared by looking at color pictures of pressure distribution and flows around a hull and keel which, in turn, could be linked to the drag of a design alternative. In contrast, tank and tunnel tests would give information about a boat's speed under specific conditions but not at the level of detail and ease provided by simulation tools. Moreover, results from scale models introduced bias when applied to full-size boats because of the chaotic nature of fluid flow, which was very sensitive to the size and shape of a surface. Simulation did not suffer from such a bias.

Of course, while models and prototypes are necessary to run experiments, they do not represent reality completely (if they did, they would be the reality they are representing!). *Fidelity* is the term used to signify the extent to which a model does represent a product, process, or service in experimentation. Perfect models and prototypes, those with 100 percent fidelity, are usually not constructed because an experimenter does not know or cannot economically capture all the attributes of the real situation and so cannot transfer them to a model even if doing so were desired. Lower-fidelity models can be useful if they are inexpensive and can be produced rapidly for "quick and dirty" feedback, which is often good enough in the early concept phase of product development, when experimentation itself is in early development. As the experimentation process itself unfolds, however, higher-fidelity models become increasingly important, first because the learning from an experiment is increasingly vital to understanding how close to a solution the effort is and second because modeling errors can be carried along.

Not surprisingly, Team New Zealand would still rely on some tank and tunnel tests because, according to chief designer Peterson, "even with all the simulation in the world, no one is going to commit $3 million to a yacht without towing it down a tank first."[16] The problem is that while simulation has proven to be quite effective at optimizing design, the team's computers weren't fast enough to simulate complex architectural changes affecting the hull of a boat. Instead, the team found simulation particularly effective at incrementally optimizing the shape of the hull and keel. For example, CFD was instrumental in improving the performance of a yacht through the design of aerodynamic wings attached to the bottom of a keel. Refining these appendages had a significant impact on overall boat speed.

At the end of the day, however, computer simulation was only as good as the team and their underlying knowledge that guided them to use the right models, as no amount of simulation could automatically result in outstanding design. The team had come up with design alternatives (step 1 of an experimentation cycle) that ultimately determined the quality of solutions pursued. Feedback from tests would provide them with opportunities to learn and find better alternatives. According to Peterson:

> *The CFD program can't design a yacht from scratch without conceptual input. It doesn't know what parameters it should be optimizing. Consider designing a golf ball to fly as far as possible off the tee. The computer won't tell you the ball should have dimples, but if you specify this as a design parameter, it will find the optimal dimple pattern and density for you.*[17]

As with the problem of biases introduced by scale models—the team built fourteen models over three iterations—the team eventually had to rely on testing the actual boat in the water: Only a third of the changes CFD suggested resulted in real performance improvements that were felt by the crew. Thus, by combining tank and tunnel tests, simulation, and tests of a full-sized boat in the water, Team New Zealand not only enjoyed the benefits of faster experimentation cycles but also eliminated problems that can arise from lower-fidelity models.

Table 3-2 lists the two classes of unexpected errors that can result from incomplete models. While type I errors can lead to wasted resources by "overdesigning" a product (designing a product for failure modes that will not occur), type II errors can have dramatic consequences and are therefore of compelling interest to experimenters. For example, the failure to detect the relationship between primary and secondary O-ring blow-by and low temperatures, in spite of extensive and documented testing, had catastrophic consequences for the *Challenger* Space Shuttle and the U.S. space program.[18] One of the most dra-

TABLE 3 - 2

Possible Outcomes from the Use of Incomplete Models

Error Classes	Description	Example	Result
Type I	Experiment detects false problem	Crash test barrier is more rigid than actual obstacle	Over design
Type II	Experiment fails to detect true problem	Crash does not test toxicity of airbag gas	Design failure

Error classes that can result from incomplete (or inaccurate) models of the object and/or environment.

matic—and highly publicized—type II errors, it was a reminder that common to all good experimentation is the development of increasingly accurate models as the process proceeds.

Less Expensive Experiments Mean More Iterations and Learning

Conducting an experimental cycle typically involves the cost and time of using equipment, material, facilities, and engineering resources. These costs can be as high as one millions dollars in the case of a fully-equipped prototype of a new car used in destructive crash testing. They can be as low as a few dollars for a chemical compound used in pharmaceutical drug development and made with the aid of combinatorial chemistry. In general, firms facing high experimentation cost are more reluctant to try radically new ideas or to depart significantly from existing know-how. They also try to economize; many design changes are combined in a single experiment, which makes learning more difficult. There are fewer errors vis-à-vis the number of trials to learn from.

Consider the four-step experimental cycle defined earlier. The cost of building (step 2) an experimentation model depends critically on the available technology, the maturity of knowledge about the phenomena, and the degree of accuracy the underlying model is intended to have.[19] For example, modern CAD tools sometimes have an interface to computer software that converts a design directly into a simulation model. In such cases, building a model is relatively inexpensive: The cost represents primarily the investment in conversion tools, which is fixed; and the time required to operate them, a variable cost. Furthermore, experimentation models can have varying degrees of fidelity to reality. As noted, the rationale for using incomplete models in experimentation is to reduce investments in real aspects that are irrelevant to the experiment and to simplify the analysis of the test results (step 4). Sometimes a model is incomplete because one cannot economically incorporate all relevant aspects of the real or because one does not know them. The incompleteness of a model, however, can result in design errors when it is replaced by higher-fidelity product or process models in the actual use environment for the first time.

The cost of analyzing (step 4) results from the run step (step 3) depends to a significant degree on access to test-related information and the availability of tools that aid in the problem-solving process. Consider the discovery of an error during prototype testing and the series of subsequent diagnostic steps to identify the error cause(s). Sometimes a designer has a thorough understanding of a tested prototype and finds the cause of the error quickly. Very often, though, subtle errors make the analysis very difficult, especially in cases of great complexity and poor knowledge of causal relationships between system inputs and outputs. As a result, designers have to rely on diagnostic tools and problem-solving methods to aid in their analysis of error symptoms. A very effective analysis tool is the use of computer simulation since it gives a designer quick access to virtually any information within the realm of the underlying simulation model. In contrast, an analysis of data from prototype testing is more difficult since access to error-related information is typically limited. As we saw in chapter 1, a real car crash happens very quickly—so quickly that it is very difficult to observe details even with high-speed cameras and well-instrumented cars and crash dummies. In contrast, a computer can be instructed to enact a virtual car crash as slowly as one likes and can zoom in on any structural element of the car to observe the forces acting on it and its response to them during a crash.

Rapid Feedback Is Critical to Efficient Learning

People learn most efficiently when their actions are followed by immediate feedback.[20] Imagine that you were learning how to play the piano, but the sound of your keystrokes took a day to be heard! How would you ever learn how to practice, much less learn how to produce anything that could be performed? Yet far too many experimenters must wait days, weeks, or months before their ideas can be turned into testable prototypes. Time passes, attention shifts to other problems, and when feedback finally arrives, momentum has been lost and the link between cause and effect severed. Moreover, time-to-market pressures don't allow people to wait around until results from an experiment become available. They usually continue with their work, and more often than not, the delayed feedback is no longer relevant or it is used primarily for verification rather than learning.

This delay is precisely what still happens in some automotive development projects where prototype build times can be several months while overall lead times are being reduced, forcing managers to make project decisions faster than ever before. From the time that design data is made available for building physical prototypes until feedback is received, the project progresses and decisions (e.g., a design freeze) have to be made (figure 3-4). In some cases, the data even come too late to contribute to planning the next round of tests. The result? Feedback contributes little to learning and improvement and is more or less used for verification that certain specifications are met. Only when test results point toward major problems (e.g., not meeting minimal government safety standards in the case of crashworthiness) do they have a major impact.

When Edison planned his new laboratory in West Orange, in 1887, he designed supply and apparatus rooms and the machine shop to be very close to the experimental rooms. The laboratory provided a larger space in which a system of experimentation could be put to work,

FIGURE 3 - 4

Long Feedback Delays Impede Learning and Improvement

With long delays in feedback from prototype experiments, the results often contribute little to learning and improvement. In this highly simplified illustration of an automotive development project, data on functional performance (e.g., crashworthiness) comes only after the design concept has been frozen by management and a second round of tests has begun.

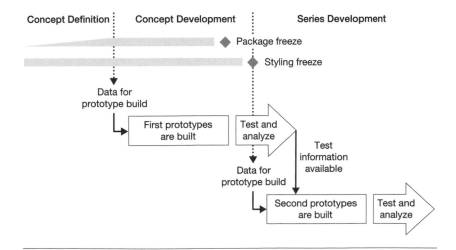

where libraries and storehouses of common and not so common materials could be established. This "workplace" design in turn helped transform Edison's approach to invention. The result was the "invention factory"—a physical arrangement that supported a more systematic and efficient definition, refinement, and exploitation of his ideas. In fact, Edison firmly believed that all material, equipment, and information necessary to carry out experiments needed to be readily available since delays would slow down his employees' work and creativity. When he or his employees had an idea, it had to be immediately turned into a working model or prototype before the inspiration wore off. The West Orange library contained 100,000 volumes so that information could be found quickly. And the facilities were designed so that experiments could flow quickly and machinists and experimenters could cooperate closely. The location of the precision machine shop next to the experimental rooms was built around the idea of speed—as ideas occurred, machinists could rapidly create models and devices that could be tested and provide feedback, which in turn led to new ideas.[21]

Similarly, Team New Zealand emphasized rapid feedback from experiments integral to its boat development process. When the hull design was robust and performance improvements in it were diminishing, the team's focus shifted toward optimizing the keel appendages for minimal drag. Through design enhancements and the placement of wings, they were hoping to increase boat speed much further. For all these experiments, they operated on a twenty-four-hour iteration cycle that guaranteed rapid feedback. The entire team generated hundreds of improvement suggestions for the keel appendages, which were analyzed by the simulation team. The most promising one or two design alternatives that emerged from simulation were prototyped overnight and tested the next day on a full-size boat by the crew. Only they could determine if in fact the boat "felt" faster and whether performance had really been improved. Their feedback also drove the generation of new improvement ideas. David Egan, one of the team's simulation experts, recalled the importance of rapid feedback:

> Instead of relying on a few big leaps, we had the ability to continually design, test, and refine our ideas. The team would often hold informal discussions on design issues, sketch some schematics on the back of a beer mat, and ask me to run the numbers. Using traditional design methods would have meant waiting months for results, and by that

time, our thinking would have evolved so much that the reason for the experiment would long since have been forgotten.[22]

More Capacity Avoids Learning Bottlenecks

The ability to provide rapid feedback to a developer is in part affected by an organization's capacity for experimentation. Not surprisingly, when the number of experiments to be carried out exceeds capacity, the waiting time grows very rapidly and the link between action and feedback is severed. What often surprises people, however, is that the waiting time in many real-world queues increases substantially even when total capacity is not being used. In fact, the relationship between waiting time and utilization is not linear: Queueing theory has shown that the waiting time gradually increases until a resource is utilized around 70 percent, and then the length of the delays surge (figure 3-5).[23]

FIGURE 3 - 5

Waiting for a Resource

According to queueing theory, the waiting time for a resource such as a central main-frame computer increases gradually as more of the resource is used. But when the utilization passes 70 percent, delays increase dramatically.

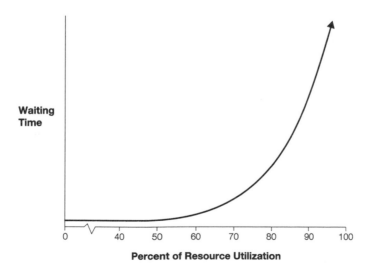

Percent of Resource Utilization

Source: Adapted with permission from Stefan Thomke, "Enlightened Experimentation: The New Imperative for Innovation," *Harvard Business Review,* February 2001, 70.

Moreover, when people expect long delays, they tend to overload queues, slowing down the system even further. More experiments are submitted in the hope that one makes it through quickly but without any sense of how it may affect the overall innovation process. Or simply, firms often lack the right incentives and organization to remove queues and speed up experimentation—an issue that is addressed in chapter 6.

Building sufficient experimentation capacity is therefore not only important but also essential for effective learning. With new technologies bringing down the cost of experimentation dramatically, the opportunities to bring capacity in line with an organization's need to experiment rapidly now exist, but they need to be taken advantage of.

Consider the changes in the world semiconductor industry.[24] In the 1980s, U.S. and European firms started to fall behind their Japanese and Korean competitors in the development of new process technologies. Having access to such technologies was especially important in the DRAM (dynamic random access memory) business where most profits were made immediately after a new technology generation was introduced. Companies such as Toshiba, NEC, and Hitachi were gaining control of the market while Motorola, Intel, and others exited the business. A six-to-twelve-month lead at mastering new equipment, processes, and production yield provided firms with a sizable competitive advantage. Not surprisingly, the ability to learn from experimentation and improve technologies and processes rapidly was very important in gaining a lead.

Research showed that by the early 1990s, U.S. firms had engineered a remarkable turnaround that erased the process technology lead of Japanese and Korean firms. The study attributed part of the success to changes in experimentation strategies; the way firms ran test batches of wafers in large process development facilities that were designed to simulate full-scale production plants. Data by TI, IBM, and Intel showed that these firms had made substantial investment into expanding their *capacity* to run millions of additional experiments, while reducing feedback time to speed-up learning. At the same time, they raised the *fidelity* of experiments by increasing the proportion of standard manufacturing equipment in their process development facilities (table 3-3). This ensured that most learning could be applied to volume production.

TABLE 3 - 3

Changes in Knowledge Generation Through Experimentation (U.S. Firms)

	1983 (1 μm technology)	1993 (0.35 μm technology)
Experimentation Capacity (wafer starts per week)	358	1015
Average Experimentation Throughput Time (in weeks)	6.3	3.4
Minimum Experimentation Throughput Time (in weeks)	1.4	0.8
Proportion of Experimentation/Manufacturing Equipment That Is the Same	62%	88%

Source: Marco Iansiti, *Technology Integration: Making Critical Choices in a Dynamic World* (Boston: Harvard Business School Press, 1998), 162.

Sequential or Parallel Experimentation Strategies Affect Learning

Most large-scale experimentation involves more than one experiment and, as we have seen, usually requires multiple iterations within projects. When the identification of a solution involves more than a single experiment, the information gained from previous trials may serve as an important input to the design of the next one. When learning from one cycle in a set of experiments is incorporated into the next cycle, experimentation has been conducted sequentially. By contrast, when there is an established plan of experimental cycles that is *not* modified by the findings from previous experiments, the experiments have been performed in parallel. For example, you might first carry out a preplanned array of design experiments and analyze the results of the entire array. You might then run one or more verification experiments, as is the case in the field of formal design of experiments (DOE) methods.[25] The experimentation cycles in the initial array are viewed as being carried out in parallel, while those in the second round have been carried out in series with respect to the initial array.

Between November 1993 and May 1994, Team New Zealand built physical prototypes for tank and tunnel testing three times, resulting in fourteen scaled-down models. There simply wasn't enough time to build and test all prototypes sequentially and feed the learning from each round into the next. The advantage of building multiple prototypes per round enabled them to test different alternatives more quickly, drop the least promising directions, and experiment further on the best alternative. Similar approaches can also be found in early car design. Most auto companies, for example, consider a large variety of styling concepts in parallel, ranging from evolutionary to revolutionary directions, and whittle them down in a sequential process where fewer and fewer parallel alternatives are built during each round until one is chosen for engineering and production.[26]

Parallel experimentation clearly can proceed more rapidly, but it does not take advantage of the potential for learning between and among trials. As a result, when parallel experimentation is used, the number of trials needed is usually much greater—but it's usually possible to get to an acceptable solution faster. In comparison, getting to such a solution takes longer with a sequential approach: The number of trials conducted depends very much on how much a firm expects to learn from each round. For example, trying 100 keys in a lock can be done one key at a time, or it can be done all keys at once as long as enough identical locks are available. Since little can be learned between experiments, a sequential strategy would, on average, require fifty trials and thus cost only half as much—but it would also take fifty times longer.[27]

Typically, parallel and sequential approaches are combined, depending on the experimentation strategy chosen. In turn, that strategy depends on many factors: cost of experiments, cost of time, the expected learning between experiments, and how firms envision the "value landscape" they plan to explore when seeking a solution for their problem (box 3-2).[28] Not surprisingly, a dramatic decrease in the cost of experimentation—the kinds of changes that new technologies provide—makes parallel strategies much more attractive to managers. The result will be a shift in many industries toward innovation processes that emphasize parallelism to explore greater experimental space and bring products and services to market more quickly, as long as managers can address some fundamental obstacles that will be discussed in the following chapters.

BOX 3-2: "VALUE LANDSCAPES" AND SEQUENTIAL AND PARALLEL EXPERIMENTATION STRATEGIES

It is very helpful to imagine experimentation strategies in terms of the "space" experimenters are to search to identify an acceptable solution to their problem and how to approach it. In other words, what is the scope of the search that an experimentation strategy is to undertake in order to begin to solve a problem? This value landscape notion is not a guarantee of a solution but only specifies the parameters of the search and effective experimental strategies—sequential and/or parallel—to employ.

Typically, a value landscape can be imagined as a flat plain with one or more "hills" rising on it. The total landscape represents the area that experimenters plan to search for solutions, with the probability of finding a solution increasing as the "hills" are ascended. So the experimenters' goal is to devise a series of experiments that will enable them to explore the hills efficiently. As they start out, experimenters may not have a lot of information about the landscape they are exploring or may hold very different theories on where to begin.[29] Indeed, one entire landscape may be jettisoned and another introduced as their work proceeds. Nonetheless, experimenters' expectations regarding the topography of the value landscape(s) they have chosen are central to their construction of efficient experimental strategies. Two extreme examples illustrate how this works.

First, suppose that the problem for which experiments are being conducted is to figure out how to open a combination lock. You, the experimenter, know that these locks typically have 10^6 (or 1,000,000) or more possible combinations, only one of which will open the lock. You also know that the combinations themselves provide no indication of how close you may be to the solution—opening the lock—as you proceed through the experimental cycle defined earlier. In imagining the value landscape for this problem, then, you would envision an absolutely flat area with a single steeply sided hill, which, when it was ascended, provided the right (and only) solution. You would like to employ a parallel approach to experimentation, therefore. The only information possible from any "trial" is either "error" or "correct." You get no further information about how to proceed in additional experiments if error is the answer. The extreme example resembles the dilemma often faced by pharmaceutical firms in

(continued)

(continued)

the search for new drugs. When only a few compounds (the keys) fit a receptor (the lock) that is hypothesized to cause a disease, a high degree of parallelism makes sense in early discovery, as long as the cost of an experiment can be kept relatively small (see chapter 1).

Consider an alternative problem, one that is amenable to ongoing clues to its solution—much like a children's game in which each participant shouts "warmer" as the one who is "it" nears the right spot. There is again only one hill in this landscape, but its sides slope down, thereby covering more of the space then did the hill in the first example. Experimenters seeking the second hill, therefore, employ a sequential strategy, because they anticipate that each cycle will yield a "warmer" result: information that will help them find the edges of the hill. The information gained from each step taken is so useful in guiding the direction of the next trial step that the correct solution is often found after only a few trials.

For more information on sequential and parallel experimentation strategies, see S. Thomke, E. von Hippel, and R. Franke, "Modes of Experimentation: An Innovation Process and Competitive Variable," *Research Policy* 27 (1998): 315–332.

More Radical Experiments Invite
Different Learning Opportunities

Not all experiments, structured or trial-and-error, are alike. Tweaking independent variables usually results in smaller changes in output—the kinds of changes that are desired in the incremental improvement of products and processes.[30] Alternatively, large variable manipulations or introducing new variables can foster a much wider search, thus increasing the probability of discovering more radical improvements and at the same inviting more failures. More radical experiments can point us in new directions and take us into unknown territories that may or may not result in more radical innovations—one has no way of knowing in advance. As a result, real-world innovation needs to strike a healthy balance between incremental and radical experimentation.

Again, Team New Zealand's yacht development process illustrates this balance very well. The team knew that experiments with its hull design could result in the biggest improvements in performance but at the risk of breaking apart under real sea conditions. After spending several months of experimenting in parallel with different hulls and testing them using scale-models in tank and tunnel tests, the improvements from each iteration started to diminish significantly. As one team member described the process:

> We were emerging with a robust design for the hull and keel. We had reduced the drag considerably over the concept design, but now, each new [round of] prototypes was giving us less and less improvement. The third set of prototypes tests, which we'd just got back, produced less than half the improvement of the second. There was a strong argument that the most improvement potential was now in the keel appendages, where a lot of enhancements can be made through the design and placement of wings. To run those experiments, however, you have to put a real yacht in the water.[31]

With the beginning of the race only eight months away, their strategy then shifted to sequential experimentation during which rapid iterations accumulated into significant changes, one small step at a time. Experimenting with different hull designs so close to the race would have been too risky since "home runs" came at the cost of "strikeouts," which cost the competitors from Australia a full-size racing yacht when their boat broke apart and sank. Therefore, Team New Zealand shifted its development strategy from more radical, parallel experiments affecting the boat's hull structure to more incremental, sequential experiments that optimized the boat's keel.

Noise Impedes Learning

A final factor, one often overlooked, is how ambiguous or excessive feedback "noise" can block learning. In a study of learning in semiconductor manufacturing, research found that production plants with low noise levels could potentially learn much more effectively from their experiments than high-noise plants.[32] Using data collected at five plants, it was estimated that the probability of overlooking a 3 percent yield improvement—a large number as first-year improvements are usually between 0.5 and 3 percent—was about 20 percent. The study concluded that brute-force statistical methods are ineffective or too expensive to deal with these high noise levels.

This noise occurs either when certain variables cannot be controlled or when too many variables are being manipulated—because the design of the experiment itself is poor or because the aim is to reduce the number of experiments overall (and too many manipulations are stuffed into one or few attempts). In either case, it's not possible to discern what is actually happening to the experiment. What is interacting with what? The sad result is that rather than being cost-cutting maneuvers, experiments loaded with too many manipulations often need to be redesigned and rerun, making the whole endeavor more expensive than it would have been in a better-designed state. Alternatively, noise can be a problem if the independent variable itself has too high a variability when observed. In this case, the experiment has limited value since the connection between cause (variable change, procedure, or policy) cannot be linked to the observed effect (change in performance). Under such circumstances, effective learning cannot take place.

The presence of noise was a big problem for Team New Zealand when it was testing changes to its racing boat under real conditions. While tank and tunnel laboratory tests and computer simulations allowed the team to control external conditions such as wind and sea movements, putting a full-sized yacht with a real crew into the sea, with constantly changing wind and weather, made learning from experiments very difficult. Racing one yacht with the design change and then racing it again without it would be possible only if all the other conditions that would affect performance could be controlled—a nearly impossible task since the crew had to detect changes on the order of two or three seconds over the entire course. A minor difference in wind speed between the two trials could easily swamp the effect of the design change and thus make the experiment worthless. The crew would have to sail multiple times to average out the effect of noisy wind, sea, and crew conditions on performance, which would have slowed down the team's experimentation cycles significantly.

To maximize learning from keel experiments and speed up iterations, Team New Zealand decided to build two yachts that could be used in combination to test iterations on the keel wings. Unique among the few teams that invested precious resources in two racing boats, Team New Zealand chose to construct two very similar boats that allowed them to test design changes side by side. With one boat as an experimental control, they could put a keel with a different wing design on each boat, race the boats, and then see how much difference there was in performance. To minimize the effect of the crew, they could swap the keels and test whether the difference still held up. The advantage of using an experimental control was that the effect of noise was now minimized since the two boats were operating under the same noisy conditions. This experimentation strategy was more costly for the team but ended up maximizing learning and performance improvement in the six months before the first race.

Experimentation and Innovation at Bank of America

Maximizing learning from experimentation matters most when companies try to become more innovative at developing and providing novel products and services, as we have seen in a number of R&D settings. To show how much it can matter to companies that have traditionally focused on service innovation or done very little R&D, consider the case of Bank of America, the second largest national bank, operating some 4,500 banking centers in twenty-one states and serving approximately 27 million households and 2 million businesses.[33]

Banks had traditionally downplayed product and service development, which was reflected by a near universal absence of R&D departments. The comforting, stolid shadow of the three-piece-suit-sporting banker, after all, still loomed over most large banks. New products and services in the banking industry, if and when they came, generally arose from marketing departments that lacked the formal processes, methodologies, and resource commitments that companies in many other industries took for granted. In fact, even inspired senior executives with sufficient initiative could, through relatively informal channels, bring their own ideas to test markets. Although banks had information technology (IT) departments, these primarily supported ongoing infrastructure changes in technology and software.

In the late 1990s, however, several converging forces led Bank of America to launch its formalized system for product and service development through its Innovation and Development (I&D) Team, a corporate unit charged with spearheading the initiative. First, along with other industries, the bank began to appreciate the value of continuous experimentation and testing in its efforts to grow through innovation. Second, Internet fever had nurtured a spirit of innovation everywhere, including the banking world. Third, banks began to realize that value creation had to be based on the voice of the customer in order to grow revenue and deepen customer relationships.

In fact, seeds of change were in the air at Bank of America when senior management decided to commit a portfolio of some two dozen real-life "laboratories" in Atlanta to experimentation. Each was a fully operating banking branch, yet in every location new product and service concepts were being tested continuously. Experiments included "virtual tellers," video monitors displaying financial and investment news, computer stations uploading images of personal checks, and "hosting stations."(See figure 3-6 for a selection of experiments carried out in a single branch.)

All these nontraditional items that customers took advantage of were, in fact, experiments. The flat-panel monitors above the tellers, for instance, represented part of the "transaction zone media" experiment (detailed in a later section); the instant retrieval of old checks was the "imageview" experiment; investment centers and complimentary coffee, too, came under experimental scrutiny. All branches closely monitored customer reactions to these innovations through a variety of means including customer satisfaction surveys and statistics on such factors as revenue growth, deposit growth, and number of services utilized by each customer.

Innovation and Development Team Vision

Every day, Bank of America processed 3.8 million transactions—including more checks than the entire Federal Reserve System. A typical noncommercial customer entered a branch every nine days and used an

FIGURE 3 - 6

Selected Experiments in a Bank of America Branch

Bank of America's Innovation & Development Market operates twenty-five branches in its portfolio, with each branch running multiple experiments like the ones show here. These "real-life" laboratories are used to test new product and service concepts that can become candidates for a franchisewide rollout.

Source: Stefan Thomke and Ashok Nimgade, "Bank of America (A)," Case 9-603-022. Boston: Harvard Business School, 2002. Copyright © 2002 by the President and Fellows of Harvard College. Reprinted by permission.

automatic teller machine (ATM) nearly three times a week. Thus, even a 99.9 percent success rate would still mushroom into over a million mistakes a year and expose consumers to problems, ranging anywhere from late paycheck deposits to bill mispayments. It was feared, therefore, that "experiment" and "mistake" would be considered synonymous. Yet if consumers wanted Swiss watch movement precision for their money, they also craved Mediterranean warmth for their service experiences. At about the same time that other banks were already creating more inviting bank branches, so was Bank of America thinking about how to experiment with the human dimension in its bank branches as well as in the human-technology interfaces. To reduce risks of large-scale failure, the bank confined experimentation to its "innovation market," the two-dozen bank branches in Atlanta.

In the controlled environment of these laboratory branches, routine transactions could be handled efficiently while customers' wishes for a good experience could be studied and experimented with. The bank could explore myriad questions: Could people's waiting time in line be made more tolerable? Was there even a need for lines? Could technology-inexperienced customers relate to using keyboards and other devices? How best could staff members coach customers about Internet banking options? The goal was to boost customer and staff satisfaction at bank branches, which would ideally boost revenue growth within a given customer base while secondarily lowering staff turnover.

The team sought to establish a process in which ideas could be generated, collated, and queued up for systematic, objective evaluation. For the few ideas that made it through this "filter," experiments would be designed and planned for the innovation market. Successful experiments—determined on the basis of consumer satisfaction or revenue growth—could then be recommended to senior management for a national rollout.

Prior to introducing these experiments into bank branches, the team actually rehearsed how the activity should occur. In a "prototype center" in Charlotte, North Carolina, people "acted out" how the host would behave as he or she handed off customers to specialists. They "choreographed" how a bank associate (not a specialist) might spend only thirty minutes with a customer to set up a mortgage. To maximize the fidelity of these prototype rehearsals, actual specialists mimicked the needed intervening steps. When all the kinks were worked out in this rehearsal process, the experiment was launched in one of the twenty-five innovation market branches in the bank's "living laboratory."

Experimentation, Learning, and Measurement

Of the many difficulties the I&D Team faced, one of the thorniest was resolving "how-to" questions. How to gauge the success of a concept, how to prioritize which concepts would be tested, how to run several experiments at once, and how to prevent the novelty factor itself from altering the experimental outcome.

The team selected concepts to be tested on the basis of available funding, business fit, and a business case. To some extent, just continuing with the evaluation process served as a natural filter for ideas. But with a very large number of ideas and concepts that needed formal testing, according to team managers, even top-priority experiments needed prioritization! As a result, the team started assigning priorities (high, medium, or low) based on an assumed impact on customers, and management made the final decisions about which product or service concepts to actually test. By May 2002, more than two hundred new ideas had been generated, of which forty made it to testing, thirty-six had been successfully implemented and were being measured, and twenty were recommended for or had already been rolled out nationally. Only four experiments eventually failed—and one of these became a "redefined" concept.

Central to their innovation process was the rate at which people could learn from experiments, and measurement played a very important role, as noted by Milton Jones, a senior executive with Bank of America: "At the end of the day, the most critical aspect of experimentation and learning is measurement. Measurements will defend you if done right; otherwise they will inhibit you."[34] The team had amassed considerable experience and mastery of the subtle factors that would affect learning, discussed throughout this chapter. More specifically, the team found the following challenges in managing these factors.

High-fidelity experiments.   The team sought to ensure that its experiments mirrored reality very closely, or possessed high "fidelity." Concepts that worked only inside their branches, after all, had little value to senior management interested in the scale effect of national rollouts. But high fidelity also meant high cost and commitment, which was hard to justify when ideas were at an early stage. Sometimes, low-fidelity tests using small focus groups gave the team an alternative during the very early stages of idea assessment. Experiments requiring minimal human intervention such as news monitors over the teller's counter, for instance, were likely to work just as well in regular branches as in innovation market branches. But not all innovations might transfer perfectly in the course of nationwide rollout. For instance, would staff in a regular branch provide the handholding and attention required to get technophobes to use a virtual teller? In such cases, the insistence by upper management that experimentation occur in a live banking situation, therefore, helped ensure high fidelity and confidence in the team's learning.

Rapid feedback.   The cycle time for any given experiment was specified at ninety days. This cycle did not include a preliminary "washout" period of a couple of weeks when the novelty factor on the parts of both staff and customers hopefully subsided. Obviously, shorter turnaround time for feedback would help experimenters learn and prepare modified experiments more rapidly. Occasionally it became quickly evident even after the first few days whether a concept would flop or succeed. Only, rarely, however, did the team remove flops prematurely. On one occasion, however, the team canceled a mortgage loan program after just a thirty-day trial primarily because the paperwork took far too long to get credit approvals. The early termination allowed for quicker revision of this experiment, leading to a successful mortgage program.

Increase experimentation capacity.   The number of experiments a single branch could run depended on available floor space and personnel, among other things. A smaller capacity for experimentation would force the team to cram more experiments into one branch. If no capacity remained, the team could be forced to do things sequentially, which in turn would slow the entire concept evaluation process. If the team succumbed to the understandable temptation of cramming too many experiments into a single branch, it would be hard to analyze the contribution of each individual experiment. A single branch might have as many as fifteen active experiments running at any given time. If customers liked a given experiment, however, it was left in the branch even after the ninety-day trial period. In the real world, after all, the branches could not simply pull the plug on something customers had grown to relish. The measurement team leader admitted: "We often worry about changing too many chemicals in the mix and wonder about which one made it explode. As bankers, we're not experts at this type of measurement."[35] The team planned to bring in a statistics expert to help sort out the effects of multiple variables. One of the bank's outside research partners had suggested moving to an entirely different market for further experiments. But the group was focused on its Atlanta market. With the customer satisfaction percentage higher than in traditional bank branches, some felt that capacity still remained for assessing additional experiments.

Minimize the effect of noise.   Isolating the effect of a particular experiment on a bank branch's performance meant being clear on what that effect was *in itself,* minus "noise" factors. Noise could arise from a variety of sources, such as seasonal performance fluctuations, changing market, or even weather conditions. To minimize the effect of noise on learning, the team made heavy use of two techniques, *repetition of trials* and *experimental controls.* First, repeating the same experiment at one branch or running it simultaneously at different branches averaged out the effect of noise and thus reduced the possibility of obscuring the changes that teams were interested in observing and measuring. It also ensured that the success of a given concept would not rely on factors unique to a given branch. A problem, however, was that repetition used up precious experimentation capacity needed for other trials. Second, pairing up two similar branches, one with an experiment (the "intervention") and the other running under normal conditions (the "control"), enabled the team to attribute differences between the branches primarily to the intervention itself. They could draw on controls from within the innovation market or from other branches in Atlanta or even from nearby regions such as North Carolina. The best controls, however, were probably the very same innovation market branches themselves in a before-and-after type of experiment; if properly done, this would help factor out the so-called Hawthorne effect. A well-documented phenomenon, the Hawthorne effect refers to the way that people who know they are under observation—such as those participating in an experiment—tend to change their behavior and thus distort the results. The team was aware that such distortion was possible, given the direct and indirect pressures on staff to perform.

More learning comes from more radical experiments.   The biggest problem with experimenting in a real-world laboratory was balancing innovation with a need for bottom-line success. Pursuing radical innovations would allow the team to explore entirely new possibilities; an incremental approach, however, allowed for improving current banking processes. Successful radical innovations would bring glory to the team.

But home runs came at the cost of strikeouts. With the future of the I&D Team not assured, the team could simply not take outrageous chances. Many tests thus ended up validating ideas that were likely to succeed. Team members readily acknowledged that this was the case for experiments such as the host stations and the transaction zone media. While the original I&D Team vision called for a 30 percent failure rate, the actual rate in the first year hovered close to 10 percent. As senior vice president Warren Butler explained, "We're trying to sell ourselves to the bank. If we have too many failures, we just won't be accepted! Currently, we may have failure *within* concepts, but not failure *in* concepts."[36]

Transaction Zone Media Experiment

A good example of the bank's new innovation process at work was the transaction zone media (TZM) experiment. Internal researchers who interviewed some 1,000 customers in bank lines noted that after about three minutes the gap between actual and perceived wait time rose exponentially. Two focus groups with sales associates and a formal analysis by the Gallup organization provided further corroboration—and the TZM experiment was born. The team hypothesized, based on published psychology literature, that entertaining clients through television monitors above the lobby tellers would reduce perceived wait-times by at least 15 percent. The team chose two similar branches for the TZM experiment and its control so that they could maximize their learning from the experiment. In the summer of 2001, the team installed monitors set to the Atlanta-based news station CNN over teller booths in the branch. The team then allowed a week's "washout" period for the novelty to wear off before measuring results for the subsequent two weeks.

Results from the TZM-equipped branch showed that the number of people who overestimated their actual wait times dropped from 32 percent to 15 percent. During the same period, none of the other branches reported drops of this magnitude. In fact, the branch used as a control saw an increase in overestimated wait times from 15 percent to 26 percent. Though these were encouraging results, the team still had to prove to senior management that the TZM could positively affect the corporate bottom line. To do so, the team relied on a model that used the easily measurable customer satisfaction index (based on a thirty-question survey) as a proxy for future revenue growth.

Prior studies indicated that every one-point improvement in a Customer Satisfaction Index corresponded to $1.40 in added annual revenue per household from increased customer purchases and retention. A banking center (branch) with a customer base of 10,000 households would thus increase its annual revenues by $28,000 should the index increase by just two points. The team carried out a statistical analysis of the test branch's results and projected that the reductions in perceived wait times would translate into a 5.9 point increase in overall banking center customer satisfaction.

While the benefits were substantial, the team now had to consider whether they outweighed the costs of buying and installing the monitors. The team determined that it would cost some $22,000 to upgrade a branch in the Atlanta innovation market but that, for a national rollout, economies of scale would bring the per-branch cost down to about $10,000 per site. Any branch with more than a few thousand households in its customer base would therefore be able to recoup the upfront cost in less than a single year. Encouraged by the program's apparent economic viability, the team recently launched a second phase to the TZM experiment, in which it is measuring the impact of more varied television programming, different sound levels, and even advertising. In the end, the team had learned much as a result of thoughtful experimentation, learning that could be directly translated into service innovations and increased customer satisfaction.

Conclusion

On the surface, the experiments run in suburban bank branches, on world-class yachts, in car companies, and in the entire integrated circuit industry could hardly look more dissimilar. Yet they share a basic iterative process of four-step experimentation cycles, as outlined in this chapter, that can be organized to maximize learning. How learning through experimentation occurs (or does not occur) is affected by seven factors: Fidelity, cost, iteration time, capacity, sequential and parallel strategies, signal-to-noise ratio, and experiment type all enhance the power of experimentation. New technologies for experimentation amplify the importance of managing these factors, thus creating the potential for higher R&D performance, innovation, and ultimately new ways of creating value for customers.

So far, it all looks easy! But it is not, as managerial biases, mental models, and organizational inertia that oppose change can get in the way. In chapter 4 we shall see how equally easily organizations can fail to unlock the potential of new experimentation technologies.

NOTES

1. Quoted from Millard (1990), page 19.

2. Ibid., page 40.

3. Garvin (2000) distinguishes between exploratory and hypothesis-testing experiments. He notes that the former are "what-if" experiments that are open-ended whereas the latter are intended to discriminate among alternative explanations.

4. For a discussion of the role of experiments in scientific discovery, see Hare (1981) and Galison (1987).

5. Over the years, many books have been written on experimental design. Montgomery's (1991) textbook provides a very accessible overview and is used widely by students and practitioners. Box, Hunter, and Hunter (1978) go much deeper into the underlying statistics of experimental design. Readers who are interested in the original works of Ronald Fisher may go to either his classic papers on agricultural science (Fisher, 1921, 1923) or his classic text on the design of experiments (Fisher, 1966).

6. Box and Draper (1969) use statistical experimentation in the incremental improvement of processes, and Box and Draper (1987) apply it to the modeling and building of "response surfaces."

7. Techniques for improving product and process robustness (also known as Taguchi methods) are discussed in Clausing (1993), Phadke (1989), and Taguchi and Clausing (1990).

8. See Allen (1966), Garvin (2000), Iansiti (1997), Leonard-Barton (1995), Marples (1961), Pisano (1997), Thomke (1998a), and von Hippel and Tyre (1995).

9. All information on Team New Zealand in this chapter comes from Enright and Capriles (1996) and Iansiti and MacCormack (1997).

10. Similar building blocks to analyze the design and development process were used by other researchers. Simon (1981, chapter 5) examined design as a series of "generator-test cycles." Clark and Fujimoto (1989) and Wheelwright and Clark (1992, chapters 9 and 10) used "design-build-test" cycles as a framework for problem solving in product development. I modified the blocks to include "run" and "analyze" as two explicit steps that conceptually separate the execution of an experiment and the learning that takes place during analysis (see also Thomke, 1998).

11. Simon (1969) notes that traditional engineering methods tend to employ more inequalities (specifications of satisfactory performance) than maxima and minima. These figures of merit permit comparisons between better or worse designs, but they do not provide an objective method to determine best designs. Since these comparisons usually happen in real-world design, Simon introduces the term "satisfice," implying that a solution satisfices rather than optimizes performance measures.

12. An example of such a change is the impotence drug Viagra, which was first identified by scientists at Pfizer's R&D laboratory in Sandwich, England. The drug was initially aimed at fighting the heart condition angina. After several clinical trials with unimpressive outcomes, the researchers were ready to shelve the project until an unexpected side effect was observed. Instead of fighting clogged heart arteries, some men with higher dosages reported improved and more frequent erections than before. Continued testing and experimentation was successful and eventually turned a "failure" into one of Pfizer's most successful drugs.

13. Quoted from Iansiti and MacCormack (1997), page 3.

14. These factors are not intended to be mutually exclusive and collectively exhaustive. Instead, the purpose is to describe a set of interdependent factors that affect how companies, groups, and individuals learn from experiments and thus need to be managed.

15. For example, Pisano (1997, chapter 2) explains why and how the representativeness of models matters in pharmaceutical production environments.

16. Quoted from Iansiti and MacCormack (1997), page 4.

17. Ibid.

18. Hauptman and Iwaki (1991) present a detailed account of the *Challenger* disaster.

19. Jaikumar and Bohn (1986) noted that production knowledge can be classified into eight stages, ranging from merely being able to distinguish good from bad processes (but only an expert knows why) to complete procedural knowledge, where all contingencies can be anticipated and controlled and production can be automated. Building models for experimentation in itself forces developers to articulate and advance their knowledge about systems and how they work, thus elevating knowledge to higher stages.

20. The importance of feedback in learning has been noted by numerous management scholars, including Garvin (2000), Leonard-Barton (1995), Senge (1990), Repenning and Sterman (2002), Sterman (1989), and Schön (1983).

21. Millard (1990), pages 9–10.

22. Quoted from Iansiti and MacCormack (1997), page 6.

23. This property of queueing systems often surprises managers even though it can be found in most operations management textbooks. For an insightful discussion of queueing theory and its application to product development, see Reinertsen (1997, chapter 3). Loch and Terwiesch (1999) have studied the resulting congestion effects in the development of a climate control system within a large vehicle development project. They found that engineering change orders can be significantly delayed (weeks or months) because of scarce capacity coupled with process variability.

24. For more details on the research on semiconductors described here, see Iansiti (1998), chapter 8.

25. Box, Hunter, and Hunter (1978), Montgomery (1991), and Fisher (1966).

26. "Set-based" design approaches advocate a similar approach where parallel alternatives are pursued simultaneously (Sobek, Ward, and Liker, 1999).

27. Loch, Terwiesch, and Thomke (2001) formally model the trade-off between sequential and parallel experimentation strategies and derive optimal policies for decision makers. Thomke, von Hippel, and Franke (1998)

show the essence of this trade-off with the following thought experiment. Consider a very simple search in which the topography of the value landscape is known to consist of n points and can be visualized as flat except for a narrow tower with vertical sides, representing the correct solution. A purely parallel experimentation strategy would require all experiments and their tests to be done at the same time. Thus, one would *not* be able to apply what one has learned from one trial to the next trial. While this approach results in a very high number of experiments (n), it also reduces the total development time significantly as all trials are done in parallel. Thus, massively parallel experimentation would be the costliest but also the fastest strategy. In contrast, a sequential strategy applied to this sample problem would allow one to learn from each experimental trial and—equipped with this new knowledge—carefully select the next one. A strategy with minimal learning (not repeating a trial that has failed) can, on average, halve the total number of experiments required but would dramatically increase total development time relative to the purely parallel approach. Of course, if there is the opportunity for greater learning from each trial, the number of trials in the series likely to be required to reach the solution (and therefore the total elapsed time) is further reduced. For example, consider a very favorable learning scenario where the n trials are arranged on a linear scale (e.g., n different pressure settings) and that after each trial, one could learn whether to move up or down on that scale. Thus one would effectively reduce the search space by 50 percent after each experimental cycle and rapidly progress toward an optimal solution. An experimenter would start with ½ (the midpoint) and move to either ¼ or ³⁄₄, depending on the outcome of the first experiment, and continue in the same fashion until the solution were found. A real-world example for such a search can be found in the practice of system problem identification: Very experienced electronic technicians tend to start in the middle of a system, find the bad half, and continue to subdivide their search until the problem is found. One can easily see that the expected number of trials until success using a serial strategy (with the kind of learning described) can be reduced to about $\log_2 n$—a dramatic reduction in cost. However, total development time would exceed that of the purely parallel strategy by the same factor.

28. The concept of a "value landscape" is related to the study of evolutionary biology that regards fitness landscapes as the distribution of fitness values across a space of entities (Kauffman and Levin, 1987; Wright, 1932). More

recently, fitness landscapes have been used in the study of organizational structure and strategy in the context of changing environments (Bruderer and Singh, 1996; Tushman and O'Reilly III, 1996; Levinthal, 1997). To distinguish between biological evolution and the design and experimentation process, the term "value landscape" is used here. (For a good explanation of value landscapes, see Baldwin and Clark (2000), pages 232–234).

29. Nelson noted the importance of prior theory in understanding the experimental search of an economic actor (Nelson, 2002). See also Nelson (1982), Nelson and Nelson (2002), and Nelson and Winter (1982, chapter 11).

30. An exception is highly nonlinear systems where small changes in independent variables can result in large changes in dependent variables. Optimizing such systems can be challenging, but experience has shown that increasing robustness, rather than a single-point performance optimization, via Monte Carlo–type methods appears to be promising (e.g., in improving automotive crash safety). However, in many areas of engineering design, applying such methods will require much more experimentation capacity than is available to development teams today.

31. Quoted from Iansiti and MacCormack (1997), page 7.

32. Bohn (1995).

33. The section draws extensively from Thomke and Nimgade (2002).

34. Ibid., page 7.

35. Ibid., pages 8–9.

36. Ibid., page 9.

4

the reality of technology

introduction

New experimentation technologies do not automatically lead to superior performance simply by being introduced into an organization. The promise of the new far too often falls disastrously short in practice. While the general problem of technology adoption is well known to both scholars and managers, the problems associated with the introduction of experimentation technology are not so familiar.[1] The tools of experimentation too often look beguilingly simple, as if, in the case of simulation, one merely substitutes the "virtual" for the "real." For instance, in chapter 3 we looked at the success of Team New Zealand, not at the efforts of its competitors. Were they asleep at the tiller? Not at all; indeed, Team New Zealand's rivals were attempting to use equally powerful experimentation technology—but clearly not with the success *Black Magic* achieved.

In this chapter we shall start with an overview of Team New Zealand's effort and then examine other organizations' attempts to adopt new technologies without thinking through how the technologies must be integrated into both experimentation processes and organizations. The question of why firms have difficulties turning technology investments into R&D performance improvements will be closely examined in the context of research findings from the global automotive industry. We shall see that *how* the technologies are being used in innovation processes limits their potential dramatically. Specifically, the chapter will show some realities that get in the way of introducing new experimentation technologies such as CAD and computer-aided engineering (CAE): Processes and people limit the impact of new technologies, excessive organizational interfaces slow down experimentation cycles, and behavior is often outpaced by technological change. Managers find that these realities prevent their companies from tapping into the changing economics of experimentation—in spite of substantial financial investments. In subsequent chapters, we'll learn how these realities can be addressed so that companies can unlock the potential.

Integrated Experimentation System of Team New Zealand

An interesting fact about the 1995 America's Cup slate of competitors is that many syndicates had larger budgets for experimentation and access to significantly better technology than did Team New Zealand.[2] The successful (United States) defender, for example, upgraded the technology that had been instrumental in its 1992 victory; moreover, its 1995 design team was led by a well-known hydrodynamics professor from MIT. Another U.S. entrant was supported by Boeing Aircraft Company and Cray Research, enabling it to run large-scale simulations on the world's fastest supercomputers while receiving feedback from experts who designed wings for supersonic jets. Every few weeks, the team ran large batches of simulations at Boeing facilities, with the results reported immediately.

Meanwhile, another competitor had forged alliances with General Motors Technical Center (for wind tunnel tests), Boeing, again (for advanced aerodynamics technical expertise and software analysis), Lockheed Space Systems (for structural design), Analytical Methods, Inc. (for computational fluid dynamics analysis), and Cray. It also employed naval architects, structural engineers, fluid dynamics experts, computer analysts, and wind tunnel and towing tank engineers.

As we saw in chapter 3, Team New Zealand elected to build two race boats so as to optimize its keel design and thus had fewer resources to spend on simulation technology (the overall budgets for teams were comparable; it was how resources were applied that differed among them). Because of that choice, the team could not afford the supercomputers that competitors were using; instead it relied on engineering workstations provided by sponsors Sun and Silicon Graphics. Critically, however, as we've seen, it *integrated*—made the best use of—its technology. The team—the "organization"—and the technology *adapted to each other and to the task at hand;* in other words, it learned from experimentation and not just improved the design of the yachts. As we saw in chapter 3, Team New Zealand's crew was pivotal in deciding how results from experimentation were or were not useful.

Team New Zealand thus turned a potential disadvantage into a plus. Instead of relying on computer simulation to drive its yacht design process, the team designed its processes, organization, culture, and management around an *integrated experimentation system.* Combining all these elements through integration took into account their respective strengths, limitations, and interdependencies so that the system promoted experimentation for learning and, ultimately, the development of a winning boat and the team to sail it. Specifically, the design team generated and simulated many keel alternatives during the day. The most promising concept was manufactured overnight, attached to the yacht, and tested in real sailing conditions by the crew on the following day. The crew, in turn, was able to provide immediate feedback— "The boat felt like it was towing a bucket!"—resulting in another round of design changes and improvements. The result was rapid experimentation cycles that increased learning and amplified the value of human experience. Experiments were successful if and only if the crew felt a difference in performance.

Workstations were installed near the dock to facilitate the interaction between teams and technology. Designers and crew members could debate alternatives, simulate the alternatives in a couple of hours, and test them the next day—a process that enhanced Blake's emphasis on openness and cooperation. By 10 May 1995, the date of the first race, thousands of design proposals had been simulated, resulting in more than fifty physical changes to the keel. Team New Zealand's design leader, Doug Peterson, estimated that these iterations alone had shaved over two minutes from their expected course time in San Diego—a significant advantage since races could be won or lost in a matter of seconds.

By comparison, Team New Zealand's competitors were unable to achieve the same level of integration between technology, process, and organization, even with much larger technology budgets. The competitor running large batches of simulations every few weeks at Boeing, for example, did not have the advantage of joint experimentation between the design team and the boat's crew. Dave Egan, Team New Zealand's simulation expert, reflected on his team's approach and pointed out the contrast:

Once simulation suggested an improvement of the keel, everyone entered a manufacturing mode. There were blueprints and plans to develop and construction work to complete. We could normally turn around a new set of wings for the keel overnight. This meant that the next day, we could try out the new design and get some immediate feedback from racing the boats. Unlike rivals using supercomputers located a few hundred miles from the dock, our crew could see the projected impact of the change we were proposing, then go sailing and see how close it was to reality.[3]

The fact that the other teams could not leverage their access to experimentation technologies as successfully as did Team New Zealand is significant for our discussion. It is surely possible that resource constraints propelled the team to embrace change and take on more risk: Designers and crew would have to be creative in their efforts to maximize the potential their new tools afforded. The question for our purposes in this chapter, however, is not simply why Team New Zealand was successful but why *all* its competitors were not. This is a matter not of who won the race per se but that the approach all the other teams took was similar yet very different from that of Team New Zealand.

In fact, what the other America's Cup teams did with their new technology resembles how technology has often been adopted: Organizations attempt to superimpose it on existing processes and procedures, failing to understand how the technology itself changes the activities. The result is that the existing system is interfered with while the potential of a new one is unrealized.

Challenges of Technology Adoption

When Nobel Laureate Robert Solow noted in 1987 that "you can see the computer age everywhere but in the productivity statistics," he drew attention to a paradox that has bedeviled scholars and managers ever since.[4] The Solow paradox, as it is often called, points towards an industry-level challenge that resembles the firm- and project-level issues addressed in this book: How does one tap into the enormous potential for innovation that new technologies provide? A recent study by the McKinsey Global Institute reports some powerful observations.[5]

The year-long McKinsey study examined, among other issues, the role of information technology and its impact on productivity between 1995 and 2000. With the help of an academic advisory committee that included Solow, the Institute studied fifty-nine economic sectors and found that there was no significant correlation between IT intensity and jumps in productivity in the United States. However, a deeper analysis of six economic sectors that drove most of the observed productivity jumps (retail, wholesale, securities, telecom, semiconductors, and computer manufacturing), combined with three sectors that failed to translate heavy IT investments into productivity gains (hotels, retail banking, and long-distance data telephony), resulted in some intriguing findings. Many of the increases in the six "jumping" sectors were explained by fundamental changes in the way firms delivered products and services, which were sometimes aided by new or old technologies. The study's authors concluded:

> [The] findings suggest that it is only when IT enables managerial innovations, facilitates the reorganization of functions and tasks into more productive approaches, and is applied in labor intensive activities, that it plays a major role in driving productivity.[6]

The potential of new experimentation technologies poses similar questions and challenges vis-à-vis higher R&D performance. The Team New Zealand case and the experiences of other firms have shown that it is possible to achieve better performance with less technology investment than that made by competitors. As painful as it is for companies to find resources to purchase new technology, doing so, in fact, is the easy part. Far more difficult is using it effectively. Doing so requires organizational changes that facilitate rapid and integrated experimentation and learning. And the challenge is by no means related only to experimental technology or to companies themselves. Consider Elting Morison's classic account of the U.S. Navy's fierce resistance to new and more advanced weapons systems:

Military organizations are societies built around and upon the prevailing weapons systems. Intuitively and quite correctly the military man feels that a change in weapon portends a change in the arrangements of his society. . . . Daily routines, habits of mind, social organization, physical accommodations, conventions, rituals, spiritual allegiances have been conditioned by the essential fact of the ship. What then happens to your society if the ship is displaced as the principal element by such a radically different weapon as the plane? The mores and structure of the society are immediately placed in jeopardy. They may, in fact, be wholly destroyed.[7]

Introducing New Technology at Eli Lilly

Eli Lilly's adoption of combinatorial chemistry and high-throughput screening illustrates the difficulty of translating new technology into performance gains when organizations have been conditioned by many years of traditional drug discovery.[8] In 1991, Eli Lilly had been one of the first large pharmaceutical firms to enter a strategic alliance with Sphinx Pharmaceuticals, an early biotechnology venture that focused on combinatorial chemistry and high-throughput screening.

As discussed in chapter 1, these technologies have significantly increased the efficiency and speed at which companies can generate and screen chemical compounds for the optimization of drug leads. Using combinatorial chemistry, researchers no longer need to painstakingly create one compound at a time. Instead, they can quickly generate numerous variations simultaneously around a few building blocks, just as locksmiths can make thousands of keys from a dozen basic shapes; they thereby reduce the cost of a compound from thousands of dollars to a few dollars or less.

In practice, however, combinatorial chemistry has disrupted well-established routines in laboratories. For one thing, the rapid synthesis of drugs has led to a new problem: how to screen those compounds quickly. Traditionally, potential drugs were tested in live animals—an activity fraught with logistical difficulties, high expense, and considerable statistical variation. So laboratories developed test-tube-based screening methodologies that could then be automated. This technology, called high-throughput screening, has required significant innovations in equipment (high-speed precision robotics, for one) and in the screening process itself to let researchers conduct many biological tests, or assays, on members of a chemical library virtually simultaneously.

The large pharmaceutical corporations and academic chemistry departments initially greeted such "combichem" technologies (combinatorial chemistry and high-throughput screening) with skepticism. Among the reasons cited was that the purity of compounds generated via combichem was relatively poor compared to traditional synthetic chemistry. As a result, several technological advances were made outside large pharmaceutical companies.

But as the technology matured, it caught the interest of large corporations like Eli Lilly, which acquired Sphinx Pharmaceuticals, one of the start-ups developing combichem, in 1994. Even then, it took Eli Lilly a few years to take the new technologies from its Technology Core group—an R&D division that supported the firm's various research activities—to its drug discovery division where the technologies could be used systematically in drug development projects.

An accidental encounter between scientists from Technology Core and drug discovery had to act as a catalyst to deploying the new technological assets in the search for a new migraine drug, but initial resistance was significant, as one director noted:

> *People felt they [researchers using combinatorial chemistry] were engaging in "voodoo science," and that the collaboration would divert valuable screening capacity. They were gutsy, taking a big gamble. Even the concept of high-throughput screening was met with skepticism. Few at Eli Lilly believed we could collapse three years of screening into three months or less. It's very easy to stop something you don't believe in.[9]*

Eli Lilly's senior management should be complimented on its willingness to invest in new technologies when there was significant uncertainty about their value to drug discovery. At the same time, however, they underestimated the internal organizational resistance they had to overcome in order to extract value from the ability to screen and refine significantly larger amounts of chemical compounds in the search for new drugs. My field research revealed that traditional chemists felt threatened by the new technology that appeared to automate many of the tasks that they had so carefully learned and refined over many years. Here was a set of new experimentation technologies that could fundamentally change drug discovery, including the role and tasks of medicinal chemists. Not surprisingly, their initial reaction was skeptical and they neither embraced nor were fully committed to improve a technology that could make them more productive.

The discrepancy between getting access to these technological assets and actually getting internal employees to use them in drug development projects was underscored by Eli Lilly's head of R&D who, rather surprised, noted in 1996 to one of his managers, "You mean not all of our chemists are using combinatorial chemistry?"[10] Management underestimated the challenges of bringing new technologies into the firm and still faced some project-level resistance about five years after its 1991 alliance with Sphinx Pharmaceuticals and after other significant investments in Eli Lilly's Technology Core group. Eventually, Eli Lilly was able to translate new technologies into improvement in discovery performance through radical measures, including making in-house screening unavailable to chemists and leaving them no other choice than to use some of the high-throughput screening capabilities at its Sphinx subsidiary. Such measures made chemists realize the potential of the new technologies and forced them to reassess their assumptions and routines.

Until now, pharmaceutical giants like Eli Lilly have used combinatorial chemistry primarily to optimize promising new drug candidates that resulted from an exhaustive search through chemical libraries and other traditional sources. But if combinatorial chemistry itself advances and achieves levels of purity and diversity comparable to the compounds in a library, companies will increasingly use it at the earlier phases of drug discovery. In fact, all major pharmaceutical companies have had to use combichem and traditional synthesis in concert; the companies best able to manage the new and mature technologies together so that they fully complement each other will have the greatest opportunity to achieve the highest gains in productivity and innovation.

Research Program on Global Automotive Development

In order to understand more deeply the management realities of deploying new experimentation technologies within firms, I now turn to some recent findings from a research program on innovation processes in the global automotive industry. Few products have changed our lives and fascinated us as profoundly as the automobile. Because of its complexity, economic significance, and pace of relentless change, the auto industry has always been the subject of much attention by scholars, managers, policy makers, and the public in general. When the publication of the 1990 book *The Machine That Changed the World* showed how Japanese firms were using so-called lean production systems to outperform Western firms, the finding caused national debates on industrial competitiveness.[11]

Meanwhile, during the mid-1980s, Kim Clark and Takahiro Fujimoto at Harvard Business School launched a landmark study of automotive development performance and organization at twenty U.S., European, and Japanese firms.[12] After interviewing managers at nearly all the world's automakers and collecting an impressive data set on twenty-nine car projects, the authors concluded that the Japanese system for product development was, on average, nearly twice as efficient as its Western counterparts and a year faster in bringing new-car concepts to market. According to Clark and Fujimoto, five patterns contributed to this performance difference. First, Japanese firms were particularly effective at leveraging supplier capabilities and simplifying project coordination. Second, the best firms applied production expertise to routine development activities such as prototyping, die making, pilot runs, and production ramp-up. Third, lead-time advantages were in part due to increased overlapping of upstream and downstream activities and better communication and hand-offs of project teams. Fourth, Japanese projects involved on average half the number of long-term participants that the U.S. and European projects used, thus leading to wider task assignments for individual engineers. And finally, the best firms employed "heavyweight" project management, leading them to excel in time, cost, and quality.[13] A follow-up study in the early 1990s showed that non-Japanese automotive firms had made significant improvement in their development performance. The narrowing gap was caused by the adoption of Japanese-style supplier management practices, higher degrees of simultaneous engineering, and stronger project management systems.[14]

In 1998, I joined forces with Fujimoto, now at the University of Tokyo, to begin a new round of automotive development research that would build on the prior two studies. Before we started to collect new project data, however, we made a significant change that resulted directly from ongoing field research and case writing in the automotive industry. Three-dimensional (3-D) CAD and CAE, such as crash safety simulations and new rapid prototyping technologies, were fundamentally revolutionizing new-car development, but these changes had not been studied systematically. Hence, we decided to include the use of new experimentation technologies as a major part of our study. Participating firms answered about 400 questions for each car project, and this information was augmented by site visits and interviews at each participating company. Because of the extensive travel and logistics, collecting all the new data took about three years. Appendix 4-1 describes how the study data were gathered.

Technology-Performance Paradox in R&D

The combined research program on global automotive development performance now consists of primary data from seventy-two new car projects that were carried out in the United States, Europe, and Japan between 1980 and 1999. To understand how performance evolved over this twenty-year period of constant change, we looked at the number of total engineering hours invested in each project and the amount of time companies needed to bring a new concept to market. The first variable, *engineering hours,* measures the level of resources required to take a concept to market introduction.[15] It includes all *internal* hours spent on design, engineering, prototype construction, and so on and *external* hours subcontracted to engineering service firms. Not only do engineering hours have a direct impact on the total cost of a project but they also tie up important resources that are not available to other projects, thus limiting a firm's R&D pipeline.

The second variable, *total lead time,* measures the calendar time a company needs to define, design, engineer, and introduce a new vehicle to the market.[16] The clock starts when a new-vehicle concept is initiated and stops with first retail sales to customers. The longer it takes to bring a product to market, the more difficult it is for companies to respond to changing customer needs and technologies, thus increasing the risk of missing a market window. Conversely, projects that are completed too hastily run the risk of providing to customers too little functionality or poor product quality.

To examine the relationship between R&D performance and the role of new experimentation technologies, we first looked at the changes in project productivity that had happened since Clark and Fujimoto's study in the 1980s. A direct comparison of the raw data was not possible because project contents (e.g., compact versus luxury cars) were different and had to be accounted for. As a result, engineering hours and lead time were adjusted for project complexity to allow for an "apples-to-apples" comparison. The resulting data, shown in figures 4-1 and 4-2, tell an interesting story: Although the transition from the 1980s to early

FIGURE 4 - 1

Actual versus Expected Engineering Hours in the World Auto Industry

This analysis is based on seventy-two development projects. The vertical axis is the difference between the actual and the expected number of project hours after controlling for project complexity. A negative value indicates better-than-expected productivity, whereas a positive value means that companies are faring worse.

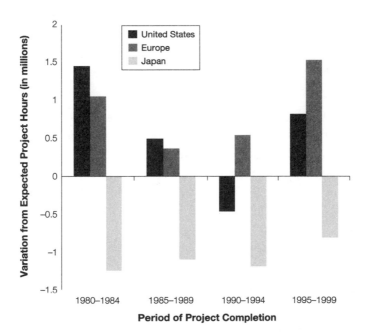

FIGURE 4 - 2

Actual versus Expected Development Time in the World Auto Industry

This analysis is based on seventy-two development projects. The vertical axis is the difference between the actual and the expected development time after controlling for project complexity. A negative value indicates better-than-expected time to market, whereas a positive value means that companies are slower.

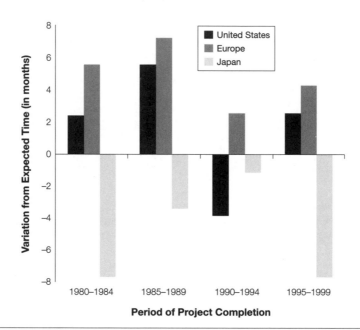

1990s can be characterized by Western firms closing the productivity gap to Japanese firms, data from the late 1990s show the gap increasing again. How do we account for this trend?

Since the graphs in the figures show only averages by region, one possibility is that companies "bought" development time by putting more engineering resources to work. It is often assumed that project tasks can be broken up further and worked on in parallel by adding engineers to a project.[17] As a result the total project should be completed more quickly. Unfortunately, managing R&D projects is not that simple. While companies can buy some time by throwing more resources at projects, adding more people also introduces organizational and task complexity. Moreover, the strategy doesn't fundamentally improve *how* new prod-

FIGURE 4 - 3

Adjusted Engineering Hours and Development Time (1980–2000)

*Adjusted development hours and time take into account differences in complexity for all
seventy-two car projects. The best-performing projects are in the lower left quadrant;
the worst projects are in the upper right quadrant. The positive correlation is statistically
significant (at the 1 percent level).*

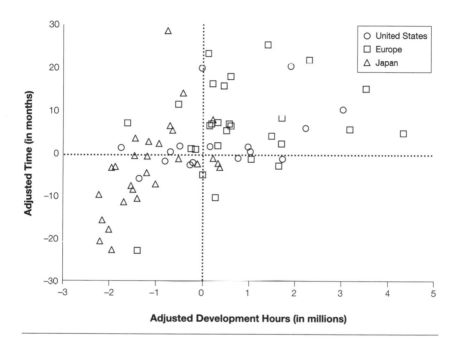

ucts are developed. Examining the relationship between adjusted engineering hours and development lead time for all seventy-two projects in
the automotive study strongly supports this notion: Companies that
brought vehicles to market more rapidly in fact needed fewer development resources (figure 4-3). It seems that the ability to organize, employ
better processes, and manage projects differently resulted in fundamental capabilities that resulted in both higher speed and more efficiency.

The most surprising finding from our research is that many development practices that accounted for performance differences in
the 1980s have converged; these practices include stronger project
management, Japanese-style supplier management practices, and the
use of simultaneous engineering. But we found that performance

differences widened again in Japan's favor during the 1990s. What was going on here?

Most certainly, there must have been other forces at work that affected automotive development performance and would have explained these "new" differences. These other forces might be the rapid advances of new technologies for CAD, CAE, and computer-aided manufacturing (CAM) and the availability of much improved rapid prototyping methods. Together, these technologies have been fundamentally changing the way developers experiment, solve problems, learn and interact with others, and manage information—and not only in the automotive industry. Senior R&D managers were in fact telling us that "digital development" has been the most significant change in their entire careers. Left with a performance gap that had to be explained, we turned to the use of advanced technology as a possible driver of the Japanese advantage.

Amazingly, however, an analysis of the most recent car projects revealed that Western firms were leading Japanese competitors in at least two very important areas. The most sophisticated CAD technologies (3-D solid and surface models) were used much more extensively in U.S. and European firms. In contrast, some Japanese firms were still relying to some degree on less sophisticated CAD technologies such as wire frames and two-dimensional (2-D) models (figure 4-4).[18]

The same pattern was found in the application of computer simulation to crashworthiness design. Project data and interviews with experts confirmed that Western firms were using both more complex models and more user-friendly tools than many of their Japanese counterparts in the mid-1990s. For example, the number of finite elements—a measure of simulation model fidelity—were higher in the United States and Europe (table 4-1). At the same time, we also found in company interviews that most Japanese firms had more recently been very aggressive at building technical capabilities in these areas.

Our analysis of the data and interviews with managers also revealed that the reasons for the widening technology and performance gap are complex. Most certainly, bureaucracy, complacency, poor planning, and short-term horizons have all played a role in some firms. The poor economic performance of some Japanese firms in the 1990s while their

FIGURE 4 - 4

The Use of Advanced Computer-Aided Design (CAD) Technologies in the Mid-1990s

An analysis of eighteen car projects shows the percentage of final component drawings that were developed using computer-aided design (CAD) tools of varying levels of sophistication. The most advanced firms were using 3D-solid models and the least advanced were using 2D or no CAD at all.

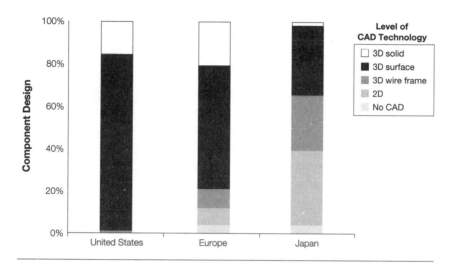

TABLE 4 - 1

Complexity of Crash Simulation Models

Complexity of Simulation Model (in thousands of finite elements)	United States (n=4)	Europe (n=4)	Japan (n=9)
During *Concept Development* (for projects reported in research study)	55	57	30
During *Concept Development* (end of 1990s)	73	110	111
During *Design Engineering* (for projects reported in research study)	84	125	48
During *Design Engineering* (end of 1990s)	118	192	115

The more finite the elements in a computer model, the more closely it simulates reality. Projects reported in research study were completed in the mid-1990s.

Western competitors posted record profits most certainly removed some of the competitive pressures that were felt in the late 1980s.

But the research supports a more fundamental reason for this apparent paradox: Leading-edge technology does not lead to quantum leaps in performance unless it is accompanied by change. Process, organization, management, and culture can easily become a bottleneck to unlocking the potential of new technologies—as has been stressed before. In fact, the Team New Zealand case and the auto industry research suggest that some firms can excel with new technology that is "good enough"—as long as they make changes that tap into the potential for accelerated learning by experimentation. One manager in our study compared the technology-performance paradox to being stuck in traffic during his morning commute. Even if he went out and bought a Ferrari sports car, his daily drive to work would not be quicker unless he found a new route that took advantage of his (substantial) investment in the vehicle. Analogously, the potential of leading-edge technologies cannot be unlocked unless new ways to experiment, learn, and manage innovation can be found.

Behind the Paradox: Understanding the Reality

When new experimentation technologies were first made available to firms, the investment decisions often focused on making *what already existed* faster or cheaper. Thus, proponents of CAE tools initially argued that substituting virtual prototypes for physical ones could, by itself, save firms millions of dollars. And indeed savings were realized for this simple act of substitution. So when news of such success became widespread, expectations across the board rose substantially. All processes and procedures could expect such results. Unfortunately, while costs could be lowered, other problems would arise.

Boeing's development of its new generation 777 aircraft is a case in point. Managers and engineers took advantage of 3-D CAD systems and in-house software to minimize physical assembly models that were often used to find design problems for the first time. However, the effective use of 3-D CAD systems required engineers to resolve design conflicts much earlier than had been necessary with physical assembly models. These engineers, it transpired, weren't even aware of each other's existence much less prepared to work together. Alan Mulally, one-time director of engineering on the 777, recalled seeing a senior structures engineer going up and down the building looking for a hydraulic designer. The engineer wanted to put a bracket on his floor beam, and he and the hydraulic designer had not come to an agreement on the location and the size of the bracket, whether it would create a problem, and so on. The furious engineer stopped Mulally and asked what the hydraulic designers looked like: "Do they have tubes in their pockets? Do they have tubes coming out of their heads?"[19] Boeing's eventual success in using 3-D CAD technology came not only from investing in it but in recognizing that leveraging its possibilities required new processes and organizational forms for teams in working together. The tubes anecdote reveals just how far the company had to go for change to happen.

Altogether, the automotive study findings (and other examples in this chapter) suggest that it is not necessarily *what* the technology is that matters but *how* it is used. Some reality lessons can be drawn from this research.

Reality 1: Technologies Are Limited by the Processes and People That Use Them

With all the excitement about new technologies, we should not forget that they don't develop new products and services—people do. As we saw in the Eli Lilly example, people follow routines and processes that they are reluctant to change, particularly if these activities have worked well for many years. As the old saying goes, "If it ain't broke, don't fix it." When e-mail, for example, was first introduced, some people saw it as a cheaper way to send letters and documents. Others, however, realized that it was a fundamentally new way to communicate and share information, which, in turn, led to innovations such as instant messaging.

The following experiences at BMW illustrate the process-and-people issue when the new kinds of technologies described in this book are made available to development organizations.[20] In the late 1990s, BMW started to feel pressured by changing market dynamics in all its product segments: Sales volumes were getting smaller for each model because changing customer demands required increasingly differentiated markets. When BMW surveyed the international arena, it found that its existing five-year development plan lagged behind those of industry competitors in Japan and the United States. While the Japanese tended to make fewer changes between consecutive models, they leveraged this shorter period to cover more market niches and market whims. To be more aggressive in all its market segments, BMW had no choice but to substantially increase the productivity of its development pipeline.

In surveying the market, BMW found that *engineering lead time,* the time required from concept freeze to product launch, had for nearly thirty years remained remarkably constant among many other European and U.S. firms: forty months. Starting in the early 1990s, therefore, top BMW managers began benchmarking visits to leading companies from other industries worldwide—for instance to Bombardier, the Canadian manufacturer of jet skis, boats, and airplanes, and to Dassault, the French company that had pioneered the widely used 3-D CAD system CATIA. Subsequently, senior management approved a bold target for slashing product development time by 50 percent. A more modest goal, such as 20 percent or even 30 percent, management felt, would have had BMW chasing a moving target. Various experimental technologies would be introduced to foster this goal, including—as we saw in chapter 1—computer simulation.

An important part of this strategy of accelerating development was working in parallel; in turn, parallel work implied coordination, with each team passing on information about the component it worked on to other teams in a timely manner. Parallel processes required the coordination of efforts themselves made possible by computerization of design. Through computer simulations, "virtual cars" that existed only in computer memory, not in the real world, could be tested in parallel with ongoing design activities. The world of virtual reality also provided a logical venue for coordinating the efforts of different functional divisions of a company such as between design and design engineering. But this coordination meant not only reorganizing the way different groups worked together but also the difficulty of changing habits that had been effective in the past.

For instance, in the traditional process, engineers were often reluctant to release less-than-perfect data.[21] To some extent, it was in each group's interest to hold back and monitor other groups' output. The earliest group to submit its data to a central database, after all, would probably have to make the most changes since it would receive the least feedback from other areas. BMW's crash simulation group, for example, traditionally found its reengineering efforts stymied because the door design group hesitated to release design data: That was the imperative (and incentive) in the days of sequential development. Only after convincing the designers that their early, rough data sufficed would the crash simulation group get the needed information, but it took six months even so. But in the new development process, a six-month delay could derail the entire program. It was incumbent on crash simulation and design engineers alike to appreciate and understand not only each other's activities but the power of the new technologies that could leverage them—something that had to be patiently built over time. This effort had to be undertaken throughout the entire development organization. BMW had a world-class crash simulation group, but unless processes were changed and people started working together in new ways, its technical leadership meant little for development performance.

BMW's experience highlights the importance of understanding the role of processes and people in the adoption and use of new experimentation technologies. A big advantage of simulated tests is that they can be used much earlier in the innovation process than can more costly physical tests. That, in turn, allows people to experiment with more design options and find problems before significant design and resource commitments are made. It also enables engineers to kill bad ideas before they take on a life of their own as formal projects. The challenge, as the BMW example clearly showed, is that unless processes are designed (or redesigned) for early experimentation and people work together to make it possible, much of the technologies' potential is wasted. Interestingly, the global automotive development data suggested that Japanese firms had an advantage precisely in this area—in spite of a technology disadvantage (table 4-2).

In crashworthiness, the first technical experiments undertaken by Japanese firms were simulated only months after vehicle layout started. Most likely, these models were far from perfect, but their creation and testing forced the technical communication and problem solving that are needed in parallel work.[22] In contrast, non-Japanese firms started

TABLE 4 - 2

Timing and Availability of Simulation and Prototypes

Important Process Milestones	United States (n=4)	Europe (n=5)	Japan (n=7)
First Crash Simulation (in months after start of vehicle layout)	11.6	9.5	4.9
First Physical Prototypes Available for Functional Testing (in months after first drawing release)	15.5	7.5	4.1

Making simulation and prototypes available earlier can lead to more experimentation and problem solving.

using simulation models months later. Similarly, firms using simulation earlier also made physical prototypes available to its developers much more quickly. These prototypes were necessary to complement computer simulation in areas where fidelity wasn't close enough to reality. The combined result was more rapid experimentation and problem solving in their R&D organizations when it matters the most: during early development.

Reality 2: Organizational Interfaces Can Get in the Way of Experimentation

As we saw in chapter 3, experimentation cycles often involve different functional groups or departments; for the process to work, their efforts must be coordinated. Engineers from different disciplines design parts of a product that has to function as a whole, while prototypes are often built by yet another group. To complete an experimentation cycle, much less conduct multiple iterations, a fluid hand-off between different groups, without the information loss and time delays that are often associated with organizational interfaces among these groups, is required.

New experimentation technologies can, by themselves, reduce some of these losses because information transfer is both reduced and standardized. But by no means is the problem eliminated. Some CAD technologies allow a single master representation whose geometry can be modified by developers, for instance. Having a single representation for a single product under development is in sharp contrast to having many models and prototypes in multiple forms, making any design change a major obstacle to getting the program underway. At the same time, these new technologies create *other* interface problems, both functional and organizational, that can get in the way of leveraging the enormous experimentation capacity implied. This is what happened in the BMW example just mentioned.

In the global automotive study, we examined organizational interfaces that could inhibit experimentation by asking how development work is divided up between technology specialists and engineers. That is, when firms employ specialists—people focused on the technology itself—the companies build up expertise in the technology; the downside is that experimentation can be slowed down when integration of this expertise is not managed well.

Recall that earlier in the chapter we saw that non-Japanese firms were using more complex CAD and CAE technologies. These companies were also employing more specialists; while these people supported engineers, they were not expert designers. Japanese engineers, by contrast, were performing more CAD/CAE work themselves, effectively reducing the number of interfaces involved overall and speeding up experimentation and problem-solving (table 4-3).

This finding is strikingly similar to what researchers discovered in the early 1990s. In a study of CAD use in U.S. and Japanese firms, it was found that employing specialists in fact *separated* engineers from design details and technology. In contrast, companies such as Toyota preferred simpler tools that were transparent to engineers[23] and lowered barriers

TABLE 4 - 3

Experimentation Interfaces in Automotive Development

CAD/CAE Use by Engineers	United States (n=4)	Europe (n=5)	Japan (n=9)
Number of CAD Specialists per Engineer	2.3	0.8	0.3
Percentage of Simulation Work Done by CAE Specialists (*not* design engineers)	75 percent	36 percent	37 percent

Less dependence on technology specialists can reduce experimentation and problem-solving interfaces for development engineers.

between groups. This strategy can also address missed opportunities when CAD specialists—as opposed to design engineers—are put in charge of system integration. When project engineers are more skilled at using design tools, they are less likely to relinquish integration to technology specialists who tend to be less familiar with system aspects of the product.

Reality 3: Technologies Change Faster than Behavior

As noted, the promise of fewer expensive prototypes has been a powerful argument for investing in new experimentation technologies since its benefit can be measured and toted up easily. Even firms that are reluctant to rethink their R&D processes should see some quick gains because development teams should be able to switch from physical to cheaper virtual models. That seems evident. But the research suggests that replacing expensive prototypes with computer simulation is hardly straightforward or simple. An analysis of physical prototypes per project shows *no* significant overall decrease in the numbers built, and, on average, Western firms build at least as many physical car prototypes as their Japanese competitors—in spite of their use of more advanced digital technology (figure 4-5).[24]

Perhaps the cost savings in prototyping were realized in new projects that were started in the very late 1990s and thus were not part of our sample. Or the increase in automotive regulation (e.g., in the crash-testing area) increased the need to test more prototypes and, as a result, even more prototypes would have been needed if digital technologies had not been available.

In my interviews with managers, I have come across another compelling explanation that should not be underestimated: The rate of technological change often exceeds that of behavioral change. When the knowledge base of an organization depends on the use of particular materials, prototypes, and technologies, engineers do not dismiss much of what they know and how they work overnight.[25] And in many cases they shouldn't. As part of our research follow-up, I presented the results of the automotive study to a management team whose firm used some of the most advanced simulation technologies but, at the same time, also built and tested the largest number of physical prototypes in our

FIGURE 4 - 5

Actual versus Average Number of Physical Prototypes

This graph shows physical prototypes that can be used in a functional test but do not include full- or partial-scale models that are built earlier. The vertical axis is the difference between the actual number of physical prototypes and the overall average; a regression analysis showed that no adjustments for project complexity are required for the sixty-five car projects shown here. A negative value indicates that fewer physical prototypes than average were built, and vice versa. Recent interviews suggest that the number of prototypes is starting to decrease, a suggestion that will be verified in future studies.

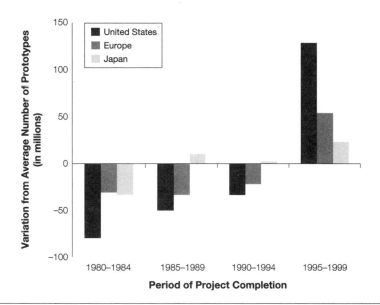

entire study sample. One manager had a surprising yet simple explanation. She explained that the majority of her test engineers were not ready to accept the results of simulated tests. When senior management increased their budget to run more computer simulations, anticipating substantial savings, the team ended up building *more physical prototypes to verify that the simulations were accurate!* The result was larger investments in *both* information technology and costly physical prototypes to verify simulated tests. In some cases, the engineer's skepticism was right on the money since virtual tests were poor substitutes of proven prototype tests. But in areas like crashworthiness, the inability to shift people's mind-sets and behaviors led to wasted resources.

Conclusion

The research on global automotive development and case studies on Eli Lilly and Team New Zealand strongly suggest that *superior technologies do not automatically translate into superior performance*. Unless technological innovation is accompanied by managerial, organizational, and process change, investing in better computers, software, and other new tools often leads to disappointing returns. A detailed study of car development projects, performance, and the use of computer-aided technologies such as CAD and CAE introduced us to some realities: Technologies are limited by the processes and people that use them, organizational interfaces get in the way of experimentation, and technologies change faster than behavior. Taken together, these realities are the result of daily routines, mind-sets, processes, and knowledge that have been built around prevailing engineering technologies and market demands. When technological change places some of these practices in jeopardy, then what has worked previously can get in the way of unlocking the potential of new experimentation technologies. In the following chapters, we will see what managers can do to address these challenges.

APPENDIX 4-1

how the automotive data were gathered

The data reported in this chapter were collected in three phases over nearly twenty years and began with Clark and Fujimoto's landmark study on automotive development performance in the 1980s.[26] During each round, field interviews and case studies led to the design of a detailed questionnaire on project-level data. All major automotive firms in the United States, Europe, and Japan were invited to participate in the study and most of them accepted. After receiving a completed questionnaire, the research team visited companies for follow-up presentations that also gave participants an opportunity to discuss and possibly correct some of their responses. Each participating company received a full feedback report with aggregate project data to ensure confidentiality.

The final data were complemented with information from public sources before the data were analyzed using rigorous statistical methods. Clark and Fujimoto collected the first-round data, David Ellison joined their team and was instrumental in the second round, and I had the fortune of joining forces with Fujimoto for the third-round study. Because of the extensive travel and logistics, each round of data collection took two to three years to complete.

In the third round, Fujimoto and I decided to expand the scope of the study and include detailed questions on the use of CAD, computer simulation, and rapid prototyping. The final questionnaire contained thirteen modules, with a total of seventy-nine major questions that each had several subsections. A fully completed questionnaire gave us about 400 data points per project. Over three years, we received data on twenty-two projects: four in the United States, five in Europe, ten in Japan, and three in Korea. Any tables or figures in this chapter that involve the use of new technologies come from the third-round study only.

Combining all projects in the global automotive development study into a single database resulted in primary data on seventy-two major car projects that were launched between 1980 and 1999. The data enabled us to analyze how development performance (productivity and time to market) and capabilities change over time, and a subset of our findings is provided in the chapter's performance data. Because of differences in project content (e.g., compact versus luxury classes), a set of control variables was determined using regression analysis and the researchers' knowledge of car design. The performance variables were adjusted to account for project complexity, which made an apples-to-apples comparison possible—particularly over such a long period of time (the adjustment is described in notes 15 and 16).

NOTES

1. Scholars have noted that there are a number of reasons why technology adoption challenges most firms. Prior research presents strong theoretical support for the notion of structural inertia (Hannan and Freeman, 1984), which increases with the age of an organization, with its size, and with low levels of differentiation in a given product space. As one would expect, structural inertia poses a considerable threat to firm survival particularly during significant shifts in the firm's environment, including the arrival of new technologies such as the ones described in this book (Tushman and

Anderson, 1986). More recently, management scholars have suggested ways to overcome these challenges. For example, Tushman and O'Reilly (1996, 1997) propose the need for ambidextrous organizations that can implement both incremental and revolutionary technology change. In a study of thirty-four projects that developed software tools to enhance internal productivity at four large electronics firms, Leonard-Barton (1995) found two managerial processes that were important in explaining successful implementations: user involvement in the design and delivery of the system and the degree of user adaptation of technology and environment. Moreover, Ettlie and Reza (1992) studied the successful adoption of process technologies in manufacturing and propose four integration mechanisms difficulties: new hierarchical structure, increased coordination between design and manufacturing, greater supplier cooperation, and new customer alliances.

2. The information on Team New Zealand comes from Enright and Capriles (1996) and Iansiti and MacCormack (1997).

3. Quoted from Iansiti and MacCormack (1997), case B, pages 1–2.

4. Research by Brynjolfsson and Hitt (1996) has argued that industry-level analysis does not fully explain the true relationship between IT investments and productivity growth. Their firm-level research does reveal a positive relationship and points toward other factors that need to be considered, such as organizational and work practices and complementary investments.

5. McKinsey Global Institute (2001).

6. Ibid., page 2.

7. Quoted from Morison (1966), page 36.

8. The information on Eli Lilly comes from Thomke and Nimgade (1997a).

9. Quoted from Thomke and Nimgade (1997a), case A, page 10.

10. Quoted from Thomke and Nimgade (1997b), case B, page 1.

11. Womack, Jones, and Roos (1991).

12. The study methods and findings were published in Clark and Fujimoto (1991).

13. While the notion of heavyweight teams was first observed in Clark and Fujimoto (1991), it has been found to be very effective in product development settings in general and was used as a general management concept in Wheelwright and Clark (1992).

14. The general findings from the second round of research can be found in Ellison, Clark, Fujimoto, and Hyun (1995) and Ellison (1996).

15. Total engineering hours are the hours spent directly on projects by engineers, technicians, and other employees. Measured activities include concept generation, product planning, and product engineering carried out in house or subcontracted to engineering firms. The numbers exclude suppliers' engineering hours, general overhead, new engines and transmission development, process engineering, and pilot production. To account for project complexity, the following variables were measured: (a) number of body types per project (e.g., two- or four-door sedans), (b) total percentage value of new parts that were designed (platform-type projects typically had values of more than 80 percent), (c) product category (micro, compact, mid-size, and luxury), and (d) the supplier contribution to design. These variables were similar to project controls used in Clark and Fujimoto's original 1991 study. A regression analysis showed that body type, new part design, and product category were very significant (at less than 5 percent) whereas supplier design contribution had significance at 12 percent. The variables' regression coefficients were used to predict the number of engineering hours for each project (given its complexity), which was then subtracted from the actual value reported by firms. Positive residual values indicated worse than expected performance and vice versa.

16. Total development time is the longest time-to-market measure, spanning the time from the initiation of concept development to market introduction. Other measures that are often used in industry journals measure the time from program or design approval to start of production, which is much shorter and was also measured as part of our study. As with engineering hours, a regression analysis was used to determine the impact of project complexity on development time. The variables new part design, suppliers' design contribution, and product category were significant (at less than 10 percent) whereas body type had significance at 18 percent. The variables' regression coefficients were used to predict development time for each project (given its complexity), which was then subtracted from the

actual value reported by firms. Positive residual values indicated worse than expected time and vice versa.

17. For a discussion of this assumed trade-off and actual empirical evidence, see Clark and Fujimoto (1991), Brooks (1982), and Pisano (1987).

18. The data shown were collected for six different subsystems of a car in eighteen projects (body in white, interior, instrument panel, seats, suspension, and engine/transmission). For simplicity, it is shown here in aggregated form by reporting only averages. Similar data were also collected for each firm's supplier base, which showed similar regional differences but also lower level of technology use by suppliers when compared to auto firms.

19. The story is reported in Sabbagh (1996), page 63.

20. This section draws extensively on Thomke and Nimgade (1998a).

21. Using research findings from the development of climate control systems at a high-end German automotive firm, Terwiesch, Loch, and DeMeyer (2002) show why and how preliminary information may or may not be exchanged between engineers.

22. Leonard-Barton (1995) and Schrage (2000) emphasize that "quick-and-dirty" prototypes are helpful if they are done early and frequently and lead to widespread experimentation within a company.

23. Daniel Whitney at MIT was kind enough to share his experiences and insights with me during informal conversations and e-mail exchanges. His extensive reports are available from his Web site: <http://web.mit.edu/ctpid/www/Whitney/papers.html> (accessed January 2003).

24. Physical prototypes in the automotive industry are usually made from metal or another material that allows for functional evaluations. In contrast, partial or full-scale models made from clay, foam, wood, or other similar materials are not reported here. As researchers, we expected the number of physical prototypes to be affected by project complexity, but the results of a regression analysis showed otherwise. The number of body types per project, the percentage value of new part design, the suppliers' contribution to design, and the product category had no effect on the number of prototypes built per project, and thus it was unnecessary to make adjustment to the reported data (the significance of the regression

analysis came out at greater than 50 percent). As a result, the total average (101 prototypes) was used as the expected value and, to be consistent with other figures in this chapter, the differences between actual prototypes and total average are shown in figure 4-5. We did observe, however, that car programs with higher expected sales volumes also ended with larger prototyping budgets which, in turn, led to more prototypes being built.

25. Allen (1977) and Vincente (1990) present good accounts of how engineers develop expertise and find technical information. Both authors find that engineers depend on experimentation and testing in the creation of new technical knowledge.

26. For details on how the data for the first study were collected, see Clark and Fujimoto (1991), page 369.

Part II

unlocking
potential
by managing
experimentation

5
experimenting early and often

In preceding chapters, we have seen that new information-based experimentation technologies have the potential to dramatically increase learning, which, in turn, can be incorporated into more rounds of experiments. These technologies have driven down the marginal costs of experimentation but also have created opportunities for innovation. That is, some technologies can make existing experimental activities more efficient, while others introduce new ways of discovering novel concepts and solutions.

Chapter 4 showed that when companies mistakenly view new technologies solely in terms of cost cutting, overlooking the vast potential for innovation, they get bogged down in confusion when attempting to incorporate the technologies into existing routines. Computer simulation doesn't simply replace physical prototypes as a cost-saving measure; it accelerates the process of experimentation, hence the learning possible and hence the potential for innovation. Just as the Internet offers enormous opportunities for innovation (far surpassing its use as a low-cost substitute for phone or postal transactions), so does state-of-the-art experimentation. But realizing the potential requires companies to adopt a different mind-set. Indeed, new technologies affect everything from the development process itself, including the way an R&D organization is structured, to how new knowledge—and learning—is created. Thus, for companies to be more innovative, the challenges are managerial as well as technical.

In this chapter we shall look explicitly at just what such new ways of experimentation—experimenting early and often—look like.[1] We'll reexamine cases that were introduced in previous chapters, particularly (but not exclusively) those of cars, software, and pharmaceuticals, where the effects of new experimental technologies are most vivid. As the chapter unfolds, however, we shall also see the organizational impact of introducing these methods. In many companies, existing systems—for example, the organization of R&D and its connections, in turn, to business processes (like incentive systems) within the firm—are set up for a far different approach to product development. It would be too blunt to say that this traditional approach essentially codifies delaying error correction until the end, thus promoting verification over experimentation. But it is true that far too many companies at least tolerate an amazing amount of cost in the form of last-minute changes: changes that because they are last minute are extremely expensive. Notwithstanding the waste that such delays entail, the fact remains that for many companies, a fire-fighting mentality prevails. Indeed, a celebrated characteristic of dot-com companies was the frantic up-all-night, night-after-night adventure of debugging code. Many dramatic accounts assured us that from founder to lowly new hire, all pitched in to ensure that the system was up and running on launch day. This was considered a good thing.

Clearly, this fire fighting was not a good thing. But the lesson isn't that investors' money was squandered by ill-conceived ventures. The lesson is that night-after-night debugging is neither inevitable nor an adventure when experimentation systems are organized to maximize early learning from experiments that are incorporated into subsequent trials: when rapid experimentation is integrated into the innovation process itself.

The fact that so many companies formed in the mid- to late 1990s failed either to understand what experimentation (described in chapter 3) is or to appreciate the experimental power of the very technologies they were often developing testifies to how entrenched innovation processes have become. Yet while tapping into the potential of new experimentation technologies is hardly simple and straightforward, there are three principles that form the core of any approach to unlocking the power of experimenting early and often: front-loading the innovation process, frequent experimentation while avoiding organizational overload, and integrating traditional and new technologies.[2]

Principle 1: Anticipate and Exploit Early Information Through Front-Loaded Innovation Processes

When important projects fail late in the game, the consequences can be devastating. In the pharmaceutical industry, for example, more than 80 percent of drug candidates are discontinued during the clinical development phases, the phases in which more than half of total project expenses can be incurred. The total investment lost to late-stage failure is significant indeed. Published results by the Tufts Center for the Study of Drug Development show that the average cost of developing a new drug was about $231 million in 1987. Results from the most recent study (2000) show that this amount has risen to $802 million compared to $318 million, which is what the cost would have been if the previous $231 million had risen only at the pace of inflation.[3] Moreover, spending increases in clinical trials exceeded preclinical (e.g., discovery) spending by a factor of 5, which means that late-stage failures had become even more costly than before. Not surprisingly, there is much value in finding potential drug failures as early as possible. Eliminating drugs with little promise before they enter expensive clinical testing would allow companies to focus and redeploy R&D resources on much stronger candidates.

Value of Early Information

Not only do companies often spend millions of dollars to correct problems in the later stages of product development, they generally underestimate the cost savings of early experimentation that could result in information and team interactions that in turn would lower downstream expenses (figure 5-1). Studies of product development have shown that late-stage problems can be more than a hundred times as costly as early-stage problems.[4] For environments that involve large capital investments in production equipment, the increase in cost can be several orders of magnitude. In addition to financial costs, companies jeopardize the value of time when late-stage problems are on a project's critical path—as they often are. In pharmaceuticals, shaving six months off drug development time means effectively extending patent

FIGURE 5 - 1

The Value of Early Information

Increasing financial and organizational commitments to activities, such as tooling in automotive manufacturing or clinical testing in pharmaceutical drug development, make late-stage problems and failures very costly and time-consuming. As a result, the average cost of solving problems can increase rapidly with time. The steeper the increase, the higher the value of finding and solving problems early via experimentation.

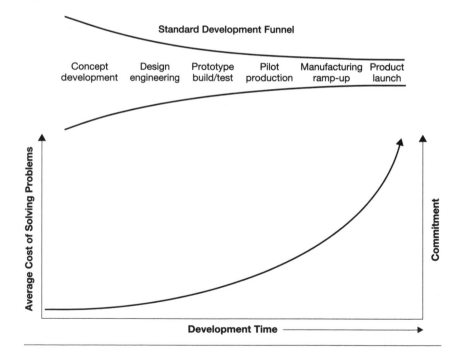

protection when it hits the market. Similarly for electronics companies: Shipping a product six months late can account for a significant reduction of the product's lifetime profits.[5]

The result for R&D managers is that as development time passes and project commitment increases, the average cost and time of making changes rises exponentially. Millions of dollars need to be spent to solve a production problem that could have been prevented upstream at a small fraction of the cost. And the steeper the increase in cost, the higher the value of experimenting and solving problems upstream.

Furthermore, managers can end up devoting an enormous amount of their time to dealing with late-stage problems—to meet launch dates, reallocate resources, unsnarl schedules, and so on. Such fire fighting is taken for granted, moreover, because most product development processes are not set up, much less optimized, for early experimentation. In addition, opportunity costs in general are hard to assess; they are invisible in most management systems used today. How much more difficult it is to measure the opportunity of *not* discovering a problem at an earlier stage in development or *not* experimenting with a more promising product design solution. In the absence of understanding the importance of these opportunities, then, the curious result is that managers have a de facto incentive to continue their last-minute "heroics"—not to create processes that can in fact leverage innovation.[6]

But when the effort is made to create such a process, the difference is striking, as the following example from Microsoft reveals.

Testing Experiences at Microsoft

Software development usually begins by creating specifications. In versions of Microsoft Office prior to its Office 95 software suite, Microsoft developers wrote specifications but did not collect them across all groups or post them in a central location. Not only were there few interfaces standardized across different Office groups (e.g., Word, Excel), there was no formal peer review process among the teams nor a process that could pinpoint problems at the earliest stage (specification writing). As a result, erroneous assumptions about, for instance, a user interface control could lead to multiple difficulties later on, all of which would require extensive and expensive rework.

As part of the overhaul of its development strategy in the mid-1990s, Microsoft brought its testing group (a group traditionally involved relatively late in software design) into the very early stages of development: It created a formal process of specification inspection. Now under document management and revision control, each specification had to follow a prescribed template and undergo two formal review steps (initial review plus final inspection and sign-off), and it had to be posted in a central location on a file-share system and then eventually to an internal Web site. In contrast to a one-sided document prepared by program management without input from others, software specifications became a contract between program managers, developers, and testers. Once through final inspection and sign-off, every word, line, and concept in the new software specification was reviewed and agreed to by groups involved in upstream and downstream development. Experienced testers were now able to provide their extensive experience on the relationships between specifications and software bugs when it mattered the most: as early as possible in the product's life cycle.

Grant George, Vice President of Testing and Operations for the Microsoft Office products, explained the new strategy of leveraging early information: "The cheapest bug in any manufacturing process is always the one found earliest. Specification inspections, just like our formalization of structured and peer reviewed tests and build verification tests, are all about catching bugs as early as possible."[7] The results were significant. According to George, about 10 to 25 percent of all late-stage problems can be found (or avoided) by following this approach. And if the increasing cost of rework is included, the cost and time savings are substantial.

Power of Using New Technologies Early

New experimentation technologies are most powerful when they are deployed to test success—and failure—early in R&D projects. We've seen how, in the automotive industry, "quick-and-dirty" (computerized) crash simulations help avoid potential problems downstream.

These simulations are not as complete or perfect as late-stage proto-types, but they are able to direct the attention of R&D managers to potential downstream risks. Suppose that an early test of a new-car concept or a new drug candidate exceeds the target threshold by a factor of 10. Even if this prediction itself is off by 50 percent or more, managers have been alerted. Maybe they should consider changing the concept before more resources are invested; maybe other possibilities are more promising, and the project should be scrapped. Rather than being locked into a seemingly inevitable and expensive development process, managers can decide among a broader array of risks what the value of going forward would be.

But the power is not simply that of an early warning system. Perhaps a more substantial benefit, one demonstrated in the Microsoft Office example, is that early experiments force organizational interactions, communication, and joint problem solving among individuals and groups that are separated in space and time. Earlier experimentation forces organizations toward earlier integration.

Solving Integration Problems Early

The use of digital mock-ups suggests how new experimentation technologies advance early problem solving and integration. One problem, for instance, that bedevils designers of complex products like cars and airplanes is "interference." That is, when different parts and/or sub-systems occupy the same coordinates in 3-D geometric space, they interfere with each other—essentially, they don't fit.[8] Yet designers are often unaware of this problem because they use the traditional method of mapping 3-D designs onto separate 2-D drawings—interference literally does not show up. Consider that complex products can involve thousands or hundreds of thousands of parts that could potentially interfere in 3-D space—designed by engineers who often do not even know each other.

When Boeing began developing its new 777 aircraft, the company also designed a new process for problem identification and correction.[9] Although increasingly refined physical prototypes (physical mock-ups) detected design problems, not all problems were discovered, and many were found very late in the development process. The interference problem was particularly acute, as one Boeing chief engineer relates:

> *You have five thousand engineers designing the airplane. It's very difficult for those engineers to coordinate with two-dimensional pieces of paper, or for a designer who is designing an air-conditioning duct to walk over to somebody who is in Structures and say, "Now, here's my duct—how does it match with your structure?" Very difficult with two-dimensional pictures. So we ended up using the [physical] mock-up and, quite honestly, also using the final assembly line to finish up the integration. And it's very costly. You end up with an airplane that's very difficult to build. The first time that parts come together is on the assembly line. And they don't fit. So we have a tremendous cost on the first few airplanes of reworking to make sure that all the parts fit together.*[10]

Because Boeing's management wanted a process that encouraged experimentation and problem solving well before final assembly, it coupled a 3-D CAD system with in-house software that enabled engineers to assemble and test digital mock-ups for interference problems.[11] Similar to physical mock-ups that detect problems of fit, digital mock-ups allow virtual assembly of a product that can be checked automatically for interferences. These automatic interference checks can be performed many times during the development process.

The result was more than early problem solving, however. The automatic checks also changed the way people interacted with each other. Not only did designers modify their designs earlier than in the past, they also relied on others to track the modifications via the new technology. Because they received immediate feedback on the technical merit of their ideas, designers were emboldened to experiment ever more—for example, by removing weight from individual parts.

To add discipline and structure to a process that made immense testing capacity available to engineers, Boeing instituted an approach divided into alternating periods of design and stabilization. During the design period, engineers were allowed to make changes. During the stabilization period, software checked for interference problems that had to be resolved before proceeding to the next design period. The resolution of these problems was no trivial task, as shown by an early interference test of twenty pieces of the 777 flap (wing section): The software made 207,601 checks, which resulted in 251 interference problems—problems that would have been very costly and time-consuming to correct during final assembly.[12]

Other firms have experienced interference benefits from similar advanced technology. A Chrysler (now DaimlerChrysler) team also discovered that 3-D CAD could help to identify interference problems before production assembly.[13] Consider, for example, their experience with "decking"—a process where the power train and its related components (exhaust, suspension, etc.) are assembled into the upper body of an automobile for the first time (figure 5-2).

When Chrysler teams developed the 1993 Concorde and Dodge Intrepid models, decking took more than three weeks and required

FIGURE 5 - 2

Interference Testing via 3D CAD

Virtual decking, where interference problems are identified and solved with the aid of digital mock-ups before physical assembly takes place.

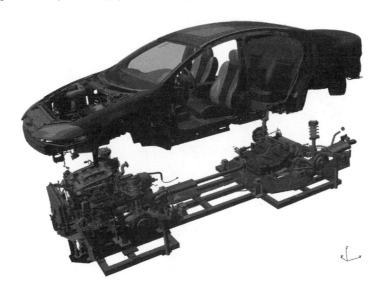

Source: Reprinted from *The Journal of Product Innovation Management* 17, S. Thomke and T. Fujimoto, "The Effects of 'Front-Loading' Problem-Solving on Product Development Performance," Copyright 2000, with permission from Elsevier Science.

many attempts before the power train could be successfully inserted. In contrast, the use of digital mock-ups in their 1998 Concorde/Intrepid models allowed them to simulate decking and to identify (and solve) numerous interference problems before physical decking took place for the first time. Rather than three weeks, the team now successfully completed the physical decking process in fifteen minutes because all decking problems had already been solved! Thus, by combining new technology with changes in the development and production planning processes, some Boeing and Chrysler teams were able to shift problem solving to phases where problems could be identified and solved at a much lower cost in money and time. And, as we learned from the automotive research in chapter 4, the overall impact on companies depends on how much these changes are driven through the entire development organization.

Putting Front-Loaded Development Processes to Work

The Microsoft example showed that front-loading can be achieved by such management strategies as the involvement of downstream testing groups in upstream decision making and planning. Most important, however, new experimentation technologies aimed at front-loading can improve performance in a number ways. As we have seen, solving problems that are identified as part of experimentation can translate into lower cost and less time, thus raising R&D productivity. Further, when more experimentation happens earlier, more ideas and concepts can be explored, which in turn can result in more innovative solutions (figure 5-3).

But how does management know if changes to a company's innovation process actually lead to early experimentation? Aggregate performance measures such as R&D cost and time don't reveal changes to development routines and can also have long lag times—in the same way that aggregate plant level measures tell us little about the changing routines of machine operators. An example of measuring front-loading directly comes from Toyota, which introduced new experimentation technologies as part of a reorganization and gradual transformation of its product development process. What triggered this effort was the need to shorten the time from when the design of body styles was approved to when the resulting vehicles were actually sold.

FIGURE 5 - 3

Solving Problems Earlier Through Front-Loaded Processes

A front-loaded process can be achieved in three ways. First, new technologies allow for earlier and faster iterations, shifting the normal problem-solving trajectory to the left (dashed-line trajectory). Second, learning from other projects reduces the number of total problems to be solved, shifting the trajectory up. Finally, the ability to carry out more diverse experiments early in development can raise product performance. The combined result is a potential improvement along time, cost, and innovation (desired trajectory).

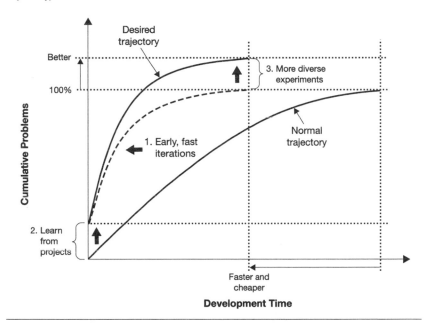

Measuring Front-Loading at Toyota

Toyota's push to accelerate its product development cycle began in the 1990s with a concerted attempt to identify and solve design-related problems much earlier than had been the case before.[14] Among the various initiatives the company undertook were to involve more manufacturing engineers during the product engineering stage, increase the transfer of knowledge between projects, make substantial investments in CAD and CAE tools, and develop rapid-prototyping capabilities. These initiatives were part of a major reorganization of development activities overall, which emphasized more effective communication and coordination among the different development groups. To measure the benefits of these actions—and to monitor the company's evolving capabilities for early problem solving—Toyota tracked problems over multiple development projects.[15] Knowing that a higher percentage of problems were being solved at earlier stages reassured Toyota's managers that they could aggressively reduce both development time and cost without risking product quality. In particular, between the first and third front-loading initiatives, Toyota slashed the cost (including the number of full physical prototypes needed) and time of development by between 30 percent and 40 percent.

Figure 5-4 shows how early problem solving evolved in the company's development organization over the years. Prior to the 1990s (two top graphs) communication between prototype shops and production engineering had been informal and unsystematic. Simultaneous engineering between body engineering and die shops, as well as engines and suspensions, had increased, but other engineering sections were still operating in the old way. In the early 1990s (center graph), the first initiatives for front-loading began. Formal, systematic efforts to improve face-to-face communication and joint problem solving between the prototype shops and production engineers resulted in a higher relative percentage of problems found with the aid of first prototypes (full-scale metal prototypes, made at stage 3). Communication between different engineering sections (e.g., between body, engine, and electrical) also improved. In the mid-1990s (second graph from bottom) the second front-loading initiative called for 3-D CAD, resulting in a significant increase of problem identification and problem solving prior to stage 3 (first prototypes). In the more recent front-loading initiative (bottom graph), Toyota was now systematically using CAE to identify functional problems even earlier in the development process. Moreover, the company had begun to transfer problem and solution information from *previous* projects to avoid "old" problems whose solutions had in fact been found.

As a result, Toyota expects to solve at least 80 percent of all problems by stage 2—that is, before the first prototypes are made. And because second-generation prototypes (stage 5) are now less important to overall problem solving, the company will be able to eliminate parts of that process, even further reducing time and cost without affecting product quality.[16]

FIGURE 5 - 4

Front-Loaded Product Development at Toyota

Front-loading (FL) capabilities are measured by the extent to which Toyota can identify and solve problems earlier in automotive development. The vertical axis measures the cumulative percentage of problems solved, whereas the horizontal axis relates to specific development stages at Toyota. S3 is first prototypes and S5 is second-generation engineering prototypes.

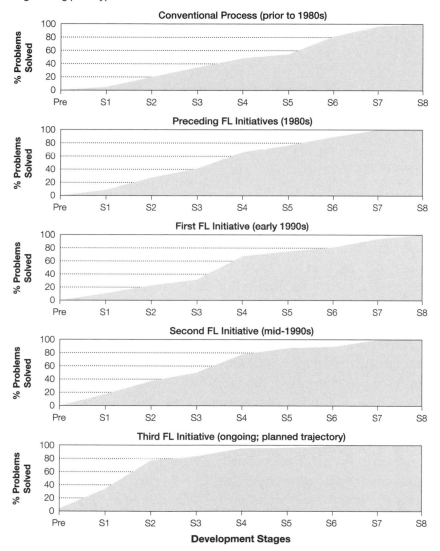

Source: Reprinted from *The Journal of Product Innovation Management* 17, S. Thomke and T. Fujimoto, "The Effects of 'Front-Loading' Problem-Solving on Product Development Performance," Copyright 2000, with permission from Elsevier Science.

Front-Loaded Processes, Experimentation, and Product Innovation

Using computer simulation to test for functionality is of critical importance—not only to reduce costs via front-loading. Using these tools explicitly as part of an experimental process invites innovation. Consider all the product functionality that such technology can affect: crashworthiness (discussed in chapter 1), acoustics, vibration, aerodynamics, thermodynamics, and complex metal forming (e.g., stamping). If these tools are used early in development, designers and engineers can receive very early feedback on innovative ideas before significant R&D commitments are made. For example, exterior styling and aerodynamic flows are interdependent, particularly at high velocities. With computational fluid dynamic (CFD) simulations, designers can have their concepts evaluated for aerodynamic performance in a matter of days and can make the necessary changes in a matter of hours. In addition to saving money, this feedback opens up new possibilities for learning and innovation. Similarly, Team New Zealand developers could go through hundreds of improvements and suggestions, analyze them via computer simulation before committing to a physical test, and then select the most promising ones for evaluation in a full-sized yacht under real sailing conditions. Having that much experimentation available before making design commitments tapped into the creativity of the entire team; not just designers but also the crew who ended up sailing the boat.

Rapid feedback is also an important objective for Millennium Pharmaceuticals and other companies in the pharmaceutical industry (see chapter 1), which incorporate such new technologies as genomics, bioinformatics, and high-throughput screening in their platforms for conducting experiments. As we have seen, evaluating potential product candidates (and rejecting others) as early as possible is particularly critical for drug discovery. For example, Millennium's technology platform enables factorylike automation that can generate and test drug candidates in minutes or seconds, compared with the days or weeks more traditional methods require. Gaining information early about, say, the toxicological profile of a drug candidate improves the ability to predict the drug's success in clinical testing and ultimately in the marketplace. Unpromising candidates could be eliminated before hundreds of millions of dollars are invested in their development (box 5-1).

BOX 5-1: NEW DRUG DISCOVERY TECHNOLOGIES
FOR EARLY EXPERIMENTATION

New drug discovery technologies can potentially provide a quick way to detect failure modes early in the drug discovery process and thus steer a company away from an unpromising avenue of research at a stage when it is still inexpensive and quick to switch course. An example of a new technology that could potentially lead to such front-loaded development is transcription profiling.[17] Drug toxicity can be one reason why drugs fail in development. To understand and assess the potential damage wrought by drug compounds in the body, we must examine the liver, since most of the body's detoxification occurs here. Liver cells, often described as the body's factory, use a variety of mechanisms to rid the body of toxins. These detoxification steps in the specific mechanism are ultimately controlled by specific genes. Toxins that cannot be removed may ultimately damage the liver itself over time, leading, for example, to the liver cirrhosis of excessive alcohol drinkers. The classic approach to examining the liver's actions against a drug involved studying drug metabolism in lab animals at the preclinical stage, a long and expensive process: Weeks or months would pass before the effects on the animal livers could be assessed. Newer methods, however, allow for exposing liver tissue slices to the test chemicals to assess for drastic effects such as cell death. In the late 1990s, this was routinely done. Through increasing biochemical finesse, however, researchers sought to discover which of the many important detoxification mechanisms in the liver were being used in order to create strategies for modifying the chemical compound to less toxic forms. A potentially powerful genomics technology for assessing toxicology is transcriptional profiling—a technology that allows for assessing what genes are active (being "transcribed" by the cell's genetic machinery into genetic messages that would serve as architectural blueprints for making proteins, the building blocks of the body). The DNA in each human cell is estimated to contain the same set—or genome—of roughly 25,000 to 40,000 genes, of which about 10 to 15 percent are active during a cell's lifetime.[18] Different combinations of genes are active in different cell types, with the highly active liver cells more likely to activate a large number of genes. To identify the set of genes in liver cells associated with detoxifying a specific class of drugs, genomics researchers

(continued)

(continued)

compare the transcriptional profile of a dormant liver cell with liver cells actively metabolizing the drugs in question. Any discrepancies probably reflect the use of genes specifically activated for ridding the body of the specific toxins. By identifying the genes most relevant for detoxifying a given compound, drug makers could potentially understand how difficult a drug might prove to detoxify much earlier in development. Whether transcriptional profiling will have a high enough fidelity to provide useful early information remains to be seen, but other promising technologies are currently under development as well.

In addition to reducing the cost and time of traditional drug development, the new technologies could also increase the ability to innovate. Specifically, pharmaceutical companies may have greater opportunities to experiment with more diverse potential drugs, including those that may initially seem improbable but might eventually lead to breakthrough discoveries.

But not only must companies master the right technologies, they must also deal with the changes and challenges to its innovation system that these opportunities require. Indeed, when Millennium's CEO Mark Levin hired Chief Technology Officer Michael Pavia, he charged him with revolutionizing the way new drugs were developed. To be twice as fast and half as expensive, Pavia understood that Millennium's technology platform wasn't sufficient: "The only way to achieve such an aggressive goal is to question everything and to hire people that challenge assumptions held by the industry for decades."[19]

Pavia's comment underscores the point that was made in the opening of this chapter: The mere introduction of new experimentation technologies does not, by itself, ensure innovation; it does not even ensure the quest for innovation. If a company like Millennium, dedicated entirely to the use—as its raison d'être—of cutting-edge technology, indicates that it must "question everything" and "challenge assumptions," imagine the difficulty for organizations with existing technology, procedures, routines, and so on of integrating such technology—much less celebrating it as a tool for innovation.

As we saw in chapter 1, an integral part of Millennium's technology platform was its increased capacity for experimentation that, in turn, would allow a developer to test more frequently. With increased testing and rapid feedback, however, management faced the next challenge: the limited ability of its scientists to assimilate and make sense of the staggering amount of information made available through more experimentation. In the pharmaceutical industry, the emergence of computer-based bioinformatics tools were aimed at addressing the challenge of potentially overloading organizations.

Principle 2: Experiment Frequently but Do Not Overload Your Organization

With the benefits of early experimentation, there remains the question of how frequently or how many experiments should be carried out. The problem for many companies is that they experiment not only too late but also too little. The quest for efficiency and cost reductions often drives out experimentation and testing until small problems become disasters or missed opportunities become competitive threats. How many corporate strategists can point toward a portfolio of forty to fifty small experiments that test new business ideas or fundamentally challenge its current business model? In the context of R&D, the challenge is in some ways remarkably similar. Realistic prototype models used in experimentation and testing can be very costly. Money can be saved, so goes the logic, by delaying experimentation and testing as long as possible and then conducting big "killer" tests.[20] However, the opportunity cost of finding problems later or not experimenting on promising ideas is not fully factored into the cost-accounting equation.

At the same time, some companies do test very frequently. For example, Microsoft runs automated tests continuously so that problems are detected right away when developers check in new software—which happens daily. Microsoft also rebuilds software systems and updates test coverage frequently to account for changes in functionality, ranging from daily prototype builds to builds every few weeks. The frequency of builds and updates depends in part on the particular needs and complexity of a project and the time required for a build. Complex software with many files and interdependencies, such as Windows and Office, have weekly or monthly build cycles, whereas single applications, such as Excel, have daily builds.[21] Microsoft commits a lot of its resources to testing, and software testers not only receive solid training in its methodology but also are offered an attractive career path. In other words, the company takes its testing activities very seriously.

Unfortunately, not all companies take experimentation and testing as seriously as Microsoft. In their research on product development organizations, Steven Wheelwright and Kim Clark suggest periodic prototyping as a way to address this problem. They note that "senior managers, functional heads and project leaders who do not fully understand and fully utilize the power of prototyping unintentionally handicap their efforts to achieve rapid, effective, and productive development results."[22]

Thus very frequent experimentation is most certainly desirable, but it probably is not for all R&D environments. For example, one would not expect automotive firms to build and test full-scale prototypes on a daily basis unless the cost and time of doing so were reduced to a small fraction of what it has been for decades. This reality may come true fairly soon for some kinds of prototypes—for example, the digital models described earlier—where the building and testing happen inside a high-speed computer. Clearly, the number and fidelity of tests are related to cost and time. So when technologies drive down these costs, by how much should developers increase their testing?

In a related research project on testing strategy, my colleague David Bell and I found a simple yet fairly robust way of addressing this question.[23] The number of tests is related to the square root of the cost. In other words, when test cost drops by a factor of 100, management should increase tests at least by a factor of 10 to fully benefit from these changes (box 5-2).

New technologies can slash the costs (in both money and time) of testing, but to reap those benefits, organizations must prepare themselves for the full effects of the technologies. Computer simulations and rapid prototyping, for example, increase not only a company's capacity to experiment frequently but also the wealth of information generated by tests; ten times as many experiments generate massive amounts of information that has to be processed, evaluated, understood, and used in the planning of a lot more experiments. This activity, however, can easily overload an organization if the organization cannot process

BOX 5-2: HOW FREQUENTLY SHOULD ONE TEST?

The fundamental challenge for managers is to balance the increasing cost of repeated experimentation and testing with the benefits of earlier information (the front-loading effect). Building a simple spreadsheet model and explicitly recognizing the value of early information already points managers halfway in the right direction—that is, to test more frequently than they currently do. Using mathematical modeling, one could try to find a more general solution that could be used as a rule of thumb. In a recent research project, my colleague David Bell and I built such analytical models and found a surprising yet robust result. A rough estimate for the number of tests is the following simple ratio:

$$\text{Number of test rounds} = \sqrt{\frac{a}{t}}$$

where a = avoidable cost if continuous testing found problems without any delay and t = the cost of one round of tests.

For example, if a company spends $1 million on total redesign (engineering changes, new tooling, etc.) and would have spent only $50,000 if all problems had been identified and solved instantly as they occurred, the avoidable cost due to delayed testing is $950,000. Now, if running one round of tests costs on average $1,000, then a rough approximation of the number of testing rounds is

$$\text{Number of test rounds} = \sqrt{\frac{950,000}{1,000}} \approx 31$$

Of course, the optimal number depends on many other factors, but this simple expression is a good starting point.

For details on our analytical model, its assumptions, development, and applications, see S. Thomke and D. Bell, "Sequential Testing in Product Development," *Management Science* 47, no. 2 (2001): 308–323.

information from each round of experiments quickly enough to be incorporated into the next round. Imagine that you are gathering biweekly feedback from your lead customers. In between, the information has to be prepared for presentation and analyzed, conclusions must be drawn, and the next round of interviews must be planned. Now imagine that feedback is suddenly arriving daily. Welcome to the testing overload! In engineering, this effect has also been referred to as the hardware swamp.[24] Prototype iterations become so frequent and overlap so much in time that the team cannot keep up any more. They become swamped by problem debugging and hardware maintenance instead of learning from experimentation and improving designs. The result is waste, confusion, and frustration. In other words, without careful and thorough planning, a new technology might not only fail to deliver on its promise of lower cost, increased speed, and greater innovation, it could actually decrease the overall performance of an R&D organization or at a minimum disrupt its operations. As a result, managers need to prepare their organizations for the full effects of more frequent experimentation so they can tap its full potential. Rapid information transfers between groups, a focus on quick decision making, and the development of new tools (e.g., in bioinformatics for drug discovery) are all examples of lowering the risk of organizational overload.

When companies manage to tap the potential for learning from early and frequent experimentation, they face one more challenge: the ability to manage a portfolio of technologies—new and traditional—for experimentation that are constantly evolving. As we shall see later in a case study on BMW, companies cannot simply substitute new for mature technologies that have been the pillars of successful innovation processes for decades. Instead, they need to learn how to integrate the new with the traditional.

Principle 3: Integrate New and Traditional Technologies to Unlock Performance

Experimentation technologies, whether those currently in use or the new approaches discussed in this book, are designed to help solve problems as part of an innovation process; they are not stand-alone techniques. To unlock their potential, a company must understand not only how new and traditional technologies can coexist within such a process but also how they enhance and complement each other.[25]

As we have seen throughout the book, some new technologies can reach the same technical performance of their traditional counterparts much more quickly and at a lower cost.[26] But the performance of a new

FIGURE 5 - 5

Integrating the New with the Traditional

A new technology will reach perhaps just 70 percent to 80 percent of the performance of an established technology. A new computer model, for instance, might be able to represent real-world functionality that is just three-quarters of that of an advanced prototype model. To avoid this performance gap, companies can use the new and old technologies in concert with each other. The optimal time for switching between the two occurs when the rates of improvement between the new and mature technologies are about the same (i.e., when the slopes of the two curves are equal).

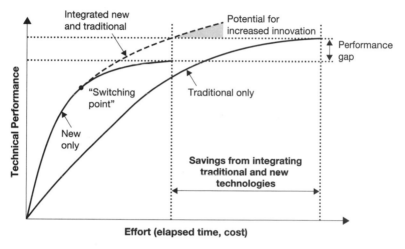

Source: Stefan Thomke, "Enlightened Experimentation: The New Imperative for Innovation." *Harvard Business Review,* February 2001, 74. Copyright © 2001 by the Harvard Business School Publishing Corporation. All rights reserved.

technology may not be more than 70 percent to 80 percent of the performance of the established technology (figure 5-5). For example, many computer models are not perfect representations of reality and thus need to be complemented by physical models. The fact is that there are still many complex phenomena than cannot be simulated with high confidence on a computer. Thus, by combining new and traditional technologies, organizations can avoid the performance gap while also enjoying the benefits of cheaper and faster experimentation.

Indeed, the true potential of new technologies often lies in a company's ability to reconfigure its processes and organization for use in concert with traditional technologies. In rare instances is the technology so advanced that it instantly displaces its traditional counterpart and all the development experience and engineering knowledge that goes with the old one. Eventually, a new technology can replace its traditional counterpart, but it then might be challenged by a newer technology that itself must be integrated.

In chapter 4, we saw the challenges of combining new combinatorial chemistry and high-throughput ("combichem") technologies with proven medicinal chemistry at Eli Lilly. These technologies significantly increased the efficiency and speed with which the company could generate and screen chemical compounds but their purity and diversity was below traditional methods. In spite of the new economics, many scientists initially greeted combichem technologies with skepticism. Only by implementing mechanisms to control how the new technologies were used in combination with medicinal chemistry was management able to have the new coexist with the traditional. For example, it temporarily limited in-house screening, leaving chemists with no choice but to use some of the new high-throughput screening capabilities and to interact with the technical staff. This practice forced chemists to learn the benefits and limitations of the new technologies.

Similarly, computer simulation needs to be complemented with real-world prototype testing, but getting internal groups to use these technologies to work together productively is and will continue to be a challenge. For example, in my research in the integrated circuit industry (chapter 2), I found that simulation groups and hardware-oriented groups were highly specialized and tended to know relatively little about the potential of the other's technologies; also, they did not share information because of biases and internal competition. Management fueled the fire between groups by viewing simulation and hardware testing as substitutes: Hardware testing was needed only when simulation engineers failed to detect problems. A successful integration, however, requires close cooperation and mutual education and information exchange between specialists so that the optimal combination of experimentation technologies can be achieved by large R&D teams. That exchange, in turn, also requires learning by doing by both specialist groups, making people exchanges between them unavoidable.

We should be careful not to confuse a knee-jerk rejection of anything new with legitimate concerns about whether the new will jeopardize current success. Most examples scattered through this chapter are of successful—even dominant—companies in their industries; they rose to prominence before integrating new experimentation technologies. The key word is "integrating." As the following BMW case suggests, simulation technologies were introduced, but applying the principles discussed in this chapter was no slam dunk.

The Principles at Work: Lessons from BMW

When managers at the German car company BMW describe the challenges that deploying new experimentation technologies involves, they speak of remarkable opportunities for process change and productivity improvement.[27] At the same time, BMW managers discovered that the right approach had to take into account the firm's culture, its routines, and most important, its product strategy. This was particularly true for managing design groups in which technologies and routines were embedded in a complex system for creative experimentation.

Competition in the World Auto Industry

According to former BMW and now Volkswagen executive chairman Bernd Pischetsrieder, "When historians look back on the motor industry in fifty years' time, they will say that the mid-1990s was a period of fundamental change."[28] This time period saw development of a consumer's market. In 1996, the European auto market, for instance, sported some fifty brand names, with about 300 different base models and virtually thousands of derivatives. The European market production capacity of 20 million overwhelmed the total yearly sales of 14 million. Customers demanded more choices but wanted to pay less. This led to a rise in secondhand and almost-new car sales along with an upsurge in generous financing schemes for new-car purchases. Car manufacturers had to respond by accelerating new model development and expanding the number of model variations.

As a response to these rapidly changing markets, automakers all over the world placed increased emphasis on speeding up development as a competitive weapon. The Japanese led the way, aiming to reduce their development lead times by over 30 percent, even though they were not known for technological advancement as much as for producing reliable cars. In the United States, auto firms tried to achieve a similar feat. By the mid-1990s, intense pressures from international competition to reduce product development time had also reached Europe and BMW.

Automobile development in the 1990s entailed literally thousands of steps involving 20,000 to 30,000 components—from screws and lamps to upholstery—all having to be coordinated among thousands of designers, skilled craftsmen, and engineers, as well as numerous specialized outside vendors. To simplify matters a great deal, an automobile can be thought of as having two major pieces: the *package* and the *skin*. The package refers to the components involved in propelling the automobile: whatever is under the hood as well as the wheels, axles, steering, climate control, and exhaust. The skin refers to what the buyer first sees in the showroom: the exterior, the seating, and the layout of the dashboard. In the initial phases of car development, design work on the package and skin can proceed in parallel, with ongoing communications and negotiations between the designers and engineers managing both processes.

BMW's Car Design Process

BMW viewed design of the exterior skin as the link between its past and its future. The head of worldwide design, Chris Bangle, declared that "a successful design is not characterized by the ability to create a brief sensation, but by the influence it exerts on subsequent designs in the years that follow."[29] Thus, company designers sought to retain a familiar resemblance among all BMW models by employing consistent styling features such as the dual circular headlights and the "double kidney" front grille. Traditionally, designing for a proposed model began with manual renderings on paper using traditional artistic media ranging from watercolor to pencil and charcoal (figure 5-6a). In this brainstorming or design concept phase, the company explicitly sought through a competitive process a large variety of concepts (which typically fell into four self-explanatory directions labeled revolutionary, evolutionary, aerodynamic, and classic) from in-house designers and sometimes external industrial designers. Next, the firm worked toward refining its design choices.

To this end, the design department made small (1:2.5) clay models of several favored initial concepts. Finally, based on feedback from senior management, the department made a few life-size models of leading contenders. These clay models were milled, with computer guidance, so precisely that, once they were painted, an inexperienced observer could not tell a finished 1:1 clay model from a real car. Clay models also served to create excitement among the people involved with auto development. Typically, it took about twelve weeks to go from initial concept to a finalized clay model, a process that was repeated at least four to five times with intermediate clay models before arriving at a final styling concept. Each 1:1 clay model cost upward of $150,000 and could be produced in about a month—and in as little as two weeks for all-stops-out emergencies.

Once the exterior design was determined ("frozen"), a scanning device would capture the geometry of the final clay model digitally, something that generally required a day or a weekend. Once captured digitally, however, the styling models could be made available to design engineering in the form of CAD models. The computer models also sped up refinements in the styling process itself. For instance, if a model maker ground down one curve or laid on more clay to build up another curve, computer guidance could ensure that corresponding changes on the other side of the car would match to within half a millimeter or so.

The Designer as Artisan

Recent advances made the power of computers available to designers in the early brainstorming phases. But even with all the advantages of computerized equipment, BMW prided itself on its handcraftsmanship. BMW's designers often came from schools of art or industrial design; model makers were skilled craftsmen who perfected their trade through many years of apprenticeship. Among their colleagues were over a dozen color and trim craftsmen and designers (including fashion designers). Working with physical models had been an integral part of designers' training; it created an emotional attachment to this process (figure 5-6b).

Designers prided themselves on the sensations that good styling would elicit: the way light sparkled off the surfaces of their cars, the way

FIGURE 5 - 6

Designers Combining Manual Renderings, CAS, and Clay Models

(a) Designer preparing hand sketches for brain-storming design concepts.

(b) Craftsman working on clay model of con-cept car.

(c) Designers using computer-aided styling (CAS) for group brainstorming.

Source: Stefan Thomke and Ashok Nimgade, "BMW AG: The Digital Auto Project (A)," Case 9-699-044. Boston: Harvard Business School, 1998. Copyright © 1998 by the President and Fellows of Harvard College. Reprinted by permission.

the lines of contour flowed. Three properties guided car styling at BMW: *Flächengenauigkeit*, the precision of the surface, *Flächenspannung*, the surface "stress," and *Reflektionslinien*, the lines of reflection. The BMW philosophy held that the contour lines should never be interrupted, even when running across transition points (e.g., from body to door). Furthermore, the company prided itself on the number of distinctive curves the side of a car possessed when viewed in cross section. While many auto makers had just one or two styling surfaces running down the side of a car, interrupted by a metal strip, BMW sought to create a subtle interplay of multiple surfaces that could not be easily created on a digital computer. All these elements created what the firm felt was the finest expression of human artistry. A customer, it was assumed, paid for a BMW not just with the wallet but also with esthetic commitment.

After exterior design was complete, the CAD data moved to body engineering. This group bore responsibility for making the exterior styling functional and manufacturable. It made the surfaces more precise by filling in gaps in styling. The group, like other BMW engineers, operated at the level of fractions of millimeters to ensure that the final assembled product would function with silky precision. It also worked with many other body engineering groups to ensure that the styling concept chosen could achieve its desired functionality in tests of crashworthiness and vehicle dynamics.

Need for Development Speed

In the early 1990s, a new development system took root at BMW, a five-year plan (five years from start of project to first sales) that was nearly 20 percent faster than its predecessor. The new system allowed for two major prototyping cycles, each cycle involving the generation of dozens of physical prototypes with increasing degrees of fidelity. (The previous plan had involved three major prototyping cycles.) A high-quality physical prototype could cost more than a million dollars and often required months of work from BMW's many prototype builders. During each prototyping cycle, functional and manufacturing problems could be identified via testing and solved while an increasing number of design and financial commitments were made to suppliers and manufacturing.

The process also started to take advantage of rapidly emerging computer simulation methods to identify potential design problems earlier in the development schedule. For example, a vehicle's crashworthiness could be simulated and improved well before the results from the first actual prototype crash test became available—a milestone that came relatively late under the old development plan. Even so, in general, the new process was merely an iteration of the old hardware-driven process, and much of the potential of computer-aided technologies remained untapped. The first cars produced through this process were the highly successful 3-Series models of 1998.

Traditionally BMW came out with new models every seven to eight years with major changes between models.[30] Contributing to this rate, which was slower than some of its competitors', was the meticulous handcraftsmanship that went into BMW products; a process that relied less on outsourcing than at other firms. Compared to other firms, BMW had higher fixed costs because of its significantly smaller volume per model. Thus it sought to squeeze sales from each model for a longer time than many other carmakers did. This strategy, however, hinged on BMW's ability to develop cars whose lives outlasted those of its competitors. With competition increasing the rate and quality at which "fresh" models were introduced, designing products with seven- to eight-year life cycles was becoming a very difficult challenge indeed.

BMW was beginning to feel the pressure of changing market dynamics in all its product segments: Sales volumes were getting smaller for each model because changing customer demands required increasingly differentiated markets. By the time BMW surveyed the international arena in the mid-1990s, it found that its five-year development process lagged behind that of Japanese and U.S. competitors. Although these other car companies tended to make fewer changes between consecutive models, their strategy emphasized the leverage of shorter development times to respond to rapidly changing markets and higher productivity to allow them to cover more market niches. To be more competitive, senior management at BMW had no choice but to substantially increase the productivity and speed of its development organization.

In the mid-1990s, senior management approved a bold target for slashing product development time by 50 percent. A more modest goal, such as 20 percent or even 30 percent, management felt, would force BMW to chase a moving target. After all, leading competitors in the United States and Japan were reported to aim at total development times of between thirty and forty months. Instrumental to such radical R&D changes were the advances in new experimentation technologies such as computer simulation and 3-D CAD.

Shortly after this decision, senior management put together a re-engineering task force to look into how to reduce lead time and cost for product development. The task force concluded that rather than think about some grand development plan for process planning, the firm should use new technologies to streamline key engineering processes. It identified five key areas—body, climate control, fuel supply, test engines (power train), and acoustics—that accounted for about 90 percent of the critical processes in the product development timeline. The reengineering effort would focus on these areas and would also, of course, entail organizational changes.

Redesigning the Development Process

To achieve this daunting new product development cycle, three changes in BMW's system would have to take place: parallel processes, more experimentation but fewer prototypes, and faster design iterations. These changes would entail increased coordination of efforts among in-house engineers and craftsmen as well as with outside suppliers.

Increased parallelization through front-loaded processes.   The challenge here was to allow development of various components of product development to proceed in parallel. Parallel processes required the coordination of efforts made possible by computerization of design. Through computer simulations, virtual cars could be tested in parallel with ongoing design activities. Parallel development, however, would entail coordinated teamwork, with each team passing on information on its component to other teams in a timely manner. It meant not only reorganizing the way different groups worked together but also the difficulty of changing habits that had worked well in the old sequential development plan.

More experimentation but fewer prototype iterations.   A process as complex as developing a new car model provides opportunities for pruning unnecessary design iterations. Moreover, the use of computer-aided testing for functionality and manufacturability would help to substantially decrease the number of physical prototypes needed. Interestingly, while the number of prototype-driven design iterations would decrease, the total number of iterations would increase substantially, counting the thousands of additional low-cost and quick iterations that could be carried out using computers. But would only one generation of prototypes before market launch—as the new plan called for—be sufficient to identify all potential design problems? Even though many auto firms were trying to achieve one major prototype generation only, BMW did not know if any of them had actually succeeded.

Speeding up design iterations.   Every development step, from design to engineering and tooling, would have to be sped up. In many cases, speed could be achieved at the tactical level through setting more stringent deadlines. For example, traditionally it took the engineering design group about ten months to get to the point of releasing data for tools manufacturing; for the new process, the goal would be six months. In many cases, the process of shortening steps involved proactively searching for problems that might arise downstream. Would a late styling change involving a taillight, for instance, cause a tooling headache several months hence? But most of all, computer simulation itself would allow engineers to iterate more quickly. For example, design-build-run-analyze cycles of a new safety concept could be carried out via crash simulation in a matter of days or weeks as opposed to the many months it had taken to design, build, and crash prototype vehicles.

Integrating New and Traditional Technologies: Computer and Clay

An important challenge in the new development system was BMW's ability to integrate new digital technologies with traditional and proven physical experimentation technologies. The integration was particularly difficult with the emergence of computer-aided styling (CAS), which had already found its application in BMW's design department; it allowed designers to visualize virtual models from a variety of angles, with the possibility of making modifications at any point (figure 5-6c). With CAS, designers could start with a virtual package and gradually overlay it with the skin. One such loop would take about a week and could involve many iterations, as opposed to the one iteration possible through physical clay models. Thus, digital design could potentially boost capacity for experimenting with alternative design concepts.

Computer-aided styling allowed for work at resolutions of hundredths of millimeters—an order of resolution greater than engineers traditionally worried about. The ability of CAS to accurately predict the course of lines of reflection also helped convince skeptics about its potential utility. In addition, a major advantage to working digitally from the very beginning was the possibility of direct data links to CAD, thus allowing for parallel development with design engineering. Working with clay models, in contrast, required laser scanners to digitize information about the clay models. This process of data conversion usually necessitated time-consuming fine corrections by hand.

Because of these advantages and the decision to slash development time, management faced much pressure to use computers in design. Already, many were talking in terms of product data management or software-driven development. Some even referred to computer-aided processes as becoming the new backbone of product development or simply the new master. On the other hand, CAS, unlike the widely used CAD systems, was still in its infancy. With only two CAS companies holding a monopolylike grip on the 1,000 to 1,500 licenses worldwide, some BMW designers saw only a limited prospect for innovation in the next five years.

It was no wonder that designers, most of whom had trained traditionally, believed that the myriad subtleties and complexities of styling that placed BMW a notch above the competition could not be fully captured through CAS models. While computers might capture at best perhaps 95 percent of a car's surface qualities, the last ineffable 5 percent might elude even the most sophisticated of CAS programs. Other car manufacturers might get away with using CAS extensively through the entire design cycle, but not BMW, they said. As evidence, they reminded management of an experiment made only a few years earlier, in which a group of designers had made a pilot attempt at designing a new 3-Series model using only CAS. Achieving the first 80 percent of styling definition proved easy, but getting up to 90 percent required many more design iterations. Getting up to BMW's high level of styling quality had required laborious hand-specified revisions. It had left many of them with serious questions about the role of digital design at BMW.

As management wrestled with issue of CAS technology adoption in its development process, they learned many lessons. Since BMW had no plans to reposition the company's high-end products, it was very clear that styling compromises would not be acceptable. In the end, BMW went with a hybrid design process that combined the time advantages of CAS with the quality benefits of clay and other traditional technologies. These traditional technologies were required to achieve the design quality demanded by BMW's strategic needs (figure 5-7).

FIGURE 5-7

Combining Computer and Clay

Computer-aided styling (CAS) and other technologies will reach perhaps 80 percent to 90 percent of the design quality of an established technology such as clay modeling. To achieve both a strategic product differentiation and development process improvements, companies can use both technologies in concert (dotted line). The degree to which technologies are used together and the resulting design processes depend on how firms want to compete and thus varies.

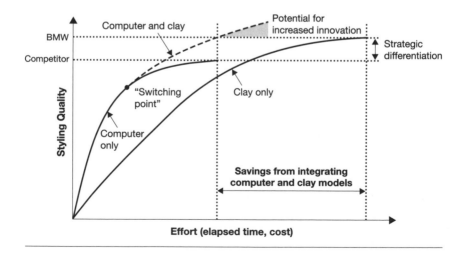

For example, BMW learned that in order to achieve the last 10 percent or so, its designers and model makers had to invest in new skills and master CAS and traditional clay models *in tandem*. However, in the end, it also required some compromises in the company's development speed and efficiency objectives, as explained in an interview with BMW's Bangle (box 5-3).

BOX 5-3: MANAGING PROCESS CHANGE AND NEW TECHNOLOGIES

AN INTERVIEW WITH CHRIS BANGLE,
HEAD OF WORLDWIDE DESIGN AT BMW

STEFAN THOMKE (ST): How would you describe the BMW way of car design?

CHRIS BANGLE (CB): The BMW way is very much rooted in the depth of a design philosophy. It follows three fundamental steps. We start with an understanding phase, followed by a phase that would best be called believing. In a company where the heart and soul is its core product, you have to believe with a fervor, like a religious fanatic. After the believing phase, we go through a phase I call seeing—you might even call it caring—because if you don't really look at it and really care, then all that love that you put into it really comes to nothing because it's not appreciated in the end. They are three very different phases. You can assign time scales to all of them. You can establish factors to speed them up. But if you skip one, you're doomed to go back and repeat it.

ST: The case study mentioned that BMW tried to reduce product development by 50 percent. How did all these issues play out within BMW? How did it affect you?

CB: The approach of reducing time to market definitely impacted all the areas of engineering, including design. Actually, we are the direct participants, let's say, in the first half of the development cycle, and everything we do drives the second half. So timewise, we're vital. Costwise, we account for maybe 1 percent of the entire development cost; we have very few people who are responsible for many projects. Because we influence half of total development time, you can imagine the perceived leverage effect that was thought to be at work if the design

(continued)

(continued)

group would change its ways of doing things. I would say the program of reducing time to market by 50 percent allowed us to look at each aspect of our process with such intensity that we realized that there are some things that we just don't want to turn the clock back on. There are some things we don't want to cut the time down on.

ST: How did BMW go about the adoption of CAS technology?

CB: The adoption of computer-aided styling into BMW and its acceptance by people came about in a number of phases. I would hesitate to say we're complete in this process, but we're probably at a point that is really wonderful. First of all, one has to look at the design process itself. It helps if you understand how cars are traditionally done—by hand, using clay tools. This creative process allows for an enormous amount of human interaction with the surfaces being developed. It means you don't have something so fixed in your head that all you are doing is execute, execute, execute. Instead, you have an idea, a direction, and you're trying to caress, love, and stroke it, and pull it out. There is truly a sensual relationship between the creator and the object that is often written about in art. The same is true in cars. It gives you time to talk to the car. It gives time for the car to talk to you. CAS basically says that we will simulate that effect and replace it with synthetic methods. Is it really the same? We used to joke: How many people would choose a wife or husband from a picture on the Internet? So there are certain tradeoffs in using a synthetic medium that are not so easy to convince people about.

At the same time, when I got to BMW there was a sense that we'll fake our way through this. We're investing in it and experimenting with it, and we've got this station this year, and next year we've budgeted for another station, and we'll increase our knowledge a little bit more. So I got there, and having come from my CAS experience in Fiat, which was very hands-on, very direct—"This puppy doesn't pay, forget it." My first experience with the team was after a few months of being there when I said, "Gentlemen, either this puppy pays within three months, or forget it, I'm going to sell the whole thing down the river." And I called up the chief engineer and said, "Wolfgang, you want to buy those computers"—the guys are standing around me while I'm doing this—"then talk to me in three months, because if they don't get their act together, the computers are gone." Now, that drove such fear into them that they just couldn't mess around with this anymore. Please note that I didn't twist the arms of the designers.

CAS is basically in the hands of the *Formgestalters* [modelers] because they're the ones who have to come to grips with it. Where the designers came into play is in the interpretive end—"Is what I see what I think it is?" So they're the ones complaining, of course, that a CAS model isn't a real-life experience. I think that many other companies believe that just by putting a designer on CAS, you will get good design. This is not what we believe. We believe that CAS is a tool that transforms surfaces to another basis than what was previously possible. Having said that, don't forget: In this case, the medium in also the message. That means a car done in clay looks different than a car done in plaster than a car done in aluminum than a car done on a computer screen. What does this medium, CAS, give us? We're still learning the answer to that question.

ST: Would you say that BMW will always go a different way with respect to design and the use of new technologies?

CB: BMW will always go a different way than other companies. Not only based on where the product is positioned in the market but also where it is in the hearts of the people who work at BMW. And you've got to ask yourself: Why do these guys do this? Why do they go through this hell? Are they doing it for a paycheck at the end of the day, or are they doing it because they really love cars? There's a really good example that illustrates this in my own personal history at BMW. Not too long ago, we had a financial officer come in and he really took me apart for spending far too much time on things that people don't see in our cars, and that we all do this stuff just for ourselves. While he was talking to me, I took him on a tour of design to show him how many different aspects there are, and we found ourselves in the color and trim group. The woman who heads that group happened at that moment to pick a middle console out of a car we were developing. She didn't realize who I was talking with, because the guy was relatively new on the job. She just came up to me and said, "Look at this. You see? This is exactly the problem we're talking about." She lifts up the arm rest, goes underneath it,

(continued)

(continued)

somewhere deep down inside a pocket, and says, "See how that surface translates from there to there? They're having a terrible time getting the same texture from there to there, and see? If you reach your hand in like that, you can actually feel a difference, and that's not good." And the financial officer is looking at me, and I know what he's thinking: "That's exactly what we're talking about." Well, at the same time I'm hearing him saying, "Don't invest that love and care into that piece that maybe one person will put his fingers into," I'm also thinking that this is what drives this woman to run her whole shop—that's the core essence of her being. That passion, that love, for everything that comes out of her group. And how can I tell her to stop caring?

If we can keep those kinds of people at the core of the company, which up until now we have, you will find that their motivation and reasons for doing this are so different than at other companies—it will always lead us down another path. My job is to communicate this to management downstream in the development process and to protect my people and—at the same time—make sure that overall objectives such as efficiency improvements are communicated to everyone.[31]

Conclusion

What we have seen in chapter 5 suggests that experimenting early and often not only makes companies more effective at innovating but also unlocks the potential of new technologies. The changes required are hardly simple and straightforward and the following three principles form their core: (1) Anticipate and exploit early information through front-loaded innovation processes; (2) experiment frequently without overloading your organization; (3) integrate new and traditional technologies. Specifically, the BMW case suggests that by combining new and established technologies, organizations can maintain or gain strategic product advantage while also enjoying the benefits of cheaper and faster development. For all their potential, new technologies can create rifts within groups and organizations and lead to resistance. Jobs and routines of designers and model makers trained in old ways are threatened by new ways of doing things as digital design disrupts well-established routines and requires investments in learning. Leadership becomes essential for management; getting some of the most respected designers, engineers, and scientists to accept new technologies and become lead adopters helps in persuading others. Some of the critical issues that managers face as part of this effort are addressed in chapter 6.

NOTES

1. This chapter draws extensively from Thomke (2001) and Thomke and Fujimoto (2000).

2. "Front-loading" refers to experimentation strategies that seek to improve development performance through early problem solving.

3. Tufts University news release, "Tufts Center for the Study of Drug Development Pegs Cost of a New Prescription Medicine at $802 Million," 30 November 2001.

4. In a study of the development of climate control systems at a high-end German automotive firm, Terwiesch, Loch, and DeMeyer (2002) found that engineering changes of components increase by a factor of 10 from one phase to the next. Similarly, in a study of several large software projects, Boehm (1981) found that the relative cost of correcting software errors (or making software changes) goes up significantly as a function of the phase in which the corrections or changes are made. He determined that a software requirements error corrected during the early specification phase consisted merely of updating the requirement specifications. A correction in the (very late) maintenance phase, however, involved a much larger inventory of specifications, code, user and maintenance manuals, training material, and, of course, revalidation. On average, he found a change in the maintenance phase to be roughly 100 times more costly than in the specification phase, not counting any indirect operational problems in the field.

5. In an article frequently cited in the electronics industry, Don Reinertsen (then a consultant with McKinsey & Company) used an economic model of new product development and commercialization to simulate the impact of faster time to market. He found that in high-growth markets with short product life cycles, shipping a product six months late can draw down its lifetime profits by 33 percent. Alternatively, late shipments in a slow-growth market with a long product life cycle creates only a 7 percent decline in profits (see Reinertsen, 1983).

6. Repenning and Sterman (2001) discuss and model a related effect in process improvement. Their research suggests that the inability of most organizations to reap the full benefits from improvement programs has little to do with the specific tool they select, but is closely related to how the program interacts with the physical, economic, social, and psychological structures within a firm. As long as "nobody ever gets credit for fixing problems that never happened," fire fighting will prevail in most organizations.

7. Quoted from personal e-mail communication from Grant George, May 2002.

8. The process of identifying the lack of fit between objects and/or contexts is central to problem-solving and testing strategies in a variety of disciplines and settings. For more details, see Alexander (1964) and von Hippel and Tyre (1995).

9. The following description of Boeing's development practice is based on Sabbagh's (1996) detailed account of the 777 aircraft project.

10. Ibid., page 59.

11. The CAD application Boeing used was the CATIA software (Computer-graphics Aided Three-dimensional Interactive Application), one of the leading CAD environments. CATIA is developed by Dassault Systemes and marketed, distributed, and supported worldwide by IBM.

12. See Sabbagh (1996), page 75.

13. Thomke and Fujimoto (2000).

14. Ibid.

15. Spear and Bowen (1999), Fujimoto (1999), and others have found that Toyota has spent decades building problem-solving capabilities, particularly in its production system.

16. Recently, the *Wall Street Journal* (2003) reported that Toyota engineers have begun developing vehicles without prototypes. Relying solely on past engineering knowledge and CAE tools, executives expect the system to save the company 30 percent in cost per vehicle. While the approach may only work for some simple derivative vehicles today, it would be nonetheless a remarkable development process achievement.

17. Thomke and Nimgade (1999).

18. The actual number of genes in the human genome is a subject of ongoing scientific debate. In 2002, the estimates were about 25,000 to 40,000 protein-coding genes, only about twice as many as in a worm or a fly. However, human genes are more complex and generate a larger number of protein products.

19. Quoted from Thomke and Nimgade (1999), page 11.

20. Reinertsen (1997), page 73.

21. Chapter 5 in Cusumano and Selby (1995) includes a detailed discussion of Microsoft's testing strategy. The information on automated testing comes from personal communications with Steven Sinofsky, a senior executive at Microsoft, February 2000.

22. Quoted from Wheelwright and Clark (1992), pages 255–256.

23. Thomke and Bell (2001).

24. See Clausing (1994), page 23.

25. Research by Marco Iansiti (1997) has already shown that, in many industries, the ability to integrate technologies into *products* is key to increasing development performance.

26. Christensen (1997) makes a similar observation for disruptive technologies and their performance in products. In this book, we are primarily concerned with innovation process performance.

27. The following section draws extensively from Thomke and Nimgade (1998a) and Thomke (2000).

28. Quoted from Thomke and Nimgade (1998a), page 4.

29. Ibid., page 5.

30. Note that product life cycles are not the same as product development time. Product development time expresses how fast a firm can bring a product concept to market. Product life cycle expresses how long the product actually stays in the market after it has been launched.

31. The following interview excerpt comes from detailed interview records that were produced during Bangle's visit to Harvard Business School in 1999. The same excerpt was published in Thomke (2000).

6
organizing for rapid iteration

Development groups and project teams tend to be organized by expertise and resource efficiency and are naturally managed for successful outcomes. No matter how much lip service is paid to the importance of learning from failure, it is a rare organization that actually carries through on this premise. What happens, then, when new experimentation technologies, like those we've examined throughout this book, work optimally when failure is actively seized? When failure is *supposed to happen*, particularly in early stages of development when many ideas and concepts need rapid feedback and modification, resource commitments are made, and unfavorable options can be eliminated at low cost? The result, all too often, is organizational and managerial confusion.

Chapter 5 introduced three principles for unlocking the power of experimenting early and often: (1) Anticipate and exploit early information through front-loading innovation processes; (2) experiment frequently but do not overload your organization; (3) integrate new and traditional technologies to unlock performance. These principles are critical to experimentation for learning and innovation. When companies begin to unlock the potential of new experimentation technologies, the importance of following these principles is even further amplified.

This chapter expands on the view that in successful innovation systems, rapid experimentation and a healthy tolerance for failure are often the source of new breakthrough products and services.[1] We shall focus on how success arises from managing failure, drawing on a set of organizational and behavioral principles. One final principle—manage projects as experiments—addresses the power of using experiments themselves to drive organizational innovation. We shall examine cases and examples that demonstrate how this principle is applied.

Principle 4: Organize for Rapid Experimentation

As we saw in chapter 3, rapid feedback is critical to effective learning. The ability to experiment quickly is also integral to innovation: As developers conceive of a multitude of diverse ideas, experiments provide the rapid feedback necessary to shape the ideas by reinforcing, modifying, or complementing existing knowledge. Rapid experimentation, however, often requires the complete revamping of entrenched routines. When, for example, certain classes of experiments become an order of magnitude cheaper or faster, organizational incentives may suddenly become misaligned, and the activities and routines that were once successful might become hindrances.

Rapid Learning Through Simulation

Recall from chapter 5 the major changes that BMW recently underwent. Only a few years ago, experimenting with novel design concepts—to make cars withstand crashes better, for instance—required expensive physical prototypes. Because the process of building prototypes took months, it acted as a barrier to innovation because engineers could not get timely feedback on their ideas. Furthermore, data from crash tests arrived too late to significantly influence decisions in the early stages of product development. So BMW had to incorporate the information far downstream, incurring greater costs. Nevertheless, BMW's R&D organization, structured around this traditional system, developed award-winning automobiles. But its success also made change difficult.

Today, thanks to virtual experiments—crashes simulated by a high-performance computer rather than via physical prototypes, as discussed in chapter 1—some of the information arrives earlier, before managers have made major resource decisions. Experimentation costs (in both money and time) are therefore lower because BMW can eliminate both the creation of some physical prototypes and the expense of potentially reworking bad designs after the company has committed itself to them. (Physical prototypes are still required much further downstream to verify the final designs and meet safety regulations.) As table 6-1 shows, the

TABLE 6 - 1

Learning by Crash Simulation and Prototype Testing*

Numbers are estimates from a project at BMW and are subject to change. Prior to starting simulation, there is a one-time fixed investment necessary to build a basic model that can be reused with modifications during the following experimentation cycles. Prototype-build cost and time are naturally a function of the magnitude and number of modifications, but even modest changes can drive up cost and time substantially. Examples of such cost drivers are tooling, material, and labor.

Experimentation Step	Simulation Only (per iteration)	Physical Prototype Only (per iteration)
1. Design	*Technical Meeting* • less than 0.5 days	*Planning and Piece Part Design* • more than 2 weeks (involves many meetings)
2. Build	*Data Preparation and Meshing* • small change: less than 0.5 days • significant change: 1 week • entire automobile: 6 weeks	*Design and Construction* • using existing model: 3 months (at $150,000 per prototype) • new model: more than 6 months (at up to $500,000 per prototype)
3. Run	*Crash Simulation* • 1 day (varies with computer hardware) at $250 per day	*Crash Physical Prototype* • 1 week (includes preparation of test area)
4. Analyze	*Post-Processing and Analysis* • less than 0.5 days	*Data Preparation and Analysis* • 1 day (crash sensor data only) • 1 to 3 weeks (data, crash films, and analysis of physical parts)
Total approximate time	**2.5 days to 6.3 weeks**	**3.8 months to more than 7 months**
Typical cost (includes effort)	**Less than $5,000**	**More than $250,000**

*The cost and times are based on data collected in 1997 and have experienced some changes in favor of simulation. For a more detailed explanation of the methods used to collect the data, see Thomke (1998b).

differences between simulation and prototype testing are very significant indeed and are likely to increase further with the decreasing cost of computational power and advances in knowledge about how to design better simulation models.

In addition, the rapid feedback and the ability to see and manipulate high-quality computer images spur greater learning and innovation: Many design possibilities can be explored in real time yet virtually, in rapid iterations. Consider that a real car crash experiment happens very quickly—so quickly that the experimenter's ability to observe details is typically impaired, even with high-speed cameras and well-instrumented cars and crash dummies. In contrast, one can instruct a

FIGURE 6 - 1

BMW's Organizational Experiment

In the standard process, teams from engineering, prototyping, and testing are each responsible for different steps of an experimentation cycle. Organizational interfaces, different incentives and knowledge bases, and costly prototyping slow down experimentation and learning cycles. In contrast, BMW's organizational experiment involves

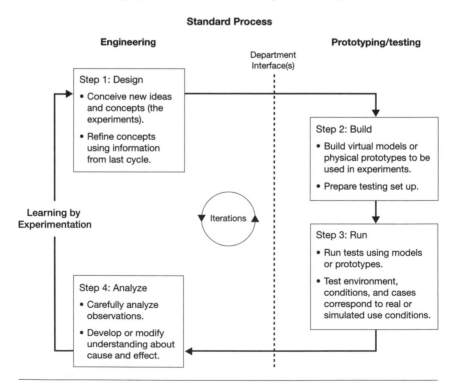

computer to enact a virtual car crash as slowly as one likes, and one can zoom in on any structural element of the car (or minute section of a structural element) that is of interest and observe the forces acting on it and its response to the forces during the virtual crash.

An Organizational Experiment

To study this new technology's impact on innovation, BMW carried out an organizational experiment that was briefly discussed in chapter 1 (figure 6-1). Several designers, a simulation engineer, and a test engineer formed a team to improve the side-impact safety of cars. Primarily

an interdisciplinary team that is organized for joint brainstorming, rapid learning, and decision making. Advanced crash simulation running on local workstations supports technical problem solving and experimentation.

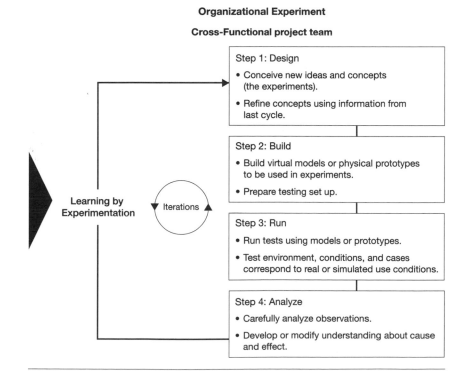

Organizational Experiment

Cross-Functional project team

Step 1: Design
- Conceive new ideas and concepts (the experiments).
- Refine concepts using information from last cycle.

Step 2: Build
- Build virtual models or physical prototypes to be used in experiments.
- Prepare testing set up.

Learning by Experimentation   Iterations

Step 3: Run
- Run tests using models or prototypes.
- Test environment, conditions, and cases correspond to real or simulated use conditions.

Step 4: Analyze
- Carefully analyze observations.
- Develop or modify understanding about cause and effect.

using computer simulations, the team developed and tested new ideas that resulted from their frequent brainstorming meetings. Traditionally, the team members had focused on work that came through their functional departments; formal interactions happened when the standard development process called for joint problem-solving sessions and design reviews. This process in turn led to interfaces between groups, which slowed down learning from cross-functional experiments. The new team structure was thus an experiment in itself since it was uncertain how car development might best benefit from computer simulation. To minimize cost, team members continued to work in their functional departments while being part of this new "virtual" team organization.

Because much of the knowledge required about safety, design, simulation, and testing resided within the small group, it was able to iterate and test new ideas and concepts rapidly. No new budgets or newly approved expenses were necessary since the cost of simulation tests was relatively low. After each round of simulated crashes, the team analyzed the results and developed new ideas for the next round of experiments. As expected, the team benefited greatly from the rapid feedback: People could accept and refine (or reject) new design solutions within days—something that had taken months before because rarely had all decision makers been in a single room or meeting and test results been available so quickly. As the trials accrued, the group members greatly increased their fundamental knowledge of the underlying mechanics, which then enabled them to design previously unimaginable experiments. In one instance, they tested and improved on a promising safety design concept that one of the engineers had picked up on at a technical conference. The low cost and short time of experimenting encouraged developers to simply try the idea and see what happened. Such what-if experiments would have been next to impossible without simulation and the integrated team structure because of the prohibitive cost of real crashes, the long feedback delays from prototypes, and the coordination usually required between functional departments.

In another instance, crash simulation completely changed the knowledge about the complex relationship between material strength and safety. The experiment involved the so-called B pillar, one of the six structural members that connect the roof of a car to the chassis below

FIGURE 6 - 2

The Side-Impact Crash Problem

The section next to the bottom of the B-pillar (see arrow) folded in crash after crash and was thus less effective as a crash barrier.

Source: Courtesy of BMW AG.

the windows. (There are three such pillars on each side of any car; from front to back, they are labeled A, B, and C.) By analyzing the records of prototype side-impact crashes from earlier development projects, engineers had found that in crash after crash, a small section of the B pillar folded. The section was next to the bottom of the pillar (shown in figure 6-2). The folding bothered them because when a pillar buckles, its value as a barrier is compromised and the probability of passenger injuries goes up.

The team members assumed that adding metal would strengthen the bottom of the pillar, making the car more resistant to penetration from the side. None of them felt that it was necessary to test this assumption since it was based on many years of experience. One team member, however, insisted on testing it, pointing out that it would be neither difficult nor expensive to run an experiment on the computer. As the team was organized for rapid experimentation and decision making, the experiment was accepted and run immediately. When the results came back, the group was shocked to discover that strengthening the folded area actually decreased crashworthiness significantly. Initially, none of the team members could explain the phenomenon because it went against their accepted knowledge base. After more experiments, careful analysis, and long discussions that drew on their diverse skills and knowledge, the team found the cause. Reinforcement of the lower part of the B pillar, they discovered, caused the pillar to be prone to folding higher up, above the reinforced area. Thus, the passenger compartment was more penetrable higher up—closer to the midsection, chest, and head area of passengers. The solution was to weaken, not strengthen, the lower area. This counterintuitive knowledge—that purposely weakening a part of a car's structure could increase the vehicle's safety—led BMW to reevaluate all the reinforced areas in the bodies of its vehicles. Significantly, the ability to change one variable at a time with simulation and the diverse skills and rapid decision making that came from the way the team was organized maximized learning from experimentation.

In summary, this small team improved side-impact crash safety by about 30 percent. It is worth noting that two crash tests of physical prototypes at the end of the project confirmed the simulation results. It should also be noted that the physical prototypes cost a total of about $300,000, which was more than the cost of all ninety-one virtual crashes. Furthermore, the physical prototypes took longer to build, prepare, and test than the entire series of virtual crashes. But to obtain the full benefits of rapid experimentation, BMW had to undertake sweeping changes in process, organization, and attitude—changes that have taken years to put in practice and are still being improved upon (described in chapter 5). Not only did the company have to reorganize the way different groups worked together, it also had to change habits that had worked well in the old sequential development process. Previously, for example, engineers were often loath to release less-than-perfect data. To some extent, it was in each group's interest to hold back and monitor the output from other groups. After all, the group that submitted its information to a central database first would quite likely have to make the most changes because it would have gotten the least feedback from other areas. However, when rapid experimentation becomes essential to increasing product development performance, such behavior becomes counterproductive, as the following example shows.

The door development team at BMW was accustomed to—and rewarded for—releasing nearly flawless data (e.g., details about the material strength of a proposed door), which could take many months to generate. The idea of releasing rough information very early, an integral part of a rapid and parallel experimentation process, was unthinkable—and not built into the incentive system. Yet a six-month delay while data were being perfected could derail a development program predicated on rapid iterations.

Thus, to encourage the early sharing of information, BMW's managers had to ensure that each group understood and appreciated the needs of other teams. The crash simulation group, for example, needed to make the door designers aware of the information it required in order to build rough models for early-stage crash simulations. That transfer of knowledge had a ripple effect, changing how the door designers worked because some of the requested information demanded that they pay close attention to the needs of other groups as well. They started to understand that withholding information was counterproductive. Going through these changes, management learned that when teams are organized for speed, other issues such as a deep understanding and appreciation of each other's information needs becomes essential to significantly slashing development time and costs and boosting innovation.

Understanding the Pitfalls That May Slow Down Experimentation

When senior management organizes teams for rapid experimentation, misaligned objectives and resource conflicts can become a major obstacle. Specifically, some managers do not fully appreciate the trade-off between response time and resource utilization. Consider what happens when companies establish central departments to oversee computing resources for performing simulations. Clearly, testing ideas and concepts virtually can provide developers with the rapid feedback they need to shape new products. At the same time, computers are costly, so people managing them as cost centers are evaluated by how much the resources are being used. The busier a central computer is, however, the longer it takes for developers to get the feedback they need. As we saw in chapter 3, the relationship between waiting time and utilization is not linear—queueing theory has shown that the waiting time typically increases gradually until a resource is utilized around 70 percent, and then the length of the delays surge (figure 3-5).[2]

An organization trying to shave costs may thus become a victim of its own myopic objective. That is, an annual saving of perhaps a few hundred thousand dollars achieved through increasing utilization from

70 percent to 90 percent may lead to very long delays for dozens of development engineers waiting for critical feedback from their tests. A huge negative consequence is that the excessive delays not only affect development schedules but also discourage people from experimenting, thus squelching their ability to innovate. So in the long term, running additional computer equipment at a lower utilization level might well be worth the investment. An alternative solution is to move those resources away from cost centers and under the control of developers, who have strong incentives for accelerating feedback.

The problem of slowing down experimentation and innovation through overutilized resources is by no means limited to computers. About two years ago, the newly appointed head of drug discovery of a major pharmaceutical firm (we'll call it Pharma to protect its identity) approached me with a dilemma. Like other senior executives who run large R&D organizations, he was trying to find new ways to make scientists more innovative. They were encouraged to experiment more with new chemical compounds that could lead to promising new drugs and at the same time eliminate unpromising candidates as early as possible. This "experiment early and often" philosophy resonated well with his staff, which had many novel ideas that simply could not be evaluated before. To follow this new approach, he had to significantly reduce the lead time that was required to test and evaluate compounds that were created by Pharma's discovery organization. More experiments early in drug discovery could be run using the combinatorial and high-throughput testing technologies described in chapter 1.

Experiments with more complex living organisms, however, fell into the hands of animal testing—a large department that was not under his control. Like many testing departments, Pharma's animal testing was run as a cost center and its performance was measured and evaluated by the extent to which management was able to utilize testing resources effectively. If everyone within animal testing were busy 100 percent of the time, Pharma would get the most out of its spending on animal testing. Right? Not so, since there was a dilemma: Management's objectives of discovery and animal testing were in complete conflict with each other. Discovery needed fast feedback on its experiments, which implied a lower resource utilization of animal testing. In contrast, a "well-managed" testing organization meant high resource utilization and long wait times, which in turn put a damper on discovery's experimentation. In fact, scientists had to wait three to four months for results from animal tests—which took a little more than a week to complete. Thus, Pharma's attempt to get scientists to experiment and innovate more, and more rapidly, could not possibly work unless its animal testing was managed very differently.

Senior management had three complementary options at its disposal. First, a solution focusing on *managerial incentives* would make sure that the objectives of animal testing were aligned with discovery. For example, the head of testing could be measured by his organization's response time (time from request to completion of test) to a request, rather than resource utilization. Second, a solution focusing on *resources* would suggest that the cost of adding testing capacity was probably less than the benefits it would bring to Pharma as a company. Not only could more compounds be evaluated for therapeutic potential, but failure modes and problems could be identified much earlier—before more resources are committed to a particular development path. The third solution would challenge the organization of all R&D: Discovery and testing are headed by the same senior executives, who could then align objectives more effectively. All three options combined would lead to more rapid experimentation.

Principle 5: Fail Early and Often but Avoid Mistakes

Experimenting with many diverse—and sometimes seemingly absurd—ideas is crucial to innovation. But when people experiment more rapidly and frequently with the aid of new technologies, the inevitable happens: many novel concepts fail. And the earlier some of the concepts are tested, the less likely they are to pass a test. Early failures are not only desirable but also necessary since unfavorable options can be eliminated quickly, letting people refocus their efforts on more promising alternatives that often build on ideas that were initially unsuccessful. In other words, failing early and often is not only desirable but necessary in order to tap into the potential of new experimentation technologies. These technologies will greatly amplify the frequency of failure on the road to success and thus challenge senior and middle management. A crash test that reveals unacceptable safety for drivers, a drug candidate that is toxic for patients, or a software user interface that confuses customers can all be desirable outcomes of an experiment—provided these results are revealed early in an innovation process where few resources have been committed, designs are still very flexible, and other design solutions can be made available for more experimentation.[3]

Note that experiments resulting in failures are *not* failed experiments. Instead, these experiments generate new information that an innovator was unable to foresee or predict—and thus can result in learning, as we have just seen in the BMW crash example. The faster the experimentation-failure cycle, the more feedback can be gathered and incorporated into new rounds of experiments with novel and potentially risky ideas. As we saw in chapter 3, these learning-by-experimentation cycles are integral to an innovative and learning organization. As opposed to emphasis on success, which relies on staying with the familiar and known and thus enhances short-term efficiency, short-term losses in experimentation can facilitate innovation and performance in the long run. Employees who prefer to work on activities where failures are more likely tend also to persevere when times get tough, engage in more challenging work, and perform better than their safety-seeking peers.[4]

The problem that organizations face is that learning from failure is difficult to manage. In my research on integrated circuit development (chapter 2), I was surprised to find that some development teams were reluctant to iterate frequently even when the cost of doing so was negligible with new programmable technologies. "Getting it wrong the first time" could in fact be the better strategy as long as people could learn quickly from their failures, make changes, and complete multiple experimentation cycles in significantly less time than it would take to plan for first-time success. The problem was that failure can lead to embarrassment and expose important gaps in knowledge, which in turn can be costly to self-esteem and an individual's standing in an organization. After all, how often are managers promoted and teams rewarded for the early exposure of failures that result in a redeployment of precious resources (i.e., when a project is killed)? This policy is especially true in environments that have adopted "zero tolerance for failure" or "error-free" work environments. The result is waste, not only the kind of waste that comes from lower productivity and longer time to market but waste from not taking advantage of the innovation potential that new technologies can provide. Thus, building the capability and capacity for rapid experimentation in early development means rethinking the role of failure in organizations.[5] It also requires a deeper understanding of and sensitivity to what it takes to promote experimentation behavior.

Failures Are Not Mistakes

Failures should not be confused with mistakes.[6] Mistakes refer to the wrong actions that result from poor judgment or inattention; they should be avoided because they produce little new or useful information and are therefore without value.[7] A poorly planned or badly conducted experiment that results in ambiguous data, forcing researchers to repeat the experiment, is a mistake. Another common mistake is repeating a prior failure or learning nothing from the experience. A familiar example is the hot stove or cooking plate that we all touched as children—in spite of our parents forbidding us to do so. The first sensation of heat on our skin teaches us the important lesson of never to touch hot objects without some kind of protective material. Although painful, it provides valuable information to us. However, the second time we touch the same object, very little new or useful information is generated, other than the fact that the pain of heat experienced in the first experiment is a certain outcome (at least for most of us). Thus, the objective is to learn from failures as quickly as possible but to avoid mistakes.

Distinguishing between failures and mistakes is desirable, but even the best organizations often lack the management systems necessary for carefully making the distinction. In fact, the ability to manage the two simultaneously requires an organization and its managers to be ambidextrous: to promote failures but to weed out mistakes. This is not an unusual requirement for firms that want to be successful at innovation. Research has shown that long-run success requires the ability to simultaneously pursue both incremental and discontinuous innovation and change, which required contradictory structures, processes and cultures—all within the same ambidextrous company.[8]

In similar fashion, firms that embrace new technologies and the sudden increase in experimentation capacity also need to be ambidextrous with respect to the management of unsuccessful outcomes. They need to encourage people to carry out experiments that result in failures early but to discourage failed experiments—those that result in mistakes and do not contribute to new learning. That practice, in turn, requires a fundamental shift in corporate cultures and attitudes that do not necessarily appreciate the role of failure in learning and innovation. This tension is underscored by a story about Tom Watson, Sr., IBM's founder and leader for several decades. A promising young executive involved in a risky new venture, so the story goes, managed to lose more than $10 million while trying to make the venture work. When the nervous man was called into Watson's office, he offered to accept the logical consequence of losing the company such a large amount of money: "I guess you want my resignation, Mr. Watson." Much to his surprise, Watson countered: "You can't be serious! We've just spent ten million [dollars] educating you."[9]

The young manager facing Watson must have felt what many people feel about their organizations today. They are told to learn from failures but most of us would rather not fail unless we feel safe to do so. A recent research project studied eight nursing teams at two urban teaching hospitals in the effort to understand differences in learning rates and their causes.[10] To measure the extent to which these teams learned, the researcher decided to follow errors: More stable teams with better leadership would learn more, thus reporting fewer mistakes. To her surprise, she found exactly the opposite: Teams of nurses with the highest reported error rates were also more comfortable with each other as well as their managers. In contrast, teams with lower reported errors were under authoritarian leadership and were not ready to take on responsibility. In follow-up research, she found that teams with greater "psychological safety" not only reported more errors but also learned more and performed better. Creating psychological safety means walking a very fine line between creating an informal, open problem-solving environment and emphasizing performance at the same time. This kind of environment is important to firms who want to be successful at experimentation and innovation and essential to unlocking the potential of new experimentation technologies.

Factors for Promoting Experimentation in Organizations

Creating a culture that takes full advantage of the potential for increased experimentation that new technologies can provide thus requires a deeper understanding of the factors that affect experimentation behavior. With this in mind, Fiona Lee and Monica Worline at the

University of Michigan and Amy Edmondson and I at Harvard Business School decided to carry out a joint research project in which we studied the extent to which organizational values, reward, and an individual's status affected experimentation.[11] These factors were particularly attractive to us because they had already been identified as important factors in other research on organizational performance and could be directly influenced by practicing managers.

Our research consisted of two studies that were designed to complement each other. In our first study, we ran, over a period of several months, a controlled laboratory study in which 185 individuals were asked to solve an electronic maze designed for management simulation exercises. Solving the task required extensive experimentation and allowed us to differentiate clearly between desirable failures and wasteful mistakes. The laboratory study also allowed us to manipulate the following factors and study their impact on experimentation behavior and performance: (1) values—encourage or discourage experimentation; (2) rewards—failures were penalized or not; (3) status—the participant had lower or higher status.

We found that low-status individuals were more willing to experiment when values and rewards gave them a consistent message that explicitly emphasized the value of learning from failures ("learn as you go") and did not penalize them for failures. Giving mixed signals, such as encouraging them to experiment while maintaining a reward system that punished failure, made things worse, leading to less experimentation than did consistently discouraging them to experiment. The mixed signals approach also demonstrates the danger of single interventions where changing only one factor (values or rewards) can make things worse. In contrast, higher-status individuals were more willing to experiment when both factors were in conflict.

We tested these findings in an empirical study of a large, Midwestern health care organization. The company was implementing a new Web-based clinical information system that integrated data from various departments within a hospital and delivered up-to-date clinical information (e.g., blood test results and medication orders). Physicians, nurses, allied health care givers (e.g., dieticians), and support staff were the primary users of the system, which could be accessed from patient floors, offices, and private homes. Since system usage was voluntary and no training was provided, the individuals' willingness to experiment was critical in the system's adoption and impact on productivity. Previously, health care workers had to use different systems to access patient information, information which was neither updated regularly, nor was it necessarily complete.

We surveyed 688 individuals throughout the health care organization, including 120 outpatient clinics, thirty health care centers and five teaching hospitals. The survey included questions about these individuals' willingness to try new information technologies, how they actually used twenty-nine different features of the new system, and their various problem-solving strategies. Status was inferred from the individual's occupation—at the highest level were physicians, followed by medical students, nurses, allied health care givers, and secretarial and administrative staff. Using these five levels, we were able to verify our earlier findings on the influence of status on experimentation.

The results of this research project were remarkably similar to our first laboratory study. We found that individuals were more willing to try out different system features when management consistently did two things: explicitly encouraged experimentation and meted out no punishment (or disincentives) for failure. As before, mixed signals resulted in confusion and mistrust, which made experimentation with the new system rarer, and lower-status individuals were much more affected by inconsistent messages as they faced the highest social costs of failure. Medical students, for example, assumed that a failed experiment—although it had no cost to patients or the hospital—could hurt their career and were much more reluctant to expose lack of familiarity with the system in front of others. By contrast, established doctors were more willing to test the new technology, even when signals about values or rewards were mixed. We also observed that learning by increased experimentation—and failure—led to better performance. Indeed, the individuals who experimented the most ended up integrating the new technology more quickly and also became the most proficient users of it. They also reported a more efficient use of their time with patients.

Experimentation Cultures Matter

To create a culture that invites the opportunities for increased experimentation and failure that new technologies provide, managers need to pay close attention to making sure that actions, statements, and rewards are clear, consistent, and unambiguously aligned with expectations. For example, 3M is known for its healthy attitude toward failure. 3M's product groups often have so-called skunkworks teams that investigate the opportunities (or difficulties) that a potential product might pose. The teams, consisting primarily of technical people, including manufacturing engineers, face little repercussion if an idea flops—indeed, sometimes a failure is a cause for celebration. When a team discovers that a potential product doesn't work, the group quickly disbands and its members move on to other projects.[12]

A healthy culture for experimentation not only requires a tolerance for failure but also an environment that invites play and self-reflection and appreciates the importance of "speaking" through models.[13] This is especially true when new technologies change the relationship between the innovator and the tools through which experiments in the virtual and real world are carried out. In his research on how professionals think and work, educator and philosopher Donald Schön once noted:

> *The therapist's use [of] transference and the architect's [use of a] sketchpad are examples of the variety of virtual worlds on which all the professionals are dependent. A sculptor learns to infer from the feel of a maquette in his hand the qualities of a monumental figure that will be built from it. Engineers become adept at the uses of scale models, wind tunnels, and computer simulations. In an orchestra rehearsal, conductors experiment with tempo, phrasing, and instrumental balance. A role-play is an improvised game in which the participants learn to discover properties of an interpersonal situation and to reflect-in-action on their intuitive responses to it. In improvisation, musical or dramatic, participants can conduct on-the-spot experiments in which, as improvisation tends towards performance, the boundaries between virtual and real worlds may become blurred. Virtual worlds are contexts for experiment within which practitioners can suspend or control some of the everyday impediments to rigorous reflection-in-action.[14]*

Before using simulation, designers at BMW had always depended on sketchpads and clay prototypes as tools for experimentation. Through drawings and prototypes, designers reflected, improvised, and communicated new ideas. This practice is not unusual, as Michael Schrage from MIT's Media Lab observed, since "within some innovation cultures, prototypes effectively become the *media franca* of the organization—the essential medium for information, interaction, integration, and collaboration."[15] To facilitate communication and feedback, BMW managers would place clay prototypes at locations within its design studio so that, in the words of a senior executive, "you couldn't walk without stumbling over these models. They were right in your face."[16]

When BMW's designers and model makers started to complement physical models with CAS images, management feared that the virtual design images would stay within the computer box in which they were created. To preserve its successful design culture, managers tried to recreate the same atmosphere by not only buying projection equipment but posting pictures of model images everywhere—right in everyone's face. This solution allowed them to tap into the experimentation potential of computers while maintaining the culture that made it one of the world's most successful auto firms.

Principle 6: Manage Projects As Experiments

As presented so far, experimentation has been shown to be part of innovation projects, where thousands or more small experiments using different technologies attempt to resolve project uncertainty about technical solutions, production possibilities, customer needs, and markets themselves. This chapter's final principle introduces a different way of thinking about experimentation: Projects themselves can be conceived of as experiments. While senior management often considers portfolios of projects in the allocation and management of resources, it rarely applies the same logic to portfolios of experiments.[17] This is somewhat surprising since projects are powerful mechanisms for managing change, learning, and the introduction of new technologies and processes.[18] Indeed, philosopher and social scientist Donald Campbell once observed that organizational reforms are often advocated as though they were certain to be successful and noted:

> *Even where there are ideological commitments to a hard-headed evaluation of organizational efficiency, or to a scientific organization*

of society, these two jeopardies lead to the failure to evaluate organizational experiments realistically. If the political and administrative system has committed itself in advance to the correctness and efficacy of reforms, it cannot tolerate learning of failure. To be truly scientific we must be able to experiment. We must be able to advocate without that excess of commitment that blinds us to reality testing.[19]

We already saw in chapter 3 that learning from organizational experiments can be maximized through specific factors that require strategic commitment on behalf of management. Similarly, senior management should have a portfolio of experimental projects that they can learn from and that are managed with the same seriousness and rigor that is applied to other business processes (figure 6-3).[20]

The power of using the project as a learning experiment and powerful change agent worked well for BMW. When the company announced

FIGURE 6 - 3

Learning from Projects As Experiments

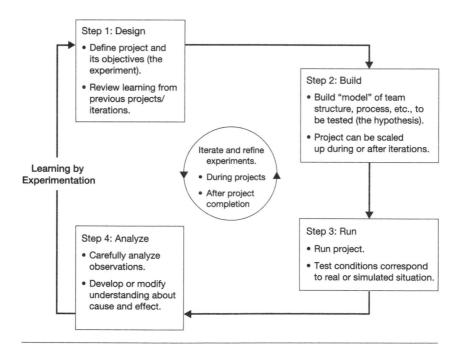

the new development process described in chapter 5, most managers and engineers found it hard to break away from daily business to press for the reengineering changes and start investing in the necessary learning by doing for the widespread use of computer-aided technologies. Functional managers in particular were simply too busy with the daily demands of development work to bring the next BMW models to life. Thus a year went by without much progress on implementing the new development system.[21]

Senior management understood how frustrated engineers and designers felt with the company struggling toward slashing development time in half while simultaneously attending to routine matters. To have meaningful change, however, they concluded that the new development system's feasibility had to be tested on a real development project. This project, they concurred, should entail so much risk and suffering that no cautious manager would ever block it! At the same time, the project should include a buffer period that would encourage people to learn by using an unproven development system that surely required many changes. After much heated discussion, the executives decided to use the latest 7-Series platform car that was already one year into development using BMW's proven five-year process. The project would serve as a psychological Rubicon—once crossed, there would be no turning back for managers and engineers. Thus, the platform project became an experiment in itself. One executive pointed out the high-stakes game the company had entered: "Developing a new product with a new process is dangerous. We didn't know how to develop a car in such a short time, but we knew the longer we waited, the longer people would find reasons not to do it!"[22] BMW felt that the risk of inaction was greater than the risk that a new development system would introduce into the organization.

The announcement to use the new process for its most important project also showed strong commitment and left little doubt about senior management's seriousness. At the same time, the project team was given additional time to learn by doing and refine a digital development system that had not been tested before. The challenge, after all, was not the procurement and installation of state-of-the-art computer hardware and software but the patient development of new capabilities and changes to processes and organization in order to leverage the opportunities that new experimentation technologies would offer.

How to Maximize Learning from Projects

When projects become experiments themselves, they require careful planning and strategic investment into an infrastructure that supports experimentation for learning. Factors such as the right fidelity, rapid feedback, controls to increase signal-to-noise ratios, and so on, which were discussed in chapter 3, now have to be elevated to another level, resulting in new questions and issues to be addressed as managers consider the factors that will increase the rate at which companies learn and improve (table 6-2).

At the same time, more information doesn't translate into learning unless it is also taken up by an organization and put into action.[23] Learning rarely takes place systematically. Precious resources are wasted because identical problems are solved over and over again in project after project.[24] Recall the situation at the end of chapter 4, where *more* physical prototypes were created to test the validity of simulation-based prototypes!

TABLE 6 - 2

Factors That Affect Learning by Projects As Experiments

Factor	Related Question when Projects Become Experiments
Fidelity of Experiments	To what extent can the project conditions and interventions be generalized to the rest of the organization?
Cost of Experiments	What is the *additional* cost (resources, opportunity costs, etc.) of running the project as an experiment?
Iteration Time (all four steps)	How quickly can we get the first feedback from the project? When will the project be completed?
Capacity	How many projects are in the experimentation portfolio? How many in the R&D portfolio are available for experimentation?
Strategy	How many projects are running in parallel and can be used as experiments?
Signal-to-Noise Ratio	Will other organizational changes obscure my variable of interest or is the "signal" (e.g., a new development system) significant enough? What projects make good experimental controls?
Type of Experiment	Is the project a breakthrough, platform, or derivative? How will this affect the experiment itself?

As one example of effective learning from projects, consider the use of postmortems in the development of computer software. Good postmortems are detailed records of a project's history and include, among other information, information on problems discovered at various stages of software development. Research at Microsoft showed that the company uses postmortem reports extensively to facilitate learning between projects and teams.[25] Development teams generally take three to six months to prepare a postmortem, which can be from under 10 to over 100 pages long. Besides accounting for people and product and scheduling issues, the postmortems also contain detailed information on number of problems (bugs) identified, problem severity, and so forth. Preparing, discussing, and reviewing postmortem reports, particularly before and/or at the beginning of a new project, has proven to be instrumental in carrying forward the knowledge from current and past projects. In many years of using postmortems, Microsoft also discovered that transferring information on problems alone is very helpful but not sufficient; they needed to understand why a problem occurred and what solutions were possible.

Postmortems are a very good example of effective learning mechanisms when the information being transferred can be easily encoded. That, however, may not always be the case. In a research study of 229 team members on twenty-five Japanese automobile projects, the researcher's findings suggest that effective knowledge transfer mechanisms have to address the kind of knowledge being transferred.[26] When information can be easily encoded, such as component-level data, it is more effective to use archival-based mechanisms (documents, drawings, and so on). However, if information is "sticky" or very costly to encode and transfer, such as tacit knowledge about the integration of components, firms performed better if they relied on face-to-face communication, people transfers, and other mechanisms that allow for an effective transfer of tacit knowledge.[27]

Aligning Incentives and Compensation

When teams take on the dual objective of meeting demanding project deadlines and organizational experimentation, it is important to send the right signals with respect to incentives and compensation.

Consider the case of Bank of America discussed in chapter 3.[28] When the bank introduced its some two-dozen life "laboratories" in Atlanta—the so-called innovation market—senior management wanted to infuse experimentation and innovation into an organization that has relied on stability and standardization. Each laboratory was a fully operating banking branch, yet in every location new product and service concepts were being tested continuously. Experiments included "virtual tellers," video monitors displaying financial and investment news, computer stations uploading images of personal checks, and "hosting stations." A thorny issue the management faced was how to motivate its staff (called associates). Could—and should—performance of these employees, who were part of continuous experimentation, be measured and rewarded conventionally?

Debate at Bank of America

In addition to the new demands on their time, Bank of America employees also faced different and sometimes conflicting incentives, which raised some hard questions about compensation. Sales associates at the branches traditionally earned between 30 percent and 50 percent of their total pay from performance bonuses tied to a point system.[29] An associate would earn points for meeting various sales quotas, and the number of points would vary according to, among other things, the products sold, the branch's customer satisfaction levels, and local market demographics.

For the first several months of the innovation market, the test branches maintained the conventional incentive scheme. Sales associates seemed to enjoy the additional activities—their involvement in the program made them feel "special" (as a number of sales associates put it), and they made extra efforts to get the experiments up and running. But their high level of motivation could not last forever, as time pressures inevitably took their toll. People soon realized that all the time they had to dedicate to meetings and training reduced their opportunities to earn bonus points. In a number of branches, moreover, associates had to take turns greeting customers as the host—an activity that, again, offered no chances to earn points. Because their monthly sales quotas hadn't changed, some associates became frustrated with the new arrangement. When acting as the host, for example, some associates would leave their post in order to help a client open an account (and to gain the associated bonus points), rather than refer the client to another specialist as the experiment's design dictated. The desire to earn points conflicted with the desire to participate in the experiments. This was an unanticipated effect of the program, and one that needed to be addressed.

In January 2001, therefore, senior management abandoned the traditional bonus system in the test branches, switching all associates to fixed incentives based on team performance. Most associates welcomed the change, which amplified their feeling of being special while also underscoring top management's commitment to the experimentation process. But, again, not all staff thrived under the new scheme. Without the lure of points, some associates lost their motivation to sell. Resentment from bank personnel outside the innovation market also intensified as a result of the special compensation program. One bank executive pointed out that "those in the innovation market branches now thought they didn't have to chin to the same level as others." Doubts about the broader applicability of test-market findings also grew. As Allen Jones, a regional executive, pointed out, "If a test is successful only under fixed-incentive schemes, then we can't roll it out elsewhere."[30]

With growing discomfort, senior management switched the staff back to the old point-based incentive system after just six months. Not surprisingly, tensions between earning bonus points and assisting in experiments quickly returned. What's more, the about-face disheartened some staffers, leading them to question management's commitment to the program. The bank's difficulties over determining incentive pay underscore the problems inherent in having employees participate in a corporate experiment while also pursuing their everyday jobs: This is a real effect of managing ambidextrous teams. A hybrid bonus system, one that includes both individual sales commissions and a fixed, team-based component, will in most cases be the best solution. But every company will likely have to go through a testing period of its own to arrive at the balance that is right for its people and that doesn't undermine the integrity of its experiments. The ambiguity of how experimentation was initially rewarded at Bank of America also affected the behavior toward risk taking and failure. Out of some forty concepts that had been tested, only four ended up as failures—resulting in a failure rate of roughly 10 percent. This was clearly not in line with the target failure rate of 30 percent that management felt was necessary to become an innovative development organization.

By experiencing two different models—one focused on in-branch operations and another on R&D-type environments—Bank of America's management learned that the dual nature of its innovation market also required a hybrid incentive system that appreciated and balanced the tension of two objectives that were often in conflict with each other. When companies manage projects as experiments, senior management needs to address similar challenges: On one hand, projects need to be completed on time and budget; on the other hand, people need some slack and incentives to take the intervention and learning aspect seriously.

Principles at Work:
Lessons from IDEO Product Development

Changing to or preserving an experimentation culture that can manage and balance the paradox of failure and success, experimentation and standardization, and ultimately, long- and short-term business pressures is neither easy nor straightforward. Senior management will be challenged—as Thomas Edison was challenged when he tried to move his organization from invention to making money; a switch akin to moving an organization predicated on *exploration* to the pressures of *exploitation*. It turns out that his shop culture prevented him from adopting mass production economies that were needed to commercially exploit his laboratory's invention. Twenty years after Edison had decided on a manufacturing strategy based on systematic cost reductions, his factories at West Orange still couldn't achieve the necessary design standardization and long production runs.[31] His factories were general purpose, with continuously changing engineering designs and relatively short production runs. The short physical proximity between the laboratory and factory that worked so well for experimentation now turned into a handicap: The demand for manufacturing products overtook finishing the design process. Historian Andre Millard summarized the challenges Edison faced:

> This was the heritage of the shop culture in which experimenting took precedence over production engineering. The hierarchy of skills

at West Orange gave the experimenter in the laboratory predomi-nance over the foreman in the [factory]. Improving the product was much higher on the list of priorities than keeping to one, stable design, and it was also a lot more rewarding for the muckers [experimenters] and their boss. Although these values suited the shop culture, they were maintained at the price of high manufactur-ing costs.[32]

Today, firms that have focused on exploitation have found that the very factors that make them successful inhibit their ability to inno-vate—in some ways, Edison's problem in reverse.[33] Managing for suc-cess, process standardization, and efficiency can get in the way of learn-ing from failure, experimentation, and innovation. This is important because the principles discussed in this chapter promote the latter but may affect the former.

In many cases, companies have decided to complement their strong exploitation capabilities through the use of outside organizations that have focused on building strong exploration capabilities. One such organization that has supported companies in balancing these conflicts, albeit at a much smaller scale, is IDEO Product Development, one of the world's leading design firms.

Company Background

For some three decades, IDEO has provided its clients and the world with thousands of products ranging from the computer mouse to the stand-up toothpaste dispenser.[34] Central to its success is a system for innovation that has evolved through continuous experimentation since the company was founded (box 6-1). Major IDEO clients have included Apple Computer, AT&T, Samsung, Philips, Amtrak, Steelcase, Baxter International, and NEC Corporation. IDEO's thirst for exploring a vari-ety of fields has led it to complete thousands of projects, including fifty projects for Apple (including its first mouse), ski goggles, the Avocet Vertech skiers' watch, and a large variety of medical instrumentation. The company has also participated in Hollywood film projects, creating scale-model submarines for *The Abyss* and a twenty-five-foot mechani-cal whale for *Free Willy*. In the 1990s, IDEO won more industry awards than any other design firm worldwide.

BOX 6-1: UNDERSTANDING IDEO'S SYSTEM FOR INNOVATION

IDEO's innovation system can best be characterized as four major elements: process, organization, management, and culture. It is the tight and balanced integration of these elements that make it so difficult to implement—although some of the pieces look deceptively simple.

ELEMENT 1: DEVELOPMENT PROCESS

Prototyping

In the early stages of a design project, perfecting a sophisticated model is considered a waste of time. Prototyping at IDEO instead follows the three Rs: rough, rapid, and right. Designers and engineers themselves create rough early prototypes from readily available material such as cardboard or clay or putty. The final R, right, refers to building several models focused on getting specific aspects of a product right. Quick-and-dirty prototyping of individual product components allows for more and faster design iterations. It helps create straw men that can be repeatedly knocked down to ultimately yield more robust designs. Prototyping also facilitates communication with clients, marketers, experts, and users by ensuring that everyone is discussing the same ideas and concepts. The entire process can be viewed as a group of serial and parallel experiments that frequently result in failures but increase learning. Prototyping is the mechanism through which experiments are carried out. Similar to Edison's labs, IDEO's prototype shop is located very close to development teams and has enough capacity for ideas to be quickly turned into physical artifacts.

Intense Brainstorming

Prototyping and brainstorming go hand in hand at IDEO, with brainstorming sessions leading to rapid prototyping or vice versa. The goal is to quickly create a whirlwind of activity and ideas, with the most promising ideas developed into prototypes in just minutes, hours, or days. While most firms employ brainstorming in their processes, IDEO's way of brainstorming is rather unique and trademarked as the Deep Dive. The approach tries to combine process with creativity by explicitly following a set of rules that aim at increasing a team's productivity in generating

(continued)

(continued)

creative ideas. Some of these rules are (1) stay focused on the topic; (2) encourage wild ideas; (3) defer judgment to avoid interrupting the flow of ideas; (4) build on the ideas of others (it is usually more productive than seeking glory for one's own insights); (5) hold only one conversation at a time to ensure that introverts also get their say; (6) go for quantity (150 ideas in thirty to forty-five minutes); (7) be visual, since sketching ideas helps people understand them. Brainstorming sessions are very intense and involve people from other projects.

Client Management

Clients come to IDEO because they expect breakthrough ideas and concepts. Quite often, large clients have internal product organizations with hundreds or thousands of developers and budgets that easily exceed IDEO's total annual revenues. As a result, the expectations are high and have to be managed carefully. Innovation outcomes are difficult to predict and so are budgets. The company charges for accomplishing milestones, at each of which clients have a choice of continuing if they are happy with the project's progress. Very frequent client meetings are required so that clients are aware of all opportunities and the costs and time involved. Again, client meetings are run with the aid of prototypes.

ELEMENT 2: ORGANIZATION

Small Units

Growing IDEO to one of the world's largest design organizations has been achieved by budding out smaller design studios whenever one appeared to grow too large. The company relies on the size of its small studios, which leaves little space for noncontributors. High-performing employees are rewarded by being given more challenging projects to lead. A self-selection process among interviewees also helps with ensuring high employee satisfaction, resulting in low turnover.

Flat, Little Hierarchy

The company is a flat organization to an extreme. All work is organized by project team, and a team forms and disbands for the life of a project (with the exception of administrative tasks). Part of the reason for constantly shuffling personnel around into different teams is to ensure diversity of team composition. There are few permanent job assignments, organization charts, titles, or promotions.

ELEMENT 3: MANAGEMENT

Low Key, Lead by Example

By David Kelley's own admission, "It is inconceivable that the head guy in any organization will know all the answers!" Management at IDEO is low key, with the primary goal of ensuring that the democratization of ideas continues undeterred. Kelley views his own role in the firm as merely creating the stage on which designers can play the leading role in creating innovative designs. Management also interfaces with the outside world, especially in helping "train" clients about the IDEO process.

Knowledge Management

The retention and transfer of project knowledge is exemplified by the so-called Tech Box, the company's giant "shoebox" for curiosities and interesting gadgets from prior IDEO projects. It is a knowledge management system that does not involve information technology and that works! At the end of projects, developers can apply to have some of their artifacts (prototypes, novel materials, and so on) become part of the company Tech Box. Being appointed curator of the box is a high honor at IDEO and people take it very seriously. When developers begin new projects, they can rummage through the Tech Box in search of inspiration and thus benefit from prior project experiences of their colleagues.

ELEMENT 4: CULTURE

Failure and Trust

The IDEO culture matches the messy and often unpredictable process of innovation that reaps many failures along the way to eventual success. People are hired carefully and are rarely fired. Trust is placed in the staff members to encourage them to take risks to create novel designs. To encourage designers to fail often in order to succeed earlier, IDEO has created an atmosphere of childlike playfulness and trust. Few formal titles, dress codes, or staid cubicles create an atmosphere that attracts and encourages self-driven individuals who are passionate about design.

(continued)

(continued)

Sharing and Respect

For the company not to sink into chaos, however, the culture strongly emphasizes idea sharing, respect for a diversity of opinions, and putting one's ego in the background. In this setting, staff members must become comfortable with confusion, incomplete information, and paradox. A prototype-driven mentality helps provide structure and communications in such an organization.

Simple Rules

IDEO's process of innovation looks deceptively simple, but it is hard to implement. To guide people's behavior, the company has devised a few simple rules that shape and reflect the company's culture. Examples are (1) enlightened trial and error; (2) the three R's of prototyping; (3) fail often to succeed sooner; (4) if a picture is worth a thousand words, a prototype is worth ten thousand. Many of these rules are posted as signs in the building and employees cite them in their daily work. They are powerful, yet simple, and they guide new recruits as well as experienced developers.

In the late 1990s, the company employed a staff of over 300 and maintained design centers in Boston, Chicago, San Francisco, London, Palo Alto, Grand Rapids, New York, Milan, Tel Aviv, and Tokyo. Although all centers operated independently, seeking business locally, they exchanged a high volume of e-mail and often shared talent as needed. Over the years, while his employees focused on designing client products, IDEO's founder David Kelley increasingly found himself designing and redesigning the company through constant experimentation. According to Kelley, "I'm more interested in the methodology of design. . . . I'm the person who builds the stage rather than performs on it."[35]

Part of this stage-building involved studying the IDEO environment in new ways. Instead of merely relying on employee surveys, the company also studied workplace interactions through suspended video cameras in order to optimize office design. IDEO also sought to improve its own design processes by reviewing all completed projects. According to Kelley, "We pick the things each client does well, and assimilate them into our methodology. We're not good at innovating because of our flawless intellects, but because we've done thousands of products, and we've been mindful."[36]

IDEO came to national prominence when it allowed ABC to televise a segment showing its designers meeting the challenge of reengineering the commonplace shopping cart—a virtually unchanged icon for the past several decades, despite its creaky and obdurate wheels and often unwieldy basket—in just five days. The IDEO design replaced the traditional large basket with a system of baskets that allowed consumers to use the shopping cart as a "base camp" for shopping. Innovative new wheels allowed greater maneuverability in the store. Hooks on the frame allowed for bagged items to be transported out to the parking lot. The absence of a central basket removed much of the incentive for stealing the shopping carts.

Rapid Experimentation Through Frequent Prototyping

Central to IDEO's design philosophy is the role of prototyping. According to Tom Kelley, general manager and David Kelley's brother, "We prototype more than our clients suspect, and probably more than our competitors do."[37] Frequent prototyping serves as the most important way for his company to communicate with clients, marketers, experts, and end users. Prototypes ensure that everyone is imagining the same design during discussions about a product. All offices have model shops in close proximity staffed by highly skilled machinists to rapidly produce both simple and sophisticated prototypes. Product developers feel that you learn just as much from a model that's wrong as you do from one that's right and thus consider perfecting high-fidelity models in the early design stages a waste of time. As a result, designers and engineers themselves create early prototypes from readily available material such as cardboard, foamcore, Legos, and Erector sets.

Rapid prototyping at IDEO follows the three Rs: rough, rapid, and right. The final R, right, refers to building several models focused on getting specific aspects of a product right. For example, to design a telephone receiver, an IDEO team would carve dozens of pieces of foam and cradle them between their heads and shoulders to find the best shape for a handset. Quick-and-dirty prototyping allows for a greater number of iterations. "By our method," David Kelley claims, "you could never design a VCR you couldn't program. [Researchers at larger companies] are afraid of looking bad to management, so they do an expensive, sleek prototype, but then they become committed to it before they really know any of the answers. You have to have the guts to create a straw man." At IDEO, straw men are repeatedly created and knocked down, a process that leaves IDEO's staffers with thick skin. "Failure," Kelley feels, "is part of the culture. We call it enlightened trial and error."[38]

In an allied process, IDEO seeks to generate as many ideas as possible early in the design process through almost daily brainstorming sessions. The entire process resembles a funnel, with several ideas at the top, three or four lower down, and only one making it all the way through. People are generally not upset if their ideas do not become the definitive solution since the act of clipping off ideas brings the entire team closer to the solution. This thinking resembles how legendary baseball batter Babe Ruth outlined his strategy: "Every strike brings me closer to the next home run." In addition, discarded ideas are archived and sometimes kept for possible future products. Sometimes in the course of a project, when progress appears to come to a standstill, the leader might call for what has come to be known as a Deep Dive approach. In this process, the team focuses intensively for an entire day on generating a large number of creative concepts very quickly, weeding out weak ideas, and starting prototyping based on the top handful of solutions. Monday show-and-tell sessions (where designers showcase their latest insights) and the Tech Box described in chapter 1 also reinforce a spirit of invention.

The company understands the need for structured development that emphasizes immersion and experimentation before locking in design solutions. In phase 0 (understand/observe), the team seeks to understand the client's business and immerses itself in finding out about the feasibility of a product. Substantial resources and time are devoted to market research for defining needs, including nontraditional means such as generating fictionalized potential users and "customer anthropology" to better understand the context in which a product might be used. In the closely related phase I (visualize/realize), the team ends up choosing a product direction based on ideas, technologies, and market perceptions. Through close coordination with the client, the team generates rough three-dimensional models of a product and a general idea of the manufacturing strategy to be utilized. In phase II (evaluating/refining), the team enhances design prototypes through testing functional prototypes. Emphasis shifts from human factors and ergonomics to engineering. Phase II culminates with a functional model as well as a "looks like" design model. In phase III (detailed engineering), the team completes product designs and verifies that the final product works and could be manufactured. By the end of this phase, the team delivers a fully functional design model, tooling databases, and technical documentation. Finally, in phase IV (manufacturing liaison) the team ensures smooth product release to manufacturing as the product moves to the client's factory lines.

Management understands that each of these phases requires very different management styles and involvement. In the early stages where creativity and ideas matter, the process resembles focused chaos with a soft, facilitative management style. Team members are encouraged to be playful, experiment with absurd ideas, and generate as many concepts as possible. The methodology emphasizes "expansion," encouraging people to go outside their traditional limits without worrying about constraints such as manufacturing. This period is then followed by a more directive style of management that emphasizes focus and generates more realistic concepts that build on earlier phases. Within these phases are many iterations with simple prototypes and sketches that communicate product ideas and concepts.

Managing Failure to Succeed Sooner

IDEO encourages its designers to fail often to succeed sooner, and the company understands that more radical experiments frequently lead to more spectacular failures. Indeed, the company has developed numerous prototypes that have bordered on the ridiculous and which were later rejected. At the same time, its innovation system has led to a host of best-sellers, such as the Palm V handheld computer, which has made the company the subject of intense media interest.

Removing the stigma of failure, though, usually requires overcoming ingrained attitudes. People who fail in experiments are often viewed as incompetent, and that attitude can lead to counterproductive behavior. As David Kelley pointed out earlier, rather than risking looking bad to management, developers will build expensive prototypes, which they are then married to despite the prototypes' relative uselessness in the end. In other words, the sleek prototype might look impressive, but it presents the false impression that the product is farther along than it really is, and that perception subtly discourages people from changing the design even though better alternatives might exist. That's why IDEO advocates the development of cheap, rough prototypes that people are invited to criticize—a process that eventually leads to breakthrough products more quickly.

Projects As Experiments

While prototyping and experimentation have been integral to IDEO's success in product innovation, the same is true for continuously evolving its system for innovation. This system was not created overnight when David Kelley founded the company. Instead, management and employees tried many organizational and system experiments over the years, some of which worked and were integrated, while many more were dismissed as failures. Critical to the quest for constant experimentation have been the projects themselves. They not only allow teams to try out new ways of organizing and managing development but also continuously challenge ingrained assumptions that over time tend to be viewed as facts.

A case in point was a new project that came from Handspring, the venture formed by former Palm executives Jeff Hawkins and Donna Dubinsky. The company's initial product, the Visor, would provide customers with flexibility through plugging in a variety of small modules. IDEO had just proven its innovation system through the development of the extremely successful Palm V handheld computer. The new challenge that Handspring posed to IDEO was a product of low price to be developed in less than half the time it took to bring the Palm V to market. Because of time and price pressures, the project implied running with only tried-and-true technology and compromises in design (e.g., plastic housing, standard batteries).

IDEO's management was not worried about meeting the deadline. What concerned them much more was having to bypass or accelerate some of the elements in its innovation system to meet the client's deadline at the possible risk of developing a product that could not match the Palm V in design excellence. It was particularly concerned about accelerating the early phases of brainstorming and experimentation where IDEO excelled many of its competitors. The project's necessary secrecy—two teams worked on competing Palm and Handspring products—also strained its culture of openness and collaboration. When IDEO decided to take on the Visor project, it was not only because it could work well with the Handspring team; IDEO also wanted to challenge the elements of its innovation system: process, organization, management, and culture. The project became an experiment that opened up a window for learning and improving its system for consistent and predictable innovation.

Conclusion

The conflicts between success and failure, standardization and experimentation, and ultimately exploration of innovative ideas and concepts and their exploitation are constantly challenging large companies such as BMW and Bank of America. Some smaller companies such as IDEO have focused instead on creating value for its clients by focusing its strategy primarily on the exploration of innovations. To succeed at innovation, however, all these companies are following the three principles introduced in this chapter: organize for rapid experimentation, fail early and often but avoid mistakes, and manage projects as experiments. New experimentation technologies amplify the importance of these principles even further as they allow increased speed and experimentation capacity but also demand more failures early in development when ideas can be discarded at little cost but are an important springboard for better products and services.

Taken together, chapters 5 and 6 have introduced six powerful principles that not only lead to more effective experimentation for learning and innovation but are also necessary for unlocking the potential of new technologies. When fully deployed, they can result in what-if experiments that were nearly impossible or impractical before: what if a car, a financial service, or a handheld device was designed and used in a particular way? As companies master these principles hand in hand with new experimentation technologies, they can tap into new breakthrough products and services as sources of value creation.

But what comes next? Throughout the book, we have focused primarily on revolutionizing product development organizations from *within*. In the next chapter, we shall see what is possible when new technologies and development processes enable companies to shift experimentation outside the firm and into the hands of customers. In some industries, this practice has fundamentally changed not only how innovation works but how value is created. In the semiconductor industry, it turned a market on its head.

NOTES

1. Some of the material in this chapter is drawn from Thomke (2001) and Thomke, Holzner, and Gholami (1999).

2. Research by Loch and Terwiesch (1999) explicitly addresses congestion effects that arise from scarce capacity and process variability when dealing with engineering change orders. Their proposed improvement strategies are aimed at reducing lead times: making capacity flexible, balancing workloads, merging tasks, pooling, and reducing set ups and batching.

3. Leonard-Barton (1995) and Sitkin (1992) have referred to these outcomes as "intelligent failures." Sitkin lists five key characteristics that contribute to failures being intelligent: They (1) result from thoughtfully planned actions, (2) have uncertain outcomes, (3) are of modest scale, (4) are executed and responded to with alacrity, and (5) take place in domains that are familiar enough to permit effective learning.

4. A discussion of the role of failure in learning and links to the research literature can be found in Sitkin (1992) and Lee, Edmondson, Thomke, and Worline (2000).

5. See also Garvin (2000, chapter 2) and Leonard-Barton (1995, chapter 5).

6. The two words *failure* and *mistake* are semantically very close to each other. Failure usually refers to a lack of satisfactory performance or an effect that results from actions taken. In contrast, mistake refers to the wrong action because of poor judgment, inattention, or simply not knowing. In this con-

text, I deliberately exaggerate the difference: Although mistakes can lead to failure, companies should focus on failure resulting from actions that may be partially correct but not good enough to meet performance expectations. Such actions are not mistakes.

7. Reinertsen (1997, page 79) makes the same point by distinguishing between two types of failures: those that generate information and those that do not. The former are very valuable to design whereas the latter only consume time and resources without producing benefit.

8. Tushman and O'Reilly (1996).

9. Quoted from Bennis and Nanus (1985), page 70.

10. Edmondson (1996).

11. The full results from the research study can be found in Lee, Edmondson, Thomke, and Worline (2000). The findings are also summarized in Lee (2001).

12. Thomke and Nimgade (1998b).

13. Leonard-Barton (1995), chapters 3 and 5.

14. Quoted from Schön (1983), page 162.

15. Quoted from Schrage (1993), page 57.

16. Personal communication from BMW management.

17. Management tools that focus on portfolio management are now being adopted by many firms. One example is the Aggregate Project Plan (APP), first introduced by Wheelwright and Clark (1992, chapter 4).

18. Scholars have long advocated that companies ought to leverage projects for purposes other than immediate deliverables. For example, Bowen, Clark, Holloway, and Wheelwright (1994) advocate that projects can be training grounds for future company leaders.

19. Quoted from Campbell (1969), page 410.

20. Lynn, Morone, and Paulson (1996) found that some companies succeeded at innovation by following a process of "probing and learning." Product solutions are changed over the years as a result of what companies have

learned through a process of experimental design and exploration. Each product development project was regarded as an experiment in itself, designed to probe initial markets and to remove uncertainty for successive projects.

21. The information comes from Thomke and Nimgade (1998a).

22. Ibid., page 12.

23. The emphasis on action in the learning process has long been advocated by Argyris (1982).

24. Watkins and Clark (1994) found that design problems were often repeated in consecutive projects. (As an example, they presented one problem that showed up repeatedly over three sequential projects.) von Hippel and Tyre (1995) observed a similar pattern and found that not only was there a lack of problem-specific information being transferred within firms but designers were sometimes unable to use the transferred information effectively.

25. The information on postmortems comes from Cusumano and Selby (1995) and Sinofsky and Thomke (1999).

26. See Aoshima (1996) for study findings and Cusumano and Nobeoka (1998) for additional research on learning between projects in the automotive industry.

27. von Hippel (1994).

28. The material on Bank of America is drawn from Thomke and Nimgade (2002) and Thomke (2003).

29. At branches in Atlanta, Georgia, Bank of America tellers earned about $20,000 a year; annual turnover averaged about 50 percent. The next step up from teller was sales associate; these people helped customers start up savings or checking accounts and fill out mortgage applications; they notarized documents and enticed customers with new services. At innovation market branches, some associates could serve as hosts—making many decisions without bringing in the branch manager.

30. From Thomke and Nimgade (2002), page 11.

31. Millard (1990), page 200.

32. Ibid., page 201.

33. Benner and Tushman (2002) address the tension between exploration and exploitation activities, as it relates to the management and control of processes.

34. The material in this section is drawn from Thomke and Nimgade (2000). For additional research and information on IDEO's innovation system, see Sutton and Hargadon (1996, 1997) and Kelley (2001).

35. Quoted from Thomke and Nimgade (2000), page 3.

36. Ibid.

37. Ibid., page 4.

38. Ibid.

7
shifting the locus of experimentation

Understanding how the potential of new experimentation technologies can be unlocked for innovation and why firms do or do not stumble in their adoption has helped us rethink how new products and services can be developed within organizations. Significantly, when new technologies for experimentation have been mastered and integrated—when process, organization, and management have been corralled to benefit from the principles introduced in this book—it is possible to explore how these new capabilities can be leveraged beyond organizations.

Maximizing learning from experimentation can and should happen throughout the value chain, and many of the principles discussed in this book hold anywhere, regardless of where experimentation happens. The mastery of experimenting early and often, organizing for rapid iterations, and managing failure while integrating new and traditional technologies matter to an innovator, whether a supplier, manufacturer, or customer. In the same way that new technologies such as computer simulation are changing how engineers develop new products, they can become new tools for collaborating with suppliers and customers. For example, manufacturers of video game consoles are providing software-based development toolkits to game suppliers while the new hardware is still under development. Outstanding toolkits can entice suppliers to design more games because they can increase productivity and experimentation—a critical success factor in the battle for console market share.[1]

In this chapter we shall look at one such possibility: how new products and service development can be shifted to customers.[2] By putting new experimentation technologies into the hands of customers, some organizations can unlock another piece of the potential for innovation (figure 7-1). In the course of studying product innovation across many industries, Eric von Hippel at MIT and I have discovered that a number of companies have adopted an intriguing approach that takes advantage of experimentation technologies discussed throughout this book.

FIGURE 7 - 1

Shifting the Locus of Experimentation to Customers

New experimentation tools and technologies not only have the potential to revolutionize a company's R&D but can also transform entire industries by shifting experimentation— and thus innovation—to customers.

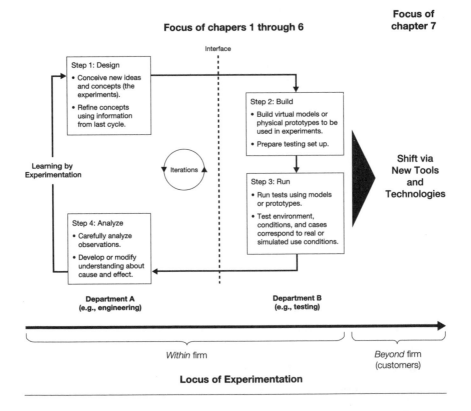

Essentially, these companies have abandoned their efforts to understand exactly what products their customers want and have instead equipped them with tools to design and develop their own new products, ranging from minor modifications to major new innovations. The user-friendly tools, often integrated into a toolkit package, deploy technologies described throughout the book (e.g., computer simulation and rapid prototyping) to make innovation faster, less expensive, and most important, better as customers run what-if experiments themselves.

A variety of industries have started to use this approach. Bush Boake Allen (BBA), a global supplier of specialty flavors to companies like Nestlé, has built a toolkit that will enable its customers to develop their own flavors, which BBA then manufactures. In the materials field, General Electric (GE) provides customers with Web-based tools for designing better plastic products. In software, a number of companies allow people to add custom-designed modules to their standard products and then commercialize the best of those components. Open-source software allows users to design, build, distribute, and support their own programs—no manufacturer required. Indeed, shifting experimentation and innovation to customers has the power to completely transform industries. In the semiconductor business, it has led to a custom-chip market that has grown to more than $15 billion.

Tapping into the innovativeness and imagination of customers— not just R&D departments—can indeed generate tremendous value, but capturing that value is hardly a simple or straightforward process. Not only must companies develop the right design toolkit, they must also revamp their business models as well as their management mindsets. When companies relinquish a fundamental task—such as designing a new product—to customers, the two parties must redefine their relationship, and this change can be risky. With custom computer chips, for instance, companies traditionally captured value by both designing and manufacturing innovative products. Now, with customers taking over more of the design task, companies must focus more intently on providing the best custom manufacturing. In other words, the location where value is created and captured changes, and companies must reconfigure their business models accordingly. This chapter offers some principles and lessons for companies that are preparing to undergo such a transformation themselves.

Development Problem Faced by Firms

Product development is often difficult because the "need" information (what the customer wants) resides with the customer and the "solution" information (how to satisfy those needs) lies with the manufacturer. Traditionally, the onus has been on manufacturers to collect the customer need information through various means, including market research and information gathered from the field. The process can be costly and time-consuming because customer needs are often complex, subtle, and fast-changing.[3] Frequently, customers don't fully understand their needs until they try out prototypes to explore exactly what does—and doesn't—work. Many companies are familiar with customers' reactions when they see and use a finished product for the first time: "This is exactly what I asked you to develop, but it is not what I now need." In other words, customers learn about their needs through informal experimentation while using new products or services. Not surprisingly, traditional product development is a drawn-out process of trial and error, often ping-ponging between manufacturer and customer.[4] First, the manufacturer develops a prototype based on information from the customer that is incomplete and only partially correct. The customer then tries out the product, finds flaws, and requests corrections. This learning-by-experimentation cycle repeats until a satisfactory solution is reached, frequently requiring many costly and time-consuming iterations.[5] When companies have to work with hundreds of customers with different needs, each requiring market research and a well-managed iteration process, it is easy to see how the companies can become overwhelmed and thus focus only on the largest and most profitable customers.

To appreciate the extent of the difficulty, consider product development at BBA (now International Flavors and Fragrances or IFF).[6] In this industry, specialty flavors are needed to bolster and enhance the taste of nearly all processed foods because manufacturing techniques weaken the real flavors. The development of the added flavors requires a high degree of customization and expertise, and the practice remains more of an art than a science. A traditional product development project might progress in the following way: A customer requests a meaty flavor for a soy product, and the sample must be delivered within a

FIGURE 7 - 2

BBA's Development Process

The "need" information (what customers want in flavors) resides with food customers and the "solution" information (how to custom design the flavors) resides with BBA. As a result, BBA and its customers go back and forth for several iterations, leading to higher cost, long development times, and low acceptance rates. Long feedback cycles and organizational interfaces (R&D, marketing, purchasing, and customer R&D) slow down experimentation significantly.

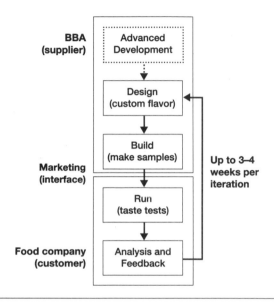

week (figure 7-2). BBA marketing professionals and flavorists jump into action and the sample is shipped in six days. A frustrating three weeks ensue until the client responds, "It's good, but we need it less smoky and more gutsy." The client knows precisely what that means, but flavorists find the request difficult to interpret. The result is more frenzied activity as BBA struggles to adjust the flavor in a couple of days. Depending on the product, BBA and the client could go back and forth for several more iterations, which can be a huge problem when a client expects BBA to get the flavor right the first time or within two or three iterations.

To make matters worse, BBA bears most of the development risk. The company collects revenue from production only after both the client and consumers are fully satisfied. R&D expenses could be just $1,000 for tweaking an existing flavor, but they could go as high as $300,000 for an entirely new family of flavors that requires not only chemists and flavorists but also sales, marketing, regulatory, and quality control expertise. On average, the client eventually accepts only 15 percent of all new flavors for full market evaluation, and only 5 percent to 10 percent make their way to the marketplace. Meanwhile, margins in the flavor industry have been falling because of increased competition and cost pressures from customers. The consequence of high development cost and low flavor acceptance rates is a business model that works as long as customers end up buying a sufficiently large production volume. Not surprisingly, customers with low-volume needs have little choice but to go elsewhere or purchase standard flavors. BBA's R&D and marketing personnel cannot reasonably be tied up with low-volume customers. The missed opportunity, however, is that there are thousands or perhaps hundreds of thousands potential customers out there whose cumulative volume needs for custom flavors are significant. In response, BBA's CEO Julian Boyden and Vice President of technology John Wright investigated the option of shifting more innovation activities to customers and thereby lowering the cost and risk of custom flavor development. The company developed an Internet-based toolkit with a computer interface that displays a profile of a standard flavor (figure 7-3). A customer can learn by experimentation through manipulating and changing the information on screen and sending it directly to an automated machine that manufactures a sample within minutes.

Larger customers could have such a machine on site whereas smaller customers could receive their samples from a regional machine operated by BBA. After tasting the sample, the customer can make any adjustments that are needed. If the flavor is too salty, for instance, the customer can easily tweak the salt parameter on the profile and have the machine immediately produce another sample. The new system could also help manage raw ingredients inventory by keeping tabs on how much of each ingredient remains. Since the starting ingredients themselves and the translation of customer designs to chemical formulations are proprietary and difficult to reverse-engineer, BBA management does not worry too much about the possibility of customers switching to competitors after completing a design.

FIGURE 7 - 3

A Design Toolkit for Customers

In this example, a customer would be designing a strawberry flavor for a dairy product using an Internet-based toolkit. Having selected in other menus cheese as the end product and strawberry as the desired flavor, the customer tweaks the "floral" dimension of strawberry by increasing lavender to 30 percent. The flavor's cost is adjusted instantly. The customer continues to tweak other dimensions until she decides to order a prototype sample, which would be produced by BBA and shipped to the customer for testing. The cycle of experimentation continues until a sample meets the customer's taste requirements.

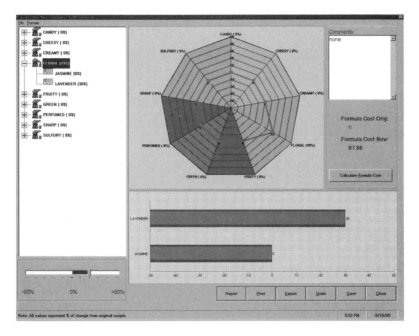

Source: Stefan Thomke and Ashok Nimgade, "Bush Boake Allen," Case 9-601-061. Boston: Harvard Business School, 2000. Copyright © 2000 by the President and Fellows of Harvard College. Reprinted with permission.

Innovation Toolkits for Experimentation

BBA wanted customers to experiment with alternative design solutions because it can be a win-win proposition for both. Instead of moving need information from customer to supplier, solution information is moved from supplier to customer via innovation toolkits (figure 7-4), which puts experimentation power into the hands of users who become an integral part of a company's innovation process.

FIGURE 7 - 4

Moving Information Between Supplier and Customers

In the traditional model, need information is primarily collected and moved from customers to suppliers via market research methods. This process can be costly and time-consuming when needs are unique, complex, and fast-changing. In the new model, the supplier's "solution" information is embodied in innovation toolkits that are moved to customers so that they can experiment and design their own products.

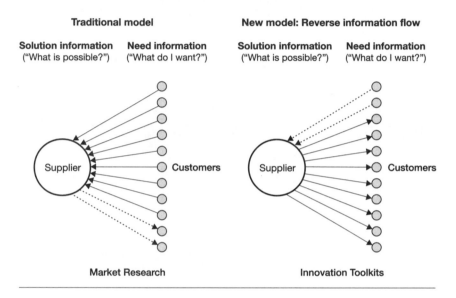

The supplier can focus on developing better solution platforms that are customized through user-friendly toolkits in the hands of customers. The customer can experiment and get feedback more rapidly, control intellectual property on the application-specific part of a design, and most important, find a solution that closely matches specified needs. It is important to note that shifting product development activities to customers does not eliminate learning by experimentation—nor should it. It does make traditional product development better and faster—for several reasons. First, a company can bypass the expensive and error-prone effort to understand customer needs in detail. Second, the trial-and-error cycles that inevitably occur during product development can progress much more quickly because the iterations are performed solely by the customer (figure 7-5).

FIGURE 7 - 5

A New Approach to Developing Custom Products

In the traditional model, suppliers take on most of the work—and responsibility—of product development. The result is costly and time-consuming iterations between supplier and customer to reach a satisfactory solution. When the locus of experimentation is shifted to customers, the supplier provides the design tools so that customers can develop the application-specific part of a product on their own. The location of the supplier-customer interface also shifts, and the iterative experimentation necessary for product development is now carried out by the customer only. The result is greatly increased speed and effectiveness.

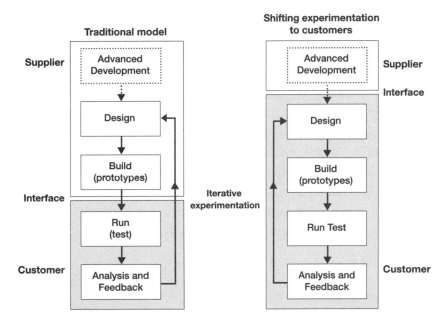

Leveraging User Innovation

Shifting experimentation to users leverages what scholars already know about the sources of innovation. Research has shown that many commercially important products are initially thought of and even prototyped by users rather than manufacturers.[7] It was also discovered that such products tend to be developed by "lead users"—companies, organizations, or individuals that are well ahead of market trends and have needs that go far beyond those of the average user.[8] Most people are already familiar with standard products that were originally developed by lead users. The prototype for protein-based hair conditioners, for instance, came from daring women in the 1950s who experimented with homemade concoctions containing beer or eggs to impart more body and shine. Similarly, antilock braking systems (ABS) that are standard on most cars today were first developed in aerospace: Military aircraft commands have a very high incentive to design ways to stop their expensive vehicles when they land before they run out of runway. Like other lead users, they opted for designing custom solutions instead of waiting for markets to become large enough before manufacturers would consider developing and selling standard products. Lead users also expect to benefit significantly from their custom solutions as they often have to overcome considerable barriers to innovating.

In other words, academic research has already shown that a small group of customers—lead users—is developing their own products, in spite of the difficulties of doing so. Now consider the fact that do-it-yourself toolkits can dramatically lower the cost of experimenting and designing custom solutions. By lowering the barriers to innovation, it is thus not surprising that the number of customers willing to participate in developing new products can be expected to rise substantially (figure 7-6).

Building a Toolkit for Experimentation

Developing the right toolkit for customers is hardly a simple matter. Specifically, toolkits must provide four important capabilities.[9] First and most important, they must enable people to iterate through the series of experimentation steps described in chapter 3: design, build, run [tests], and analyze. Computer simulation, for example, allows customers to quickly try out ideas and design alternatives without having to manufacture the actual products. When the simulation technology lacks the desired accuracy, it can be supplemented with rapid prototyping methods. As customers carry out experimentation cycles with the help of user-friendly tools, learning and improvement can take place locally, without having to involve the supplier.

FIGURE 7 - 6

The Shift Toward Custom Products Developed by Users

Lead users have needs that are well ahead of a market trend and create custom solutions for themselves (before). Development toolkits lower the cost of designing such custom solutions and thus can significantly shift innovation activity toward customers (after).

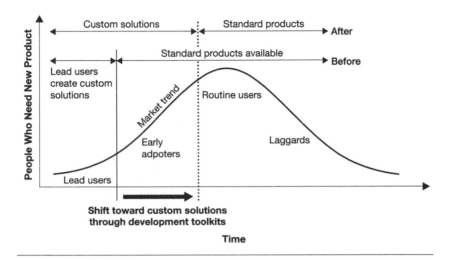

Second, toolkits must be user-friendly. Customers should be able to operate them using their existing skills; they should not need to learn an entirely new design language. (Flavorists, for example, think in terms of formulations and chemical compounds, whereas customers think of tastes such as smoky, sweet, fresh, etc.) Third, they must contain libraries of useful components and modules that have been pretested and de-bugged to save customers from having to reinvent the wheel and permit them to focus their efforts on the truly novel elements of their design. Fourth, toolkits must contain information about the capabilities and limitations of the production process that will be used to manufacture the product to ensure that a customer's design will in fact be producible.

Putting toolkits into the hands of customers, however, is hardly an easy or straightforward process, as BBA senior management realized after its R&D personnel certified its toolkit as functional. After CEO Boyden briefed his senior managers one by one about the project and

possible rollout plans, marketing and the overseas division were anything but excited. One senior executive recalled feeling "sick as a dog"
after the possibility of giving customers access to the toolkit was announced. More specifically,

> *The first time I heard of the [toolkit], we were waiting for a cab
> together and Boyden said, "What about this as an idea. . . ." After lis-
> tening, I said, "I think it's a fine idea." It's a great idea to use the
> [toolkit] for flavor production. We do need faster compounding. If we
> can feed in a formula at one end and out pops the compound, that's
> great! From an ownership point of view, where the machine is kept
> entirely centrally with us, I'm one hundred percent behind [it]. But
> for outside uses I have reservations. . . . Our industry has made our
> customers lazy! Our competitors have a team of salespeople virtually
> camped on the lawn of our most important customers. So even if we
> give one of our largest clients a machine, our traditional competitors
> will still probably give samples faster. On top of that, I don't know if
> we have customers clever enough to do it; but we'll have customers
> who think they're clever enough to do it. If the customer feels that
> making flavors is easy, they'll devalue the worth of our flavorists. Pro-
> moting client-based machines might be like the turkeys voting for
> Thanksgiving or Christmas.[10]*

As a result of the objections raised, BBA considered a range of
options for deploying the new design and experimentation toolkit.
The first proposal—strongly favored by the international division and
marketing—would keep the toolkit technology in-house. Management
efforts would focus on leveraging the system to link BBA development
centers around the world and provide them with rapid flavor development capabilities. Customers would still go through traditional sales
channels but get samples more quickly, thereby increasing service quality. No customer would have direct access to the toolkit technology. The
proposal would significantly boost the efficiency of an organization
marked by two decades of decentralization.

The second proposal involved physically placing a flavor prototyping
machine with some large customers and allowing them to design their
own flavors via the toolkit technology. These customers would have full
control over their flavor development process and BBA would support

them only on a per-need basis. Because customers would have to go through BBA's Web site to access the flavor design tools, the company could closely monitor outside development activities. Moreover, only BBA's R&D would know how to translate design parameters (e.g., "fruity," "cheesy," "creamy") into chemical formulations that would be needed to make prototype samples—know-how that was difficult for competitors to imitate. It was unclear, however, which customers should be signed up and how the cost and maintenance of the prototyping machine would be divided between BBA and the customers. The proposal implied that sales and R&D increasingly would focus on smaller and less profitable customers who would not have access to the toolkit technology.

The third and most radical proposal would abandon the current business model altogether. The new technology would be available to anyone anywhere who needed flavors, and BBA would yield 100 percent development control to customers. The company would establish sample prototyping centers around the world, putting flavor samples within 24-hour shipping distance to any customer. New customers would be able to design flavors through BBA's Web site and automatically receive sample shipments from the nearest prototyping center. Marketing's role in this proposal was still unclear and there were numerous unresolved issues around how it would affect BBA's current business model.

The three options illustrate the struggles that companies can go through when a toolkit for experimentation becomes first available. Particularly when companies relinquish some fundamental design tasks to customers, the value shifts are felt throughout the organization and possibly entire industries, as we shall see later.

As BBA was developing new business models to leverage its toolkit technology, it was acquired by industry leader IFF. Today, senior management is exploring the new technology's fit with the business model of its current owner who enthusiastically supports the project.

When Toolkits for Experimentation Work Best

Companies will continue to develop many great products using a deep understanding of customer needs and well-managed development processes. The new model of development described in this chapter

makes most sense when products require a high degree of design customization and the need information is costly to transfer, as was the
case for BBA's specialty flavors. When companies intend to develop
standard products with little customization, other approaches will continue to work very well as long as markets are sufficiently large. For
example, some sophisticated methods such as emphatic design or the
Zaltman Metaphor Elicitation Technique (ZMET) can explore basic
and potentially common need areas at a deep level; the results can be
used to minimize unnecessary product features.[11]

To see how other approaches relate to innovation toolkits, one needs
to consider two important need dimensions (figure 7-7). The first

FIGURE 7 - 7

Complementary Approaches to Addressing Customer Needs

*Different approaches are appropriate to addressing customer needs. When needs are
relatively homogenous, it usually makes sense for suppliers to learn about these needs
via market research techniques that vary in sophistication and cost. In contrast, when
needs become heterogeneous and information is difficult to transfer, making solution
information available to customers and allowing them to design themselves can be
more effective.*

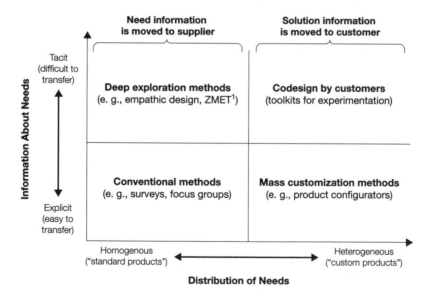

[1]ZMET (Zaltman Metaphor Elicitation Technique) identifies common deep-level needs that often drive
observable secondary needs in products.

dimension—need distribution—characterizes the degree to which a set of needs is common within a market segment. At one extreme, all needs are shared and can be satisfied with a standard product. At the other extreme, all needs are unique and require full custom products ("markets of one").[12] The second dimension characterizes the need itself and the ease or difficulty of getting to the information. Again, at one extreme, the needs are unarticulated and perhaps unknown to customers themselves (in short, tacit), which requires very sophisticated and often costly market research techniques.[13] At the other extreme, customers can easily express what they want if one simply asks them. Depending where a supplier ends up in these dimensions, different techniques turn out to be most useful. However, many business-to-business settings that we have examined in our research involve a high degree of customization and difficulty in getting the "right" customer requirements in place as they often change over the course of a development project. Thus the attractiveness of the toolkit approach.

More specifically, we have identified the following major signs that an industry may be ready for the approach described in this chapter:

- Market segments are shrinking, and customers are increasingly asking for customized products. As suppliers try to respond to those demands, their costs increase, and it is difficult to pass the costs on to customers.

- Customers need many experimental iterations with suppliers before their needs are satisfied. Some customers are starting to complain that suppliers have gotten the product wrong or that they are responding too slowly. Suppliers are tempted to restrict the degree to which their products can be customized, and smaller customers must make do with standard products or find a better solution elsewhere. As a result, customer loyalty starts to erode.

- Suppliers use high-quality computer-based simulation and rapid prototyping tools internally to develop new products. They also have computer-adjustable production processes that can manufacture custom products. (These technologies could form the foundation of a toolkit that customers could use to develop their own designs.)

Transforming an Industry

To understand the major impact that shifting design and experimentation to customers can have, consider the integrated circuit industry once more (see also chapter 2). Its history holds several profound lessons about how the right toolkit can turn a market on its ear. During the late 1970s, suppliers of custom chips experienced the same types of market dynamics that BBA more recently encountered. At the time, a typical customer of specialized semiconductors, such as a toy manufacturer that needed circuitry to operate its new robotic dog, might have hired a chip supplier to develop a custom design. Because that process was complicated and costly, the chip company could afford to undertake only projects for high-volume customers. Smaller customers were turned away and had no choice but to use standard circuit components. That, in turn, limited the extent to which they could develop products that were smaller, better in performance, lower in cost, or simply more innovative. In other words, there was a very large unfilled demand for custom chips because the dominant suppliers couldn't economically serve smaller customers (figure 7-8).

FIGURE 7 - 8

New Markets Need New Models for Innovation

Because the process of developing custom products is complicated and costly, customers below a high sales threshold are turned away and have to use standard components. This creates an unfilled demand because a supplier cannot economically serve smaller customers.

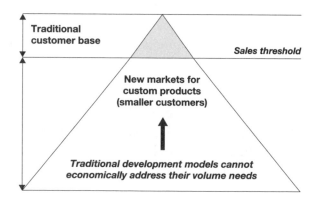

Then a handful of start-ups turned everything upside down. New firms like LSI Logic and VLSI Technology provided both large and small customers with do-it-yourself tools that enabled them to design their own specialized chips. As Wilf Corrigan, LSI's CEO and principal founder, recalled:

> *Having decided to start a semiconductor company, I spent quite a few months visiting people I knew in the computer industry, both in the United States and in Europe. A pattern started to emerge: most of these companies needed custom circuits. I had flashbacks of when I was at Fairchild and good customers would ask me, "Would you do a custom program for us?" At Fairchild [Semiconductor], I always said no, but in retrospect, I should have recognized that over the previous few years there was an opportunity bubbling up in custom circuits. . . . Custom circuits—the big guys don't want to mess with them, the customers seem to need them, yet there don't seem to be any viable sources in spite of increasing demand.*[14]

Corrigan's inability to respond while working at Fairchild, a leading semiconductor firm in the 1960s and 1970s, was certainly not because he lacked influence: he was its CEO from 1974 to 1980. In fact, many members of LSI's founding team and its design tool expertise came from Fairchild, which had abandoned its custom IC efforts because it was losing money for the firm. With LSI's new development system, customers could benefit by getting what they wanted through their own experimentation, and the fledgling chip firms could profit by manufacturing the customer designs. The win-win solution was right on the money. Between the 1980s and 2000, the market for such custom integrated circuits has soared from virtually nothing to more than $15 billion, with the number of customers growing from a handful of high-volume buyers to hundreds of thousands of firms with very diverse user applications.

One of the keys to that market is the toolkit technology. In principle, outsourcing custom design to customers can help slash development times and costs, but customers are not experts in a supplier's R&D or production process. So how can customers possibly be expected to create custom designs that are producible on a manufacturer's sophisticated process equipment? The answer to that was found in a major shift that had been taking place in the semiconductor industry.

Traditionally, specialized information used by a manufacturer to design and build custom products has been locked in the minds of the company's development engineers. This knowledge accumulates over decades of experience. In recent years, companies have been able to incorporate a considerable amount of this human expertise into computer-based tools. As we have seen throughout the book, these CAD, CAE, and CAM programs have grown increasingly sophisticated, and many now contain libraries of tested and debugged modules that people can simply plug into a new design. The best tools also enable rapid testing through computer simulation and provide links to automated equipment that can build prototypes quickly. This leading-edge technology, which manufacturers had been using internally to increase R&D productivity and innovation, has become the basic building block for toolkits geared to customers.

When LSI was founded in 1981, R&D engineers at large semiconductor companies were already using many elements of the customer toolkit, but there was no integrated system that less skilled customers would be comfortable with. So LSI bought some of the pieces, made them customer-friendly by adding graphical user interfaces, and integrated them into a package called the LSI Development System (LDS; figure 7-9). The result was a packaged toolkit that enabled customers to design their own chips with little support from LSI.

The brilliant insight that made possible a toolkit for less-skilled customers was that the design of the chip's fundamental elements, such as its transistors, could be standardized and could incorporate the manufacturer's solution information of how semiconductors are fabricated. Then all the information the customer needed about how the chip would function could be concentrated within the electrical wiring that connected the fundamental elements. In other words, this new type of chip, called a gate array, had a novel architecture created specifically to separate the manufacturer's solution information from the customer's need information. As a result, all customers had to do was use a toolkit that could interconnect a gate array based on their specific needs. For its part, LSI had to rethink how to make its production processes more flexible so that it could manufacture the custom chips at low cost.

Customer toolkits based on gate-array technology offer the four major capabilities described earlier. They contain a range of tools, including those to test a design, that enable users to create their own proto-

FIGURE 7 - 9

LSI's Development Toolkit for Custom Chips (circa 1984)

Source: Courtesy of LSI Logic.

types via trial and error. They are customer-friendly in that they use Boolean algebra, which is the design language commonly taught to electrical engineers. They contain extensive libraries of pretested circuit modules. And they also contain information about production processes, so users can test their designs to ensure that they can be manufactured.

Interestingly, more recent technology—integrated circuits called field-programmable logic devices (FPLDs), described in chapter 2— enables the customer to become both the designer and the manufacturer. FPLDs are a family of programmable chip technologies where links between components are either created, "melted," in the case of fuse technologies, or programmed, in the case of field-programmable gate arrays (FPGAs). Suppliers such as Xilinx, Inc. or Altera Corporation prefabricate these chips and sell them to customers who use their design and simulation software and equipment to program chips for themselves. Suppliers do not have to be involved in the design process, and physical prototypes can be prepared by customers at little cost or time (see chapter 2 for a more detailed description of different custom IC technologies).

Benefits and Challenges

Well-designed customer toolkits, such as those developed for the design of custom semiconductor chips, offer several major advantages. First, they are significantly better at satisfying subtle aspects of customer need because customers know what they need better than manufacturers do. Second, designs are usually completed much faster because customers can experiment at their own site, with minimal supplier involvement. Third, if customers follow the rules embedded in a toolkit (and if all the technological bugs have been worked out), their designs can be manufactured the first time around.

And there are ancillary benefits. Toolkits enable a company to retain small customers that might have been prohibitively expensive to work with before, thus expanding the accessible market—and the number of product innovations. By serving smaller clients, toolkits also reduce the pool of unserved, frustrated potential customers who might turn to competitors or to new entrants into the market. Furthermore, they allow companies to better serve their larger, preferred customers. That's a benefit most suppliers wouldn't expect, because they'd assume that their bigger customers would prefer the traditional hand-holding to which they're so accustomed. Experience shows, however, that large customers are often willing to use a toolkit especially when fast product turnaround is crucial.

Of course, toolkits do not satisfy every type of customer. For one thing, they generally cannot handle every type of design. Also, they create products that are typically not as technically sophisticated as those developed by experienced engineers at a manufacturer using conventional methods. So manufacturers may continue to design certain products (those with difficult technical demands) while customers take over the design of other products (those that require quick turnarounds or a detailed and accurate understanding of the customer's need). And if homogenous markets require standard products, the traditional approach of deep market research probably works better.

The business challenges of implementing a toolkit can be daunting. Turning customers into innovators requires no less than a radical change in management mind-set (box 7-1). Pioneers LSI Logic and VLSI Technology were successful because they abandoned a principle that had long dominated conventional management thinking at leading companies like IBM, Intel, and Fujitsu. For many years, these companies had assumed that their interests would best be served by keeping design expertise, tools, and technologies away from customers. In contrast, LSI and the other industry upstarts understood that they needed to do just the opposite: Put robust, user-friendly toolkits into customers' hands.

Such a dramatic shift in mind-set required a thorough rethinking of entrenched business practices. In essence, a company that shifts experimentation to customers is outsourcing a valuable service that was once proprietary, and the change can be traumatic if experimentation has been a major competitive advantage. For example, a common problem is resistance from sales and marketing departments, which have traditionally been responsible for managing relationships with customers and providing them with first-class service. With toolkits, computer-to-computer interactions replace intense person-to-person contact during product development. In other words, customers who design products themselves have little need for a manufacturer's sales or marketing department to determine what they need. If this change affects the compensation of sales representatives in the field, it could easily derail any efforts to alter the company's business model. As a result, senior management needs to face these issues head on—for example, by determining how the sales and marketing functions should evolve and by using specific incentives to induce employees to support the transformation.

To better understand these issues, consider GE Plastics, which recently made the bold move of introducing some elements of a Web-based customer toolkit.[15] Doing so required GE Plastics to rethink its sources of competitive advantage and to develop new business models

BOX 7-1: IMPORTANT STEPS FOR SHIFTING EXPERIMENTATION AND INNOVATION TO CUSTOMERS

1. Develop a user-friendly toolkit for customers.

   - The toolkit must enable customers to run repeated trial-and-error experiments and tests rapidly and efficiently on their own.

   - The technology should allow customers to work in a design language that is familiar to them. This will make it less expensive for customers to adopt your toolkit.

   - The toolkit should include a library of standard design modules that customers can use to create a complex custom design rapidly.

   - The technology should be adapted to your production processes so that customer designs can be sent directly to your manufacturing operations without extensive tailoring.

2. Increase the flexibility of your production processes.

   - Your manufacturing operations should be retooled for fast, low-cost production of specialized designs developed by customers using your toolkits.

3. Carefully select the first customers to use the toolkit.

   - The best prospects are customers who have a strong need for developing custom products quickly and frequently, who have

that forced major changes, including the ways in which its sales and marketing staff acquired new customers. The company's story holds several valuable lessons.

GE Plastics does not design or manufacture plastic products but sells resins to those who do, and the properties of the resins must precisely match that of both the product (e.g., a cell phone) and the process used to manufacture the product. With the formation of the Polymerland division in 1998, GE Plastics allowed customers to order plastics online and later took the bold step of making thirty years of its in-house knowledge available on a Web site. Registered users were given access to company data sheets, engineering expertise, and simulation software skilled engineers on staff, and who have little experience with traditional customization services. These customers are likely to stick with you during the inevitable shakedown period when you are working out the bugs of the new system.

4. Evolve your toolkit continually and rapidly to satisfy your leading-edge customers.

   - Customers at the forefront of technology will always bump up against the limitations of your toolkit and will push for improvements. Investments in the advancements they need are likely to pay off because many of your customers tomorrow will need what leading-edge customers desire today.

5. Adapt your business practices accordingly.

   - Outsourcing product development to customers will require you to revamp your business models to profit from the shift. The change might, for instance, make it economically feasible for you to work with smaller, low-volume customers.

   - Toolkits will fundamentally change your relationship with customers. Intense person-to-person contact during product development will, for example, be replaced by computer-to-computer interactions. Prepare for these changes by implementing incentives to reduce resistance from your employees.

Source: Thomke and von Hippel (2002).

(figure 7-10). Customers could use that knowledge and technology to conduct their own trial-and-error experiments to investigate, for example, how a certain grade of plastic with a specific amount of a particular type of reinforcement would flow into and fill a mold. The approximate cost of bringing such sophisticated tools online: $5 million.

GE Plastics, of course, did not make the investment simply to be magnanimous. Through the Web site, the company identifies and tracks people likely to become customers. The information is then relayed to an e-marketing staff. By 2002, the Web site attracted about a million visitors per year who are automatically screened for potential sales; the information accounts for nearly one third of all new customer leads,

FIGURE 7 - 10

GE Plastic's Customer Toolkit

GE Plastics customers can download the latest tools (material selectors, datasheets, simulation tools) that assist them with the development of plastic products. The resins for those products can be purchased from GE.

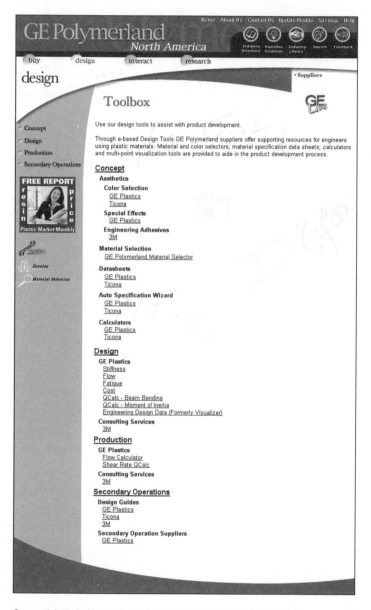

Source: Adapted with permission from <http://www.gepolymerland.com>.

thus fueling much of GE Plastic's growth. And because the cost of acquiring new business has decreased, GE Plastics can now go after smaller customers it might have ignored in the past. Specifically, the sales threshold at which a potential customer becomes attractive to GE's field marketing has now dropped by more than 60 percent.

The online tools have also enabled GE Plastics to improve customer satisfaction at a lower cost. Before the Web site, GE Plastics received about 500,000 customer calls every year. The availability of online tools has slashed that number in half. In fact, customers use the tools more than 2,000 times a week. To encourage the rapid adoption of its toolkit, GE Plastics runs about 400 e-seminars a year that reach roughly 8,000 customers interested in learning about its tools and products. The company hopes that this effort will help encourage product engineers to design parts made of plastic (and GE resins) when they could have chosen metal or other materials.

Creating and Capturing Value

Perhaps the most important lesson to be learned from GE Plastics and others is that a company that wants to shift experimentation and innovation to customers must adapt its business accordingly. In fact, adopting the new approach is neither easy nor straightforward. We have found that because the value of customer toolkits tends to migrate, a company must continually reposition itself to capture the value. When a supplier introduces a toolkit, the technology first tends to be company specific: The designs can be produced only in the factory of the company that developed the toolkit. This creates a huge short-term advantage for the pioneering supplier, which can reduce its custom design costs because they are partially outsourced to customers. This advantage, in turn, enables the supplier to serve more customers. And because the customer's designs must be produced on the supplier's system, the supplier doesn't risk losing any business.

But the loss of leverage by customers represents a fundamental shift. Traditionally, in the field of specialized industrial products, companies interested in a customer's business must develop a custom design and submit it for evaluation. The customer picks the proposal from one supplier, and the others are saddled with a loss for their time and investment. A toolkit tied to a single supplier changes that dynamic: A customer who develops a design using the toolkit cannot ask for competing quotes because only one company can manufacture it. Of course, customers would prefer the advantages of a toolkit without the associated loss of leverage. In the long run, this type of solution tends to emerge: Customer pressure induces third parties to introduce toolkits that can create designs to fit any supplier's manufacturing process. Or, in a slight variation, customers complain until a company that owns a dominant toolkit is forced to allow a spin-off to evolve the technology into a supplier-neutral form. Then customers are free to shop their designs around to competing manufacturers.

In other words, the long-term result of customer toolkits is that manufacturers lose a portion of the value they have traditionally delivered. But if the conditions are ripe for the technology to emerge in a given industry and if customers will benefit from it—and our research shows that they will—then suppliers really don't have a choice. Some company will eventually introduce a toolkit and reap the short-term advantages. Then, others must follow. In the case of custom integrated circuits, the lessons are striking. Fujitsu initially resisted making its in-house design technology available to customers, thinking that the move was too risky. Aspects of this dilemma are neatly captured by a conversation between Wilf Corrigan, LSI's cofounder and CEO, and Mr. Yasufuku, a senior executive at Fujitsu. Corrigan explained to Yasufuku LSI's strategy of shifting design and experimentation to customers. (At the time of this conversation, LSI was a start-up and Fujitsu was an established major player in the custom integrated circuit market with a major market share.) "We are going into the gate array business with software tools which our customers will have in their own hands." Yasufuku responded: "That is a brilliant strategy. If you do that and the software is good, you will win." Corrigan then asked, "Why don't you do that?" (Fujitsu had developed an excellent set of internal design tools.) The answer: "Our software is so valuable that if we expose it to outsiders, they will steal it." Fujitsu hadn't even transferred their tools to its U.S. subsidiary because they were afraid of losing control of it.[16]

But the outcome in the custom integrated circuits market showed that the choice facing firms in that marketplace really was only one of timing. After LSI introduced its toolkit and design methodology to the marketplace, customers showed that they greatly preferred the option of "doing it themselves" by moving business to LSI. Faced with eroding market share,

Fujitsu and other established suppliers were forced also to adopt the toolkits approach. The cost of delay: LSI had been given a window in which to grow from an insignificant start-up into a major player and, together with competitors such as VLSI Technology, captured much of the value of the underserved market for custom chips. With continued developments such as field-programmable technologies offered by firms such as Xilinx and Altera, LSI's move transformed the industry and created billions of dollars worth of new value (figure 7-11). In chapter 2, we already saw why some managers prefer programmable technologies in their projects: more flexibility and higher development process performance.

Even major firms such as Intel considered the custom integrated circuit business in 1971, but their spectacular growth and success came

FIGURE 7 - 11

Creating Value by Shifting Experimentation to Customers

In the electronics market, suppliers have traditionally been the designers of full-custom and application-specific integrated circuits (with compound annual growth rate (CAGR) of 12 percent). During the 1990s, toolkits based on gate-array and standard-cell technologies (CAGR of 13 percent) enabled customers and third parties to also become chip designers. With field-programmable technology (CAGR of 29 percent), customers take on primary responsibility for custom circuit design, creating great value in the industry. The total shaded area equals the cumulative billings of these technologies over time.

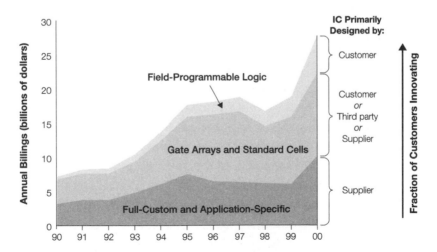

Source: Figures are from World Semiconductor Trade Statistics for custom metal oxide semiconductor (MOS) logic, a dominant technology for digital circuits. Adapted with permission from Stefan Thomke and Eric von Hippel, "Customers as Innovators: A New Way to Create Value." *Harvard Business Review*, April 2002, 10.

from standard integrated circuits sold in large volumes. LSI's new approach to the development of custom chips didn't fit Intel's model. Then in 1985, Intel started to lose business to firms providing custom and application-specific chips (e.g., LSI) because customers now had the choice of not using standard integrated circuits. As a result, Intel decided to enter the custom chip business. After extensive research, Intel realized that the secret to success was excellent design tools, quick-turnaround manufacturing, and cell libraries that could be used by customers. Because Intel didn't have all these capabilities in house, they licensed IBM's tools, libraries, and process (IBM was the largest supplier and customer of custom IC's in the world). The only problem: IBM's design methodology was too rigid, the tools were not user friendly, and in some cases, the technology was not up to date. While Intel learned much from the experience and used it to improve internal development capabilities, the efforts were discontinued in 1988 when Intel realized that it was losing ground to now established firms such as LSI and VLSI and ran into some supplier disputes with IBM.[17]

What Comes Next

Predicting where value will migrate—and knowing how to capture it—will be crucial as customer toolkits become more widespread. So far, the approach introduced in this chapter has mainly emerged in the business-to-business field, but numerous signs indicate that it is also spreading to the business-to-consumer arena. Many companies already offer so-called product configurators that enable consumers to obtain a mass-customized version of a standard product.[18] Dell Computer customers, for example, can select various components (disk drive, monitor, memory modules, etc.) from a menu to assemble the computer best suited to their needs. Eyeglass frames, automobiles, and even Barbie dolls can be similarly configured. In fact, no application seems too trivial. General Mills is planning to introduce a Web site that will allow consumers to mix and match more than 100 ingredients to create their own breakfast cereal. Although such product configurators are currently limited in what they can do (for one thing, they don't allow a user to experiment with design solutions through either a prototype or a computer simulation), future versions could approach the functionality of true customer toolkits and allow for radically new innovations (box 7-2).

BOX 7-2: WHAT MASS CUSTOMIZATION IS— AND WHAT IT ISN'T

Imagine a mass manufacturer that could customize products for each of its customers. Economically, customization would require two things: first, learning how to design specialized products efficiently (the R&D problem), and second, learning how to manufacture the products cheaply and quickly (the production problem).

The second problem has been addressed by the popular concept of mass customized production. In that approach, computerized process equipment or flexible assembly procedures can be adjusted quickly and inexpensively to enable companies to make single-unit quantities of one-of-a-kind products at a cost that is reasonably competitive with the manufacture of similar mass-produced items. The classic example is Dell Computer: Consumers can buy a Dell computer by picking the major components they want (the size of the hard drive, the kind of monitor, the number and types of memory modules, etc.) from a menu on a Dell Web site, and the company will assemble and deliver the custom product in days.

But Dell's mass customization approach does not address the first problem: how to design novel custom goods efficiently. The company's customers have only a limited number of standard components and combinations to choose from, leaving them little room for creativity or real innovation. What if someone wants a computer that cannot be assembled from the standard components, or what if a person is uncertain that a certain product will actually fulfill her needs? For instance, will the computer she's assembled be able to run the latest game software without crashing? Unless customers can test a computer design that they've assembled before placing the order, they can't perform the trial-and-error experiments needed to develop the product best suited to their needs. In other words, with mass customization, the cost of manufacturing unique products has dropped, but the cost of designing them has not.

Source: Thomke and von Hippel (2002).

Producers of information products, especially software, will perhaps feel the biggest impact. Companies like Microsoft have long relied on customers to beta-test new products.[19] Now other companies have taken that concept to the next level. Stata, which sells a software package for performing complex statistical analyses, encourages its customers to write software add-on modules for performing the latest statistical techniques; the company then adapts and incorporates the best of the add-ons into its next release.

The danger to software companies is that production is essentially free, so the customer might one day mass-distribute copies of a custom program with the simple press of a button. If that practice becomes widespread, a truly effective toolkit might itself become the product, forcing companies to adapt quickly to the dramatic change. Or users might abandon their status as customers altogether, collaborating to design and build their own toolkits as well as their own specialized programs. The growing popularity of open-source software could touch off such a revolution. Consider what has happened to companies that sell software for Linux, an operating system that is virtually free. Recently, IBM took the bold step of placing $40 million of in-house tools for developing software into the public domain to encourage people to write programs that run on Linux. IBM is hoping that the move will help make Linux a widespread standard and that the company will make money by selling specialized Linux software applications, the hardware to run them, and consulting services. Other Linux companies like Red Hat are focusing on packaging, distribution, and support.

Conclusion

Throughout the book, we have learned about the importance of experimentation to the creation of great products and services and how companies can benefit from organizing the process to invite innovation. But the cost of experimentation has often limited innovation. New technologies, such as computer modeling and simulation, are lifting the constraint by changing the economics of experimentation and are creating the potential for higher R&D performance and innovation. We have also learned how changing the processes, organization, and management of innovation can unlock this potential within companies and their R&D departments.

In this chapter, we have seen how taking experimentation and new technologies *beyond* organizations can open up additional opportunities for innovation and value-creation. In the form of user-friendly toolkits, the technologies enable management to tap into possibly the largest source of dormant experimentation capacity: the customer. Not only could shifting experimentation to customers result in faster development of products better suited to their needs, but it could generate innovations that suppliers simply cannot imagine today. The approach thus holds the power to turn markets topsy-turvy, as we have seen in integrated circuits, creating and shifting value at three separate levels: the industry as a whole, companies that implement the technology, and customers that take advantage of it. Exactly where the value will be generated and how it might best be captured are the multimillion dollar questions facing companies competing in businesses that are being transformed by the potential of new technologies.

NOTES

1. For example, see Thomke and Robertson (1999) on the role of toolkits in Sega's Dreamcast project.

2. This chapter draws extensively from Thomke and von Hippel (2002), where our joint research was reported. Other related publications are von Hippel (2001) and von Hippel and Katz (2002).

3. Recent research has aimed at making market research and testing more rapid and cheaper through the use of "virtual" techniques that leverage the Internet. For example, see Dahan and Srinivasan (2000) and Dahan and Hauser (2001).

4. In part, the back and forth is caused by information transfer costs, which can be high when such information is "sticky" or difficult to encode. For a discussion of interaction patterns between user and manufacturer as a result of information stickiness, see von Hippel (1994).

5. "Learning by doing" often has iterative experimentation as part of the doing. For example, see Pisano (1997) and von Hippel and Tyre (1995).

6. All the information on Bush Boake Allen in this chapter comes from Thomke and Nimgade (2000).

7. Research on users as an important source of innovations can be found in von Hippel (1988), whose pioneering work has changed how we view the way innovation happens.

8. Lead users can be an important source of new product concepts and were identified as part of von Hippel's research on user innovation (von Hippel, 1988). Many firms, such as 3M, have tapped into the expertise of lead users and their prototype solutions. For an explanation of how lead users can be tapped, see von Hippel, Thomke, and Sonnack (1999).

9. von Hippel (2001) provides a detailed description of how toolkits work.

10. Quoted from Thomke and Nimgade (2000), page 8.

11. For more information on empathic design techniques, see Leonard-Barton (1995). Alternatively, ZMET was developed by Gerald Zaltman, and more information can be found in Zaltman (2002). For a comprehensive summary of market research in product development, see Urban and Hauser (1993).

12. Gilmore and Pine (2000).

13. The notion of "tacit" information has been used extensively in innovation and knowledge management research. For example, see Polanyi (1958) and Nonaka and Takeuchi (1995).

14. Quoted from Walker (1992), page 47.

15. The information on GE comes from personal interviews with executives and has been previously published in Thomke and von Hippel (2002).

16. Quoted from Walker (1992), pages 79–80, where the story is told by Wilf Corrigan.

17. IBM's attempts to get into the custom chip market are described in Walker (1992), pages 219–225.

18. For a good overview of the ideas and applications around mass customization, see Pine (1993).

19. For a detailed description of Microsoft's beta testing, see Cusumano and Selby (1995), pages 309–313.

epilogue

On 19 November 2002, the *Wall Street Journal* reported that IBM would build two new supercomputers for the U.S. Department of Energy (DOE).[1] Valued at $290 million, the computers plan to leapfrog the world's fastest computer, the Earth Simulator made by Japan's NEC Corporation and used for simulating weather patterns and earthquakes, and have a combined peak speed of up to 467 trillion calculations per second. The first of the two supercomputers, named ASCI Purple, will primarily simulate the "button to bang" of nuclear weapons, since the United States has abandoned its physical testing program.[2] Thus, simulation capabilities have come full circle: First developed to aid in the design of the country's nuclear weapons, advanced simulation has now become a complete substitute for physical testing of nuclear weapons.

Indeed, advances in simulation can be found everywhere. When I studied the companies described in the book, I was struck by the excitement and enthusiasm for the new technologies and the questions they might answer. What if a technology, product, or service were designed and deployed in a particular way? Now, not only can more experiments be run, but the kinds of experiments possible are also expanding. General Motors recently announced that it has increased computer simulation capacity by 1,200 percent to digitize its car development process.[3] DaimlerChrysler is using a $20-million full-motion driving simulator in Berlin not only to test new vehicle configurations during engineering but also to evaluate the impact of medication, alcohol, and fatigue on driver responsiveness—experiments that would be too dangerous to perform in real vehicles.[4] The learning that development engineers and managers gain from seeing what works and what doesn't work is used in the design of new electronic safety systems that already assist drivers in dangerous situations.

Not only are experimentation and innovation intimately linked, but it is through the process of experimentation that new technologies can generate higher R&D performance, innovation, and new ways of creating value for customers. Mastering and integrating new technologies also pose grave challenges. Unlocking their potential requires changes in the processes, organization, and management of innovation. These changes are captured throughout the book and emphasize that in experiments, learning what doesn't work is as important as learning what does. In consequence, most of the findings, summarized here, are about management, not technology. They address how people reflect on, improvise with, and evaluate and implement new ideas.

First, an organization's ability to innovate relies on a process of experimentation whereby new products and services are created and existing ones are improved. Traditionally, the high cost of experimentation has limited innovation. Statistical methods for designing experiments have helped companies get more out of each experiment—make them more efficient. Alternatively, new technologies like computer simulation and modeling are lifting the cost constraint by changing the economics of experimentation. These technologies slash the cost and time to free up testing capacity as well as make possible what-if experiments that in the past have been either prohibitively expensive or nearly impossible to carry out. They amplify the impact of learning, thus creating the potential for higher R&D performance and breakthrough products. However, managers must understand both the power of new technologies for experimentation and how they impact the processes, organization, and management of innovation.

Second, the integrated circuit industry makes a compelling case for the importance of new experimentation technologies and how they can fundamentally change product development. Significantly, my research has shown that new programmable technologies have not only lowered the cost and time of prototype iterations but also given rise to differences in development strategy, process, and performance. In the past, change was deemed risky and "frozen" specifications drove incremental experiments. We have seen that this *specification-driven* development is a rational response to the constraints that technology—in this case, gate arrays and standard cells—poses: Changes are costly and should be avoided. Once flexible, programmable technologies were introduced, however, changes were considered natural and experimentation was invited in as a way of rapidly resolving uncertainty. This *experimentation-driven* development starts with a specification that is good enough and uses computer simulation combined with frequent prototype iterations to address and solve problems quickly—which, in turn, requires a fundamental rethinking of how the process and the organization are designed.

Third, all experiments, regardless of technologies deployed, share a four-step basic iterative process and can be organized to maximize learning. How learning through experimentation occurs (or does not occur) is affected by seven factors: Fidelity, cost, iteration time, capacity, sequential and parallel strategies, signal-to-noise ratio, and experiment type all enhance the power of experimentation. New technologies for experimentation amplify the importance of managing these factors, thus creating the potential for higher R&D performance, innovation, and ultimately new ways of creating value for customers. Managerial biases, mental models, and organizational inertia, however, can get in the way.

Fourth, research underscores the point that superior technologies do not automatically translate into superior performance. Unless technological innovation is accompanied by managerial, organizational, and process change, investing in better computers, software, and other new tools can lead to disappointing returns. A detailed study of the global auto industry and its use of computer-aided technologies (e.g., CAD and CAE) introduced us to some realities: Technologies are limited by the processes and people that use them, organizational interfaces get in the way of experimentation, and technologies change faster than behavior. Taken together, these realities are the result of daily routines, mind-sets, processes, experience, and knowledge that have been built around existing engineering technologies and market demands. When technological change places some of these practices in jeopardy, then what worked previously can itself become a barrier to unlocking the potential of new experimentation technologies.

Fifth, six principles capture how learning by experimentation does and does not occur. The first three address the need for experimenting early and often: (1) Anticipate and exploit early information through front-loaded innovation processes; (2) experiment frequently without overloading your organization; (3) integrate new and traditional technologies. Specifically, by combining new and established technologies, organizations can maintain or gain strategic product advantage while also enjoying the benefits of cheaper and faster development. For all their potential, new technologies can create rifts within groups and organizations and lead to resistance. Jobs and routines of designers and model makers trained in old ways are threatened by new ways of doing things as digital design disrupts well-established routines, and they require investments in learning. Leadership becomes essential; getting some of the most respected designers, engineers, and scientists to accept the new technologies and become lead adopters helps in persuading others.

Sixth, the second three principles emphasize how to succeed at innovation and handle the constant conflict between learning from success and failure: (4) Organize for rapid experimentation; (5) fail early and often but avoid mistakes; (6) manage projects as experiments. Experiments resulting in failure are not failed experiments—they reveal what does not work, which is critical to learning what will work. Their value, as such, is maximized when they are revealed early in an innovation process, when few resources have been committed, decision making is still flexible, and other approaches can be experimented with quickly. New experimentation technologies amplify the importance of these principles even further; they allow for increased speed and experimentation capacity but also encourage more failures early in development when the attrition of ideas comes at little cost to organizations but are important springboards for better approaches.

Seventh, taking new experimentation technologies *beyond* organizations can open up additional opportunities for innovation and value creation. In the form of user-friendly toolkits, these technologies enable management to tap into possibly the largest source of dormant experimentation capacity: the customer. Not only can shifting experimentation to customers result in faster development of products better suited to their needs, but it may generate innovations that companies simply cannot imagine today. The approach thus holds the power to turn markets topsy-turvy, creating and shifting value at three separate levels: the industry as a whole, companies that implement the technology, and customers that take advantage of it.

By learning from *Experimentation Matters,* managers and their organizations are poised to confront the challenges of introducing new experimentation technologies into their innovation systems and unlock their potential. Indeed, many companies have really just begun exploiting this new power. The next decade will bring advances in knowledge, products, and technologies that are possible because of the changing economics of experimentation. And as these technologies are transforming how innovation happens, the success of this revolution will be measured in the value they create for companies and the lives they improve.

NOTES

1. See W. Bulkeley (2002).

2. According to the *Wall Street Journal,* ASCI Purple is the fifth generation of the Energy Department's decade-old Advanced Simulation and Computing Initiative (in short, ASCI). The other generations were named after colors as well.

3. See *Technology Review* (2002).

4. See Weisshaar (1996).

bibliography

Abernathy, W. (1978). *The Productivity Dilemma: Roadblock to Innovation in the Automobile Industry.* Baltimore, MD: Johns Hopkins University Press.

Abernathy, W., and K. B. Clark (1985). "Innovation: Mapping the Winds of Creative Destruction." *Research Policy* no. 14: 3–22.

Abernathy, W., and R. Rosenbloom (1968). "Parallel and Sequential R&D Strategies: Application of a Simple Model." *IEEE Transactions on Engineering Management* EM-15, no. 1: 2–10.

Abernathy, W., and J. M. Utterback (1978). "Patterns of Industrial Innovation." *Technology Review* 80, no. 7: 2–9.

Adler, P. (1986). "New Technologies, New Skills." *California Management Review* 29 (Fall): 9–28.

Adler, P. (1990). "Shared Learning." *Management Science* 36 (August): 938–957.

Adler, P., and K. B. Clark (1991). "Behind the Learning Curve: A Sketch of the Learning Process." *Management Science* 37 (March): 267–281.

Agarwal, A. (1999). "Raw Computation." *Scientific American,* August, 60–63.

Alexander, C. (1964). *Notes on the Synthesis of Form.* Cambridge: Harvard University Press.

Allen, T. J. (1966). "Studies of the Problem-Solving Process in Engineering Design." *IEEE Transactions on Engineering Management* EM-13, no. 2: 72–83.

Allen, T. J. (1977). *Managing the Flow of Technology.* Cambridge: MIT Press.

Allen, T. J. (1986). "Organizational Structures, Information Technology and R&D Productivity." *IEEE Transactions on Engineering Management* EM-33, no. 4: 212–217.

Amabile, T. (1983). *The Social Psychology of Creativity.* New York: Springer-Verlag.

Amabile, T. (1997). "Motivating Creativity in Organizations: On Doing What You Love and Loving What You Do." *California Management Review* 40, no. 1: 39–58.

Anderson, P., and M. L. Tushman. (1990). "Technological Discontinuities and Dominant Designs: A Cyclical Model of Technological Change." *Administrative Science Quarterly* 35: 604–633.

Aoshima, Y. (1996). *Knowledge Transfer across Generations: The Impact on Product Development Performance in the Automobile Industry.* Ph.D. dissertation, Massachusetts Institute of Technology.

Argyris, C. (1977). "Double-Loop Learning in Organizations." *Harvard Business Review,* September–October, 116–124.

Argyris, C. (1982). *Reasoning, Learning, and Action.* San Francisco: Jossey-Bass.

Argyris, C., and D. Schön (1978). *Organizational Learning.* Reading, MA: Addison-Wesley.

Arrow, K. (1962). "The Economic Implications of Learning by Doing." *Review of Economic Studies* 29: 155–173.

Baba, Y., and K. Nobeoka (1998). "Towards Knowledge-Based Product Development: The 3-D CAD Model of Knowledge Creation." *Research Policy* 26, no. 6: 643–660.

Bacon, G., S. Beckman, D. Mowery, and E. Wilson (1994). "Managing Product Definition in High Technology Industries: A Pilot Study." *California Management Review* 36, no. 3: 32–56.

Baldwin, C. Y., and K. B. Clark (2000). *Design Rules: The Power of Modularity.* Cambridge: MIT Press.

Barley, S. "Technology as an Occasion for Structuring Evidence from Observations of CT Scanners and the Social Order of Radiology Departments," *Administrative Science Quarterly* 31, no. 1 (1986): 78–109.

Basili, V., R. Selby, and D. Hutchens (1986). "Experimentation in Software Engineering." *IEEE Transactions on Software Engineering* SE-12, no. 7: 733–743.

Bell, P. (1995). "An Experimental Investigation into the Efficacy of Visual Interactive Simulation." *Management Science* 41 (June): 1018–1038.

Bell, P. (1987). "Visual Interactive Simulation: History, Recent Developments, and Major Issues." *Simulation* 49, 3: 109–116.

Benner, M., and M. Tushman (in press). "Exploitation, Exploration, and Process Management: The Productivity Dilemma Revisited." *Academy of Management Review.*

Bennis, W., and B. Nanus (1985). *Leaders: Strategies for Taking Charge.* New York: HarperCollins.

Boehm, B. (1981). *Software Engineering Economics.* Englewood Cliffs, NJ: Prentice Hall.

Boehm, B., T. Gray, and T. Seewaldt (1984). "Prototyping versus Specifying: A Multiproject Experiment." *IEEE Transactions on Software Engineering* SE10, no. 3: 290–302.

Bohn, R. (1987). "Learning by Experimentation in Manufacturing." Working paper 88-001. Harvard Business School, Boston.

Bohn, R. (1994). "Measuring and Managing Technological Knowledge." *Sloan Management Review* 36, no. 1: 61–73.

Bohn, R. (1995). "Noise and Learning in Semiconductor Manufacturing." *Management Science* 41 (January): 31–42.

Bowen, K., K. B. Clark, C. Holloway, and S. Wheelwright (1994a). "Make Projects the School for Leaders." *Harvard Business Review,* September–October, 131–140.

Bowen, K., K. B. Clark, C. Holloway, and S. Wheelwright (1994b). *The Perpetual Enterprise Machine.* New York: Oxford University Press.

Box, G., and N. Draper (1969). *Evolutionary Operations: A Statistical Method for Process Improvement.* New York: John Wiley & Sons.

Box, G., and N. Draper (1987). *Empirical Model-Building and Response Surfaces.* New York: John Wiley & Sons.

Box, G., W. Hunter, and S. Hunter (1978). *Statistics for Experimenters.* New York: John Wiley & Sons.

Brenner, A. (1996). "The Computer Revolution and the Physics Community." *Physics Today* 46: 24–39.

Brooks, F. (1982). *The Mythical Man-Month: Essays on Software Engineering.* Reading, MA: Addison-Wesley.

Brown, J. S., and P. Duguid (2000). *The Social Life of Information.* Boston: Harvard Business School Press.

Brown, S., and K. Eisenhardt (2000). *Competing on the Edge: Strategy as Structured Chaos.* Boston: Harvard Business School Press.

Bruderer, E., and J. Singh (1996). "Organizational Evolution, Learning, and Selection: A Genetic-Algorithm-Based Model." *Academy of Management Journal* 39, no. 5: 1322–1349.

Brynjolfsson, E., and L. Hitt (1996). "Paradox Lost? Firm-Level Evidence on the Returns to Information Systems Spending." *Management Science* 42, no. 4: 541–588.

Bucciarelli, L. (1994). *Designing Engineers.* Cambridge: MIT Press.

Bulkeley, W. (2002) "IBM Computer Will Outpace Japanese Rival," *Wall Street Journal* 19 November.

Burgelman, R. A. (1994). "Fading Memories: A Process Theory of Strategic Business Exit in Dynamic Environments." *Administrative Science Quarterly* 39: 24–56.

Burns, T., and G. M. Stalker (1961). *The Management of Innovation.* London: Tavistock.

Campbell, D. (1960). "Blind Variation and Selective Retention in Creative Thought as in Other Knowledge Processes." *Psychological Review* 67: 380–400.

Campbell, D. (1969). "Reforms as Experiments." *American Psychologist* 24: 409–429.

Casti, J. (1997). *Would-Be Worlds: How Simulation Is Changing the Frontiers of Science.* New York: John Wiley & Sons.

Champion, D. (2001). "Mastering the Value Chain: An Interview with Mark Levin of Millennium Pharmaceuticals." *Harvard Business Review,* June, 109–115.

Chandler, A. (1990). *Scale and Scope: The Dynamics of Industrial Capitalism.* Cambridge: Belknap Press of Harvard University Press.

Chesbrough, H. (2003). *Open Innovation: The New Imperative for Creating and Profiting from Technology.* Boston: Harvard Business School Press.

Christensen, C. M. (1992). "Exploring the Limits of the Technology S-Curve. Part I: Component Technologies." *Production and Operations Management* 1, no. 4: 334–357.

Christensen, C. M. (1992). "Exploring the Limits of the Technology S-Curve: Part II: Architectural Technologies." *Production and Operations Management* 1, no. 4: 358–366.

Christensen, C. M. (1997). *The Innovator's Dilemma: When New Technologies Cause Great Firms to Fail.* Boston: Harvard Business School Press.

Christensen, C. M., and R. Rosenbloom (1995). "Explaining the Attacker's Advantage: Technological Paradigms, Organizational Dynamics, and the Value Network." *Research Policy* 24: 233–257.

Clark, K. B. (1985). "The Interaction of Design Hierarchies and Market Concepts in Technological Evolution." *Research Policy* 14 (October): 235–251.

Clark, K. B., and T. Fujimoto (1980), "Lead Time in Automobile Development: Explaining the Japanese Advantage," *Journal of Technology and Engineering Management* 6: 25–58.

Clark, K. B., and T. Fujimoto (1991). *Product Development Performance: Strategy, Organization, and Management in the World Auto Industry.* Boston: Harvard Business School Press.

Clark, K. B., and T. Fujimoto (1989). "Lead Time in Automobile Development: Explaining the Japanese Advantage," *Journal of Technology and Engineering Management* 6: 25–58.

Clausing, D. (1994). *Total Quality Development: A Step-by-Step Guide to World Class Concurrent Engineering.* New York: ASME Press.

Cockburn, I., R. Henderson, and S. Stern (2000). "Untangling the Origins of Competitive Advantage." *Strategic Management Journal* 21: 1123–1145.

Cohen, W., and D. Levinthal (1990). "Absorptive Capacity: A New Perspective on Learning and Innovation." *Administrative Science Quarterly* 35, no. 1: 128–152.

Collins, H. M. (1982). "Tacit Knowledge in Scientific Networks." In *Science in Context: Readings in the Sociology of Science,* edited by B. Barnes and D. Edge. Cambridge: MIT Press.

Cooper, R. G. (1983). "A Process Model for Industrial New Product Development." *IEEE Transactions on Engineering Management* EM-30, no. 1: 2–11.

Cooper, R. G. (1986). *Winning at New Products.* Reading, MA: Addison-Wesley.

Cusumano, M. (1992). "Shifting Economies: From Craft Production to Flexible Systems and Software Factories." *Research Policy* 21, no. 5: 453–480.

Cusumano, M., and K. Nobeoka (1992). "Strategy, Structure and Performance in Product Development: Observations from the Auto Industry." *Research Policy* 21, no. 3: 265–293.

Cusumano, M., and K. Nobeoka (1998). *Thinking Beyond Lean: How Multi-Project Management Is Transforming Product Development at Toyota and Other Companies.* New York: Free Press/Simon & Schuster.

Cusumano, M., and R. Selby (1995). *Microsoft Secrets.* New York: Free Press.

Dahan, E., and J. Hauser (2001). "The Virtual Customer." Working paper, MIT Sloan School of Management, Cambridge, MA.

Souder, W. (1987). *Managing New Product Innovations.* Lexington, MA: Lexington Books.

Dahan, E., and V. "Seenu" Srinivasan (2000). "The Predictive Power of Internet-Based Product Concept Testing Using Visual Depiction and Animation." *Journal of Product Innovation Management* 17, no. 2: 99–109.

Datar, S., C. Jordan, S. Kekre, S. Rajiv, and K. Srinivasan (1996). "New Product Development Structures: The Effect of Customer Overload on Post-Concept Time-to-Market." *Journal of Product Innovation Management* 13: 325–333.

Datar, S., C. Jordan, S. Kekre, S. Rajiv, and K. Srinivasan (1997). "New Product Development Structures and Time-to-Market." *Management Science* 43, no. 4: 452–464.

Davies, K. (2001). *Cracking the Genome: Inside the Race to Unlock Human DNA.* New York: Free Press.

DiMasi, J., R. Hansen, H. Grabowski, and L. Lasagna (1991). "Cost of Innovation in the Pharmaceutical Industry." *Journal of Health Economics* 10: 107–142.

DiMasi, J. A., R. W. Hansen, H. G. Grabowski, and L. Lasagna (1995). "Research and Development Costs for New Drugs by Therapeutic Category." *Pharmaco-Economics* 7, no. 2: 152–169.

Doerner, D. (1996). *The Logic of Failure.* Reading, MA: Addison-Wesley.

Dougherty, D. (1992). "Interpretive Barriers to New Product Development in Large Firms." *Organization Science* 3, no. 2: 179–202.

Drews, J. (2000). "Drug Discovery: A Historical Perspective." *Science* 287: 1960–1964.

Duncker, K. (1945). "On Problem Solving," translated by L. S. Lees. *Psychology Monographs* 58, no. 270: 1–112.

Economist (1998a). "A Survey of the Pharmaceutical Industry." *Economist.* 21 February, 9–10.

Economist (1998b). "Millennium's Bugs." *Economist.* 26 September, 70.

Edmondson, A. (1996). "Learning from Errors is Easier Said than Done: Group and Organizational Influences on the Detection and Correction of Human Error." *Journal of Applied Behavioral Science* 32, no. 1: 5–32.

Eisenhardt, K., and B. Tabrizi (1995). "Accelerating Adaptive Processes: Product Innovation in the Global Computer Industry." *Administrative Science Quarterly* 40, no. 1: 84–111.

Ellison, D. (1996). *Dynamic Capabilities in New Product Development: The Case of the World Auto Industry.* Ph.D. dissertation, Harvard University.

Ellison, D., K. Clark, T. Fujimoto, and Y. Hyun (1995). "Product Development Performance in the Auto Industry: 1990s Update." Working paper 95-066. Harvard Business School, Boston.

Enright, M., and A. Capriles (1996). "*Black Magic* and the America's Cup: The Victory." Case 796-187. Boston: Harvard Business School.

Enriquez, J. (2001). *As the Future Catches You: How Genomics and Other Forces Are Changing Your Life, Work, Health and Wealth.* New York: Crown Business.

Eppinger, S. (1991). "Model-Based Approaches to Managing Concurrent Engineering." *Journal of Engineering Design* 2, no. 4.

Eppinger, S., D. Whitney, R. Smith, and D. Gebala (1994). "A Model-Based Method for Organizing Tasks in Product Development." *Research in Engineering Design* 6, no. 1:1–13.

Ettlie, J. E., W. Bridges, and R. O'Keefe (1984). "Organizational Strategy and Structural Differences for Radical vs. Incremental Innovation." *Management Science* 30: 682–695.

Ettlie, J. (2000). *Managing Technological Innovation.* New York: John Wiley & Sons.

Ettlie, J., and E. Reza (1992) "Organizational Integration and Process Innovation." *Academy of Management Journal* 34, no. 4: 795–827.

Fisher, R. (1921). "Studies in Crop Variation: I. An Examination of the Yield of Dressed Grain from Broadbalk." *Journal of Agricultural Science* 11: 107–135.

Fisher, R. (1923). "Studies in Crop Variation: II. The Manurial Response of Different Potato Varieties." *Journal of Agricultural Science* 13: 311–320.

Fisher, R. (1966). *The Design of Experiments.* 8th ed. Edinburgh: Oliver and Boyd.

Fleming, L. (2001). "Recombinant Uncertainty in Technological Search." *Management Science* 47, no. 1: 117–132.

Foster, R. (1986). *Innovation: The Attacker's Advantage.* London: Macmillan.

Freeman, C. (1982). *The Economics of Industrial Innovation.* London: Frances Pinter.

Friedel, R., and P. Israel (1987). *Edison's Electrical Light: Biography of an Invention.* New Brunswick, NJ: Rutgers University Press.

Frischmuth, D., and T. Allen (1969). "A Model for the Description and Evaluation of Technical Problem Solving." *IEEE Transactions on Engineering Management* EM-16, no. 2: 58–64.

Fujimoto, T. (1999). *The Evolution of a Manufacturing Systems at Toyota.* New York: Oxford University Press.

Galbraith, J. (1973). *Designing Complex Organizations.* Reading, MA: Addison-Wesley.

Galison, P. (1987). *How Experiments End.* Chicago: University of Chicago Press.

Galison, P. (1997). *Image and Logic.* Chicago: University of Chicago Press.

Garvin, D. (1993). "Building a Learning Organization." *Harvard Business Review,* July–August, 78–91.

Garvin, D. (2000). *Learning in Action: A Guide to Putting the Learning Organization to Work.* Boston: Harvard Business School Press.

Garvin, D. (2002). "A Note on Corporate Venturing and New Business Creation." Note 302-091. Boston: Harvard Business School.

Gilmore, J., and J. Pine, (2000). *Markets of One: Creating Customer-Unique Value through Mass Customization.* Boston: Harvard Business School Press.

Glaser, B., and A. Strauss (1970). *The Discovery of Grounded Theory: Strategies for Qualitative Research.* Chicago: Aldine, 1970.

Gomory, R. (1983). "Technology Development." *Science* 220: 576–580.

Griffin, A., and J. Hauser (1992). "Patterns of Communication Among Marketing, Engineering, and Manufacturing—A Comparison between Two New Product Teams." *Management Science* 38, no. 3: 360–373.

Griffin, A., and J. Hauser (1993). "The Voice of the Customer." *Marketing Science* 12, no. 1: 1–27.

Halliday, R., S. Walker, and C. Lumley (1992). "R&D Philosophy and Management in the World's Leading Pharmaceutical Companies." *Journal of Pharmaceutical Medicine* 2: 139–154.

Hamel, G. (2000). *Leading the Revolution.* Boston: Harvard Business School Press.

Hannan, M., and J. Freeman (1984). "Structural Inertia and Organizational Change." *American Sociological Review* 49: 149–164.

Hannan, M. T., and J. Freeman (1989). *Organizational Ecology.* Cambridge: Belknap Press of Harvard University Press.

Hare, R. (1981). *Great Scientific Experiments.* Oxford: Phaidon Press.

Hauptman, O., and G. Iwaki (1991). "The Final Voyage of the Challenger." Case 691-037. Boston: Harvard Business School.

Hayes, R., S. Wheelwright, and K. B. Clark (1988). *Dynamic Manufacturing: Creating the Learning Organization.* New York: Free Press.

Henderson, R. (1994). "The Evolution of Integrative Capability: Innovation in Cardiovascular Drug Discovery." *Industrial and Corporate Change* 3, no. 3: 607–630.

Henderson, R., and K. B. Clark (1990). "Architectural Innovation: The Reconfiguration of Existing Systems and the Failure of Established Firms." *Administrative Science Quarterly* 35, no. 1: 9–30.

Henderson, R., and I. Cockburn (1994). "Measuring Competence: Exploring Firm Effects in Pharmaceutical Research." *Strategic Management Journal* 15: 63–84.

Hofstadter, D. (1989). *Gödel, Escher, Bach: An Eternal Golden Braid.* New York: Vintage Books.

Holland, J. (1995). *Hidden Order: How Adaptation Builds Complexity.* Reading, MA: Addison-Wesley, 1995.

Huber, G. (1991). "Organizational Learning: The Contributing Processes and the Literatures." *Organization Science* 2, no. 1: 88–115.

Iansiti, M. (1995a). "Shooting the Rapids: Managing Product Development in Turbulent Times." *California Management Review* 38: 37–58.

Iansiti, M. (1995b). "Technology Integration: Managing the Interaction between Applied Science and Product Development." *Research Policy* 24, no. 4: 521–524.

Iansiti, M. (1997). *Technology Integration: Making Critical Choices in a Dynamic World.* Boston: Harvard Business School Press.

Iansiti, M., and A. MacCormack (1997). "Developing Products on Internet Time." *Harvard Business Review,* September–October, 108–117.

Iansiti, M., and A. MacCormack (1997). "Team New Zealand (A), (B) and (C)." Cases 697-040, 697-041, and 697-042. Boston: Harvard Business School.

Jaikumar, R., and R. Bohn (1986). "The Development of Intelligent Systems for Industrial Use: A Conceptual Framework." *Research on Technological Innovation, Management and Policy* 3: 169-211.

Kanter, R. M. (1997). *Rosabeth Moss Kanter on the Frontiers of Management.* Boston: Harvard Business School Press.

Kauffman, S. (1993). *The Origins of Order: Self-Organization and Selection in Evolution.* New York: Oxford University Press.

Kauffman, S., and S. Levin (1987). "Towards a General Theory of Adaptive Walks on Rugged Landscapes." *Journal of Theoretical Biology* 128: 11–45.

Katz, R. (1982). "The Effects of Group Longevity on Project Communication and Performance." *Administrative Science Quarterly* 27: 81–104.

Katz, R., (1985). "Organizational Issues in the Introduction of New Technologies," In *The Management of Productivity and Technology Manufacturing,* edited by P. Kleindorfer. New York: Plenum Press, 275–300.

Kelley, T. (2001). *The Art of Innovation.* New York: Doubleday.

Krishnan, V., S. Eppinger, and D. Whitney (1997). "A Model-Based Framework for Overlapping Product Development Activities." *Management Science* (Special Issue on Frontier Research in Manufacturing and Logistics) 43, no. 4: 437–451.

Kuhn, T. (1962). *The Structure of Scientific Revolutions.* Chicago: University of Chicago Press.

Lawler, E., III (1977). "Adaptive Experiments: An Approach to Organizational Behavior Research." *Academy of Management Review* (October).

Lawrence, P., and J. Lorsch (1967). *Organization and Environment.* Boston: Harvard Business School Press.

Lee, F. (2001). "The Fear Factor." *Harvard Business Review,* January, 29–30.

Lee, F., A. Edmondson, S. Thomke, and M. Worline (2000). "Promoting Experimentation in Organizations: Effects of Values, Rewards and Status." Working paper 00-087, Harvard Business School, Boston.

Leonard-Barton, D. (1988). "Implementation as Mutual Adaptation of Technology and Organization." *Research Policy* 17, no. 5: 251–267.

Leonard-Barton, D. (1992a). "Core Capabilities and Core Rigidities: A Paradox in Managing New Product Development." *Strategic Management Journal* 13: 111–125.

Leonard-Barton, D. (1992b). "The Factory as a Learning Laboratory." *Sloan Management Review* 34, no. 1: 23–38.

Leonard-Barton, D. (1995). *Wellsprings of Knowledge: Building and Sustaining the Sources of Innovation.* Boston: Harvard Business School Press.

Leonard-Barton, D., and W. Kraus (1985). "Implementing New Technology." *Harvard Business Review,* November–December, 102–110.

Levinthal, D. (1997). "Adaptation on Rugged Landscapes." *Management Science* 43, no. 7: 934–951.

Levinthal, D., and J. March (1993). "The Myopia of Learning." *Strategic Management Journal* 14: 95–112.

Liker, J., J. Ettlie, and J. Campbell, eds. (1995). *Engineered in Japan: Japanese Technology Management Practices.* New York: Oxford University Press.

Liker, J., and M. Fleischer (1989). "Implementing Computer-Aided Design: The Transition of Non-users." *IEEE Transactions on Engineering Management* 36, no. 3: 180–190.

Liker, J., M. Fleischer, M. Nagamachi, and M. Zonnyville (1992). "Designers and Their Machines: CAD Use and Support in the U.S. and Japan." *Communications of ACM* 35, no. 2: 76–95.

Loch, C., and C. Terwiesch (1998). "Communication and Uncertainty in Concurrent Engineering." *Management Science* 44, no. 8: 1032–1048.

Loch, C., and C. Terwiesch (1999). "Accelerating the Process of Engineering Change Orders: Capacity and Congestion Effects." *Journal of Product Innovation Management* 16 (March): 145–159.

Loch, C., C. Terwiesch, and S. Thomke (2001). "Parallel and Sequential Testing of Design Alternatives." *Management Science* 47, no. 5: 663–678.

Lynn, G., J. Morone, and A. Paulson (1996). "Marketing and Discontinuous Innovation: The Probe and Learn Process," *California Management Review* 38, no. 3: 8–37.

MacCormack, A., R. Verganti, and M. Iansiti (2001). "Developing Products on Internet Time: The Anatomy of a Flexible Development Process." *Management Science* 47, no. 1: 133–150.

Mansfield, E. (1968). *Industrial Research and Technological Innovation: An Econometric Analysis.* New York: W. W. Norton.

March, J. (1991). "Exploration and Exploitation in Organizational Learning." *Organization Science* 2, no. 1: 71–87.

March, J., and H. Simon (1958). *Organizations*. New York: John Wiley & Sons.

March, J., L. Sproull, and M. Tamuz (1991). "Learning from Samples of One or Fewer." *Organization Science* 2, no. 1: 1–13.

Marples, D. (1961). "The Decisions of Engineering Design." *IRE Transactions on Engineering Management* (June): 55–71.

McDonough, E., III, and G. Barczak (1992). "The Effects of Cognitive Problem-Solving Orientation and Technological Familiarity on Faster New Product Development." *Journal of Product Innovation Management* 9: 44–52.

McGrane, S. (1999). "For a Seller of Innovation, a Bag of Technotricks." *New York Times*. 11 February.

McKinsey Global Institute (2001). *US Productivity Growth: Understanding the Contribution of Information Technology Relative to Other Factors*. Washington, DC: McKinsey Global Institute (October).

Millard, A. (1990). *Edison and the Business of Innovation*. Baltimore, MD: Johns Hopkins University Press.

Montgomery, D. (1991). *Design and Analysis of Experiments*. New York: John Wiley & Sons.

Morison, E. (1966). *Men, Machines, and Modern Times*. Cambridge: MIT Press.

Mowery, D., and N. Rosenberg (1991). *Technology and the Pursuit of Economic Growth*. Cambridge: Cambridge University Press.

Nayak, P., and J. Ketteringham (1997). "3M's Post-it Notes: A Managed or Accidental Innovation?" In R. Katz, *The Human Side of Managing Technological Innovation*. New York: Oxford University Press.

Nelson, K., and R. Nelson (2002). "On the Nature and Evolution of Human Know-How." *Research Policy* 31, no. 5: 719–733.

Nelson, R. (1961). "Uncertainty, Learning, and the Economics of Parallel Research and Development Efforts." *Review of Economics and Statistics* 43: 351–364.

Nelson, R. (1982). "The Role of Knowledge in R&D Efficiency." *Quarterly Journal of Economics* (August): 453–470.

Nelson, R. (2002). "Bounded Rationality, Cognitive Maps, and Trial and Error Learning." Working paper, Columbia University, New York.

Nelson, R., and S. Winter (1982). *An Evolutionary Theory of Economic Change*. Cambridge: Belknap Press of Harvard University Press.

Nelson, W. (1990). *Accelerated Testing: Statistical Models, Test Plans, and Data Analysis*. New York: John Wiley & Sons.

Newell, A., and H. Simon (1972). *Human Problem Solving*. Englewood Cliffs, NJ: Prentice-Hall.

Nonaka, I., and H. Takeuchi. (1995). *The Knowledge-Creating Company*. New York: Oxford University Press.

Norman, D. (1988). *The Design of Everyday Things*. New York: Doubleday Currency.

Pavitt, K. (1984). "Sectoral Patterns of Technical Change: Towards a Taxonomy and a Theory." *Research Policy* 12, no. 6: 343–373.

Peters, T. (1988). *Thriving on Chaos.* New York: Alfred A. Knopf.

Peters, T., and R. Waterman (1982). *In Search of Excellence.* New York: Harper & Row.

Petroski, H. (1992). *To Engineer Is Human: The Role of Failure in Successful Design.* New York: Vintage Books.

Petroski, H. (1996). *Invention by Design: How Engineers Get Thought to Thing.* Cambridge: Harvard University Press.

Phadke, M. (1989). *Quality Engineering Using Robust Design.* Englewood Cliffs, NJ: Prentice Hall.

Pine, J. (1993). *Mass Customization: The New Frontier in Business Competition.* Boston: Harvard Business School Press.

Pisano, G. (1996). "Learning before Doing in the Development of New Process Technology." *Research Policy* 25, no. 7: 1097–1119.

Pisano, G. (1997). *The Development Factory: Unlocking the Potential of Process Innovation.* Boston: Harvard Business School Press.

Pisano, G., A. Leamon, K. Slack, and R. Martinez (2002). "Discovering the Future: R&D Strategy at Merck." Case 601-086. Boston: Harvard Business School.

Pisano, G., and S. Wheelwright (1995). "The New Logic of High-Tech R&D." *Harvard Business Review,* September–October, 93–105.

Plunkert, M., and J. Ellman (1997). "Combinatorial Chemistry and New Drugs." *Scientific American,* April, 68–73.

Polanyi, M. (1958). *Personal Knowledge: Towards a Post-Critical Philosophy.* Chicago: University of Chicago Press.

Prahalad, C. K., and V. Ramaswamy (2000). "Co-opting Customer Competence." *Harvard Business Review,* January–February, 79–87.

Reinertsen, D. (1983). "Whodunit? The Search for New-Product Killers." *Electronic Business.* July, 62–66.

Reinertsen, D. (1997). *Managing the Design Factory.* New York: Free Press.

Repenning, N., and J. Sterman (2001). "Nobody Ever Gets Credit for Fixing Problems that Never Happened: Creating and Sustaining Process Improvement." *California Management Review* 43 (Summer): 64–92.

Repenning, N., and J. Sterman (2002). "Capability Traps and Self-Confirming Attribution Errors in the Dynamics of Process Improvement." *Administrative Science Quarterly* 47: 265–295.

Rifkin, G. (2002). "GM's Internet Overhaul." *Technology Review* (October): 62–67.

Rogers, E. (1983). *Diffusion of Innovations.* New York: Free Press.

Rosenberg, N. (1982). *Inside the Black Box: Technology and Economics.* New York: Cambridge University Press.

Sabbagh, K. (1996). *Twenty-First Century Jet: The Making and Marketing of the Boeing 777.* New York: Charles Scribner's Sons.

Sachs, E., et al. (1992). "CAD-Casting: Direct Fabrication of Ceramic Shells and Cores by Three Dimensional Printing." *Manufacturing Review* 5, no. 2: 117–126.

Schön, D. (1967). *Technology and Change.* New York: Delacorte Press.

Schön, D. (1983). *The Reflective Practitioner: How Professionals Think in Action.* New York: Basic Books.

Schrage, M. (1993). "The Culture(s) of Prototyping." *Design Management Journal* 4, no. 1: 55–65.

Schrage, M. (2000). *Serious Play: How the World's Best Companies Simulate to Innovate.* Boston: Harvard Business School Press.

Science (1998). "Breakthrough of the Year." *Science* 282, no. 5397: 2156–2161.

Schumpeter, J. (1934). *The Theory of Economic Development.* Cambridge: Harvard University Press.

Scott-Morton, M. (1967). "Computer-Driven Visual Display Devices." Ph.D. dissertation, Harvard Business School.

Seidel, R. (1996). "From Mars to Minerva: The Origins of Scientific Computing in the AEC Labs." *Physics Today* (October): 33–39.

Senge, P. (1990). *The Fifth Discipline: The Art and Practice of the Learning Organization.* New York: Doubleday.

Shannon, C., and W. Weaver (1963). *The Mathematical Theory of Communication.* Chicago: University of Illinois Press.

Simon, H. A. (1969). *The Sciences of the Artificial.* Cambridge: MIT Press.

Sinofsky, S., and S. Thomke (1999). "Learning from Projects: Note on Conducting a Postmortem Analysis." Note 600-021. Boston: Harvard Business School.

Sitkin, S. (1992). "Learning Through Failure: The Strategy of Small Losses." *Research in Organizational Behavior* 14: 231–266.

Slywotzky, A. (1996). *Value Migration: How to Think Several Moves Ahead of the Competition.* Boston: Harvard Business School Press.

Smith, P., and D. Reinertsen (1991). *Developing Products in Half the Time.* New York: Van Nostrand Reinhold.

Smith, R., and S. Eppinger (1997). "A Predictive Model of Sequential Iteration in Engineering Design." *Management Science* 43, no. 8: 1104–1121.

Sobek, D., A. Ward and J. Liker (1999). "Toyota's Principles of Set-Based Concurrent Engineering." *Sloan Management Review* 40, no. 2: 67–83.

Souder, W. (1987). *Managing New Product Innovations.* Lexington, MA: Lexington Books.

Spear, S., and K. Bowen (1999). "Decoding the DNA of the Toyota Production System." *Harvard Business Review,* September–October, 96–106.

Sterman, J. (1989). "Modeling Managerial Behavior: Misperceptions of Feedback in a Dynamic Decision-Making Experiment." *Management Science* 35, no. 3: 321–339.

Sutton, R., and A. Hargadon (1996). "Brainstorming Groups in Context: Effectiveness in a Product Design Firm." *Administrative Science Quarterly* 41, no. 4: 685–718.

Sutton, R., and A. Hargadon (1997). "Technology Brokering and Innovation in a Product Development Firm." *Administrative Science Quarterly* 42, no. 4: 716–749.

Sze, S. M. (1988). *VLSI Technology,* 2d ed. New York: McGraw-Hill.

Taguchi, G., and D. Clausing (1990). "Robust Quality." *Harvard Business Review,* January–February, 65–75.

Taubes, G. (2002). "The Virtual Cell." *Technology Review* (April): 63–70.

Technology Review (2000). "The Bell Labs of Biology." *Technology Review* (March–April): 94–98.

Teece, D. (1986). "Profiting from Technological Innovation: Implications for Integrating, Collaborating, Licensing, and Public Policy." *Research Policy* 15, no. 6: 285–305.

Teece, D., G. Pisano, and A. Shuen (1997). "Dynamic Capabilities and Strategic Management." *Strategic Management Journal* 18, no. 7: 509–533.

Terwiesch, C., C. H. Loch, and A. DeMeyer (2002). "Exchanging Preliminary Information in Concurrent Engineering: Alternative Coordination Strategies." *Organization Science* 13, no. 4: 402–419.

Thomke, S. (1997). "The Role of Flexibility in the Development of New Products: An Empirical Study." *Research Policy* 26, no. 1: 105–119.

Thomke, S. (1998a). "Managing Experimentation in the Design of New Products." *Management Science* 44, no. 6: 743–762.

Thomke, S. (1998b). "Simulation, Learning and R&D Performance: Evidence from Automotive Development." *Research Policy* 27, no. 1: 55–74.

Thomke, S. (2000). "Managing Digital Design at BMW." *Design Management Journal* 12, no. 2: 20–28.

Thomke, S. (2001). "Enlightened Experimentation: The New Imperative for Innovation." *Harvard Business Review,* February, 66–75.

Thomke, S. (2003). "R&D Comes to Services: Bank of America's Pathbreaking Experiments." *Harvard Business Review,* April.

Thomke, S., and D. E. Bell (2001). "Sequential Testing in Product Development." *Management Science* 47, no. 2: 308–323.

Thomke, S., and T. Fujimoto (2000). "The Effect of 'Front-Loading' Problem-Solving on Product Development Performance." *Journal of Product Innovation Management* (March): 128–142.

Thomke, S., M. Holzner, and T. Gholami (1999). "The Crash in the Machine." *Scientific American,* March, 92–97.

Thomke, S., and W. Kuemmerle (2002). "Asset Accumulation, Interdependence and Technological Change: Evidence from Pharmaceutical Drug Discovery." *Strategic Management Journal* 23, no. 7: 619–635.

Thomke, S. and A. Nimgade (1997a). "Eli Lilly and Company: Drug Development Strategy (A) and (B)." Cases 9-698-010 and 9-698-011. Boston: Harvard Business School.

Thomke, S. and A. Nimgade (1997b). "Note on New Drug Development in the United States." Note 698-028. Boston: Harvard Business School.

Thomke, S. and A. Nimgade (1998a). "BMW AG: The Digital Auto Project (A) and (B)." Cases 699-044 and 699-045. Boston: Harvard Business School.

Thomke, S. and A. Nimgade (1998b). "Innovation at 3M Corporation (A)." Case 9-699-012. Boston: Harvard Business School.

Thomke, S. and A. Nimgade (1999). "Millennium Pharmaceuticals, Inc. (A)." Case 600-038. Boston: Harvard Business School.

Thomke, S. and A. Nimgade (2000). "Bush Boake Allen." Case 601-061. Boston: Harvard Business School.

Thomke, S. and A. Nimgade (2002). "Bank of America (A) and (B)." Cases 603-022 and 603-023. Boston: Harvard Business School.

Thomke, S., and D. Reinertsen (1998). "Agile Product Development: Managing Development Flexibility in Uncertain Environments." *California Management Review* 40, no. 1: 8–30.

Thomke, S. and A. Robertson (1999). "Project Dreamcast: Serious Play at Sega Enterprises Ltd. (A)." Case 600-028. Boston: Harvard Business School.

Thomke, S. and E. von Hippel (2002). "Customers as Innovators: A New Way to Create Value." *Harvard Business Review,* April, 74–81.

Thomke, S., E. von Hippel, and R. Franke (1998). "Modes of Experimentation: An Innovation Process and Competitive Variable." *Research Policy* 27: 315–332.

Tripsas, M. (1997). "Unraveling the Process of Creative Destruction: Complementary Assets and Incumbent Survival in the Typesetter Industry." *Strategic Management Journal* 18 (Summer Special Issue): 119–142.

Tufts Center for the Study of Drug Development (2001). "Tufts Center for the Study of Drug Development Pegs Cost of a New Prescription Medicine at $802 Million." *Press Release,* 30 November.

Tushman, M., and P. Anderson (1986). "Technological Discontinuities and Organizational Environments." *Administrative Science Quarterly* 31, 3: 439–466.

Tushman, M., and C. O'Reilly (1996). "The Ambidextrous Organization: Managing Evolutionary and Revolutionary Change." *California Management Review* 38, no.4: 8–31.

Tushman, M. and C. A. O'Reilly (1997). *Winning Through Innovation: A Practical Guide to Leading Organization Change and Renewal.* Boston: Harvard Business School Press.

Tushman, M., and L. Rosenkopf (1992). "Organizational Determinants of Technological Change: Toward a Sociology of Technological Evolution." *Research in Organizational Behavior* 14: 311–347.

Tushman, M., and W. Smith (2002). "Organizational Technology." In *The Black-well Companion to Organizations,* edited by J. Baum. Oxford: Blackwell, 386–414.

Ulrich, K. (1995). "The Role of Product Architecture in the Manufacturing Firm." *Research Policy* 24, no. 3: 419–440.

Ulrich, K., and S. Eppinger (1994). *Product Design and Development.* New York: McGraw-Hill.

Upton, D. M. (1997). "Process Range in Manufacturing: An Empirical Study of Flexibility." *Management Science* 43, no. 8: 1079–1093.

Urban, G., and J. Hauser (1993). *Design and Marketing of New Products.* 2d ed. Englewood Cliffs, NJ: Prentice Hall.

Utterback, J. (1996). *Mastering the Dynamics of Innovation: How Companies Can Seize Opportunity in the Face of Technological Change.* Boston: Harvard Business School Press.

Vincente, W. (1990). *What Engineers Know and How They Know It.* Baltimore, MD: Johns Hopkins University Press.

von Hippel, E. (1988). *The Sources of Innovation.* New York: Oxford University Press.

von Hippel, E. (1990). "Task Partitioning: An Innovation Process Variable." *Research Policy* 19, no. 5: 407–418.

von Hippel, E. (1994). "Sticky Information and the Locus of Problem-Solving: Implications for Innovations." *Management Science* 40 no. 4: 429–439.

von Hippel, E. (2001). "Perspective: User Toolkits for Innovation." *Journal of Product Innovation Management* 18, no. 4: 247–257.

von Hippel, E., and R. Katz (2002). "Shifting Innovation to Users via Toolkits." *Management Science* 48, no. 7: 821–833.

von Hippel, E., S. Thomke, and M. Sonnack (1999). "Creating Breakthroughs at 3M." *Harvard Business Review,* September–October, 20–27.

von Hippel, E., and M. Tyre (1995). "How 'Learning by Doing' Is Done: Problem Identification in Novel Process Equipment." *Research Policy* 24, no. 1: 1–13.

Walker, R. (1992). *Silicon Destiny: The History of Application Specific Integrated Circuits and LSI Logic Corporation.* Milpitas, CA: C.M.C. Publications.

Wall Street Journal (2003). "Japan Auto Makers Train Their Sights on the U.S. Again." *Wall Street Journal,* 6 January.

Watkins, M., and K. Clark (1994). "Strategies for Managing a Project Portfolio." Working paper 93-004. Harvard Business School, Boston.

Weick, K. (1979). *The Social Psychology of Organizing.* New York: McGraw-Hill.

Weisshaar, T. (1996). "Freie Fahrt im Dom." *Mercedes—Das Magazin für mobile Menschen,* no. 4.

Wernerfelt, B. (1984). "A Resource-Based View of the Firm." *Strategic Management Journal* 5: 171–180.

Wheelwright, S., and K. Clark (1992). *Revolutionizing Product Development.* New York: Free Press.

Whitney, D. (1988). "Manufacturing by Design." *Harvard Business Review,* July–August, 83–91.

Womack, J., D. Jones, and D. Roos (1991). *The Machine That Changed the World.* New York: Harper Perennial.

Wright, S. (1932). "The Roles of Mutation, Inbreeding, Crossbreeding and Selection in Evolution." *Proceedings of the 11th International Congress of Genetics* 1: 356–366.

Zaltman, G. (2003). *How Customers Think: Essential Insights into the Mind of the Market.* Boston: Harvard Business School Press.

Ziman, J. (2000). *Technological Innovation as an Evolutionary Process.* Cambridge: Cambridge University Press.

index

about the author

Stefan Thomke is an associate professor of technology and operations management at Harvard Business School, where he has been a faculty member since 1995. His research and writing focus on the management of technological innovation, product development, and experimentation strategies. An important part of his work has been examining the impact of new and rapidly advancing technologies (e.g., computer simulation and rapid prototyping) on the economics of innovation in general and R&D performance and management in particular. Prior to 1995, Thomke worked in medical electronics and semiconductor fabrication and later was with McKinsey & Company in Germany. He has worked with U.S. and European firms on product and technology development and on organizational and strategic issues.

Thomke has written or cowritten more than three dozen academic papers, articles, cases, and notes, which have been published in leading journals such as the *California Management Review, Harvard Business Review, Journal of Product Innovation Management, Management Science, Research Policy, Scientific American,* and *Strategic Management Journal.* Professor Thomke holds a Ph.D. in electrical engineering and management from the Massachusetts Institute of Technology (MIT).